THALBERG

THALBERG

THE LAST TYCOON
AND THE
WORLD OF M-G-M

ROLAND FLAMINI

CROWN PUBLISHERS, INC.   NEW YORK

Published by Crown Publishers, Inc., 201 East
50th Street, New York, New York 10022.
Member of the Crown Publishing Group.

Random House, Inc. New York, Toronto, London,
Sydney, Auckland

Crown is a trademark of Crown Publishers, Inc.

Manufactured in the United States of America

Design by June Bennett-Tantillo

Library of Congress Cataloging-in-Publication Data

Flamini, Roland.
    Thalberg: The last tycoon and the world of
M-G-M / Roland Flamini.—1st ed.
    Includes bibliographical references and index.
    1. Thalberg, Irving G., 1899–1936. 2. Motion
picture producers and directors—United States—
Biography. 3. Metro-Goldwyn-Mayer.
    I. Title.
    PN1998.3.T467F63   1993
    791.43'0232'092—dc20   93-2523
    [B]   CIP

ISBN 0-517-58640-1

10 9 8 7 6 5 4 3 2 1

First Edition

For my son, Christopher

ACKNOWLEDGMENTS

This book owes a lot to the cooperation, encouragement, and memories of many people, and in some notable cases the contact goes back over a period of years. When I finally began writing the book, I was able to return to some of my earlier Thalberg sources, but a number of his contemporaries were no longer here to speak about him. After all, if Thalberg were alive today, he would be over ninety. For the readiness with which they agreed to talk on the record, I am grateful to the late: Brian Aherne, Barry Brannen, Howard Dietz, Ava Gardner, Lee Garmes, Helen Hayes, Eddie Lawrence, John Lee Mahin, Samuel Marx, Lilly Messenger, Coleen Moore, Daniel O'Shea (David Selznick's partner), Howard Strickling and his wife Gail, and Minna Wallis.

My thanks are also due to J. J. Cohn, Lucinda Ballard Dietz, Philip Dunne, Kitty Carlisle Hart, Deborah Pellow (Mrs. Irving Thalberg, Jr.), Norma Pisar, Maurice Rapf, Mickey Rooney, Ann Straus, David Thompson, Emily Torchia, and William Wyler.

A full list of books consulted appears in the bibliography, but I am greatly indebted to three of my fellow writers: Neal Gabler, author of the seminal work on the role of Jews in Hollywood, *An Empire of Their Own*; Gavin Lambert, whose biography of Norma Shearer has become the essential source of information on Thalberg's wife; and David Thompson, because of his wonderful biography of Thalberg's generally friendly rival, David O. Selznick.

In California, I owe a great debt to Deborah Edler Brown for her invaluable help with additional documentary research. I am also grateful to Ned Comstock of the University of Southern California Movie and Television Library in Los Angeles, to the Margaret Herrick Library at the Academy of Motion Picture Arts and Sciences, and to Turner Entertainment. In London, I would like to thank the Research Library staff at the British Film Institute Library.

Lastly, I have a number of professional and private debts. Lino Cassar read through the finished book (more than once) with a knowledgeable eye and made many helpful suggestions. At Crown Publishers, my editor Betty A. Prashker saw the potential of the subject and provided stimulating guidance and commentary; and Kimberley Reilly pressed the deadlines patiently and effectively. I am also indebted, as always, to Helen Brann, my agent, and—also as always—to my wife, Diane, for her inexhaustible supply of calmness, encouragement, and forbearance.

CONTENTS

INTRODUCTION

My interest in Irving Thalberg goes back to the 1960s, when I was writing a book about the filming of *Gone With the Wind*. For Thalberg, Louis B. Mayer's partner at Metro-Goldwyn-Mayer Studios, this was the picture that got away. As Hollywood's foremost studio, M-G-M was automatically first on the list whenever the film rights of a new novel or Broadway play were on offer; thus Mayer and Thalberg had first option of purchasing Margaret Mitchell's soon-to-become-best-selling novel. Mayer wanted to buy it, Thalberg didn't. "Forget it, Louis. No Civil War picture ever made a nickel," he said. It was left to Mayer to pronounce the final sentence. "Well, that's it," Mayer said. "Irving knows what's right." Since M-G-M was run on the principle that Irving always knew what was right, the offer of *Gone With the Wind* was turned down, leaving the way clear for producer David Selznick, who was Mayer's son-in-law, to step in, buy the book, and make what has become the most famous motion picture of all time. Later, Selznick was forced to surrender the distribution rights of his picture to M-G-M in return for the loan of Clark Gable to play Rhett Butler. But by then Thalberg was dead.

Thalberg's refusal to buy the novel raises a curious, nagging question. He was Hollywood's Boy Wonder. He was handsome, literate, and, to the movie community that stood in awe of him, infallible—incapable of failure and a miracle healer when it came to repairing flawed movies. Yet if he was so smart, why had he not recognized *Gone With the Wind* for the surefire blockbuster that it was?

In search of an answer, I sent a message to Thalberg's widow, Norma Shearer, asking for an interview. At the time, I was a journalist in Los Angeles, and I had met her on a couple of occasions. A few days later I received a telephone call from her second husband, Marti Arrouge, to say that his wife was ill and could not see me. There had, in fact, been rumors that her eyesight was failing, and she was becoming increasingly reclusive. I thought I had drawn a blank. But then Norma herself came on the line and proceeded to give her views on why Thalberg had turned down *Gone With the Wind*.

Irving's health had been a factor, she said. He'd already had his hands full with *Marie Antoinette* as well as other productions, and the prospect of adding the massive novel to his list of projects must have seemed too daunting. Besides, she added, "Irving had to see a picture in his mind. If he didn't see it, he didn't make it." When told what Thalberg had said to Mayer about the novel, Norma replied that Irving had indeed believed Civil War pictures were not good box office. So much for infallibility.

And so began my quest for Irving Thalberg. I started a process sometimes known in journalism as "collecting string"—that is, gathering information on a specific topic intermittently, as it becomes available, with the intention of writing about it at some future time. Over the years I questioned several of Thalberg's Hollywood friends and collaborators and between 1969 and 1972 had a couple of short but illuminating conversations about him with Norma Shearer. By the time I started work in earnest on this biography in 1991, she had died and so had several of my original sources, but my "string" provided a sound basis for the further research that was required.

It was harder than usual to peel away the incrustations of myth and legend to get to the man underneath. It was harder because the transition from real person to mythic character following his death had been rapid and effective. Thalberg's death at thirty-seven, while he was still a major figure in Hollywood's Golden Age and not some old recluse with a distinguished but dimly remembered past, ensured his quick transition from Irving the Boy Wonder to Irving the Saint.

Even in dying he was the right man in the right place. By the close of the thirties, motion picture production was the nation's third largest industry. The introduction of sound technology had given films a timely boost, and high-quality color was around the corner. Hollywood films had carved out a huge world market, projecting a seductive image of American life brimming with vitality and rooted in democracy and personal freedom. In short, the movies in America had reached a stage of maturity where the emergence of a hero seemed not only appropriate but desirable. On March 8, 1938, seventeen months after his death, the Academy Awards presentations included for the first time the Irving G. Thalberg Award, "for the most consistent high quality of production achievement by an individual producer based on pictures he had personally produced during the preceding year."

The award is still given most years, and today millions of people who watch the televised Academy Awards presentations are familiar with the name Irving Thalberg. Yet how many know anything about him beyond the fact that he was a movie producer in the 1930s and clearly a Hollywood icon?

Thalberg himself bears some responsibility for this lack of definition. For one thing, he was by all accounts a guarded man who revealed little of himself. He had few friends outside his circle of movie associates, and he remained something of an enigma even to them. For another, he never put his name on a picture because he believed that his productions bore his unmistakable imprint and therefore did not need labels. Successive generations continue to enjoy *Mutiny on the Bounty, A Night at the Opera, Camille, Grand Hotel, The Big Parade, Mata Hari, Queen Christina, Marie Antoinette,* and dozens of other Metro-Goldwyn-Mayer movies from the studio's heyday without being aware that, in a very real sense, they were made by Irving Thalberg. And although Thalberg closely supervised the making of more pictures than any other producer in Hollywood's history, the credit "Produced by Irving Thalberg" never appeared on the screen during his lifetime and only one time after his death.

In a community overpopulated with egos, this remarkable act of self-denial alone makes him unique, but there are other reasons why Thalberg deserves greater attention. He was the archetype of the creative producer, and he embodied all the virtues and vices of that particular system of filmmaking. He spent half his life as a top film executive, and when he died the *New York Times* gave a clear indication of his stature by publishing an editorial calling him "the most important force" in the motion picture industry. He set the pace and others followed, the paper said, because his way combined style, glamour, and profit.

His was not so much a career as a saga, and he had an extraordinary talent for sounding conservative and acting radical. In many ways he was a revolutionary in a gray flannel suit. When he became head of Universal Studios at the age of twenty, he made an immediate impact by dismissing the director Erich von Stroheim from the picture *Merry-Go-Round* in the middle of filming in a dispute over production costs. News of the incident stunned the motion picture community. Von Stroheim was autocratic, overbearing, and notorious for his unbridled extravagance, but no director had ever before been fired from a picture. More important, Thalberg won the clash of wills. Von Stroheim attempted to go over the young executive's head to the owner of the studio, but he stayed fired. For Hollywood producers it was the dawn of a new age, for directors the end of a period of wide creative freedom.

At twenty-three Thalberg joined forces with Louis B. Mayer to merge three small studios into the greatest studio of them all, Metro-Goldwyn-Mayer. As vice president in charge of production at M-G-M, one of the pictures he inherited in the merger was *Ben-Hur*. The epic was careening toward disaster on location in Rome at a cost of millions, and the new management team's first thought was to dump the production and cut its losses. But Thalberg recognized the picture as an opportunity to make an immediate impact. He scrapped much of the original Italian footage and started afresh on the M-G-M back lot in Culver City, lavishing even more millions on massive new sets, including the Circus Maximus for the exciting chariot race. His calculated gamble paid off. The enormous success of *Ben-Hur* focused attention on the new studio and its new production head, adding to his growing reputation for bold, decisive action.

Today it is taken for granted that the director creates the movie and the producer handles the financing and logistics. But Thalberg did it all, from choosing Tarzan's electronically produced yell to writing Garbo's first words on the screen. Until 1933, when overwork forced him to renounce his supervising post, take a long vacation, and return to vastly reduced activity, he largely originated, cast, helped write, edited, and reedited every film that was shown with the trademark of M-G-M's roaring lion.

As far as Hollywood was concerned, he invented retakes, the costly practice of putting a picture back into production for additional filming after its completion (although he used to say retakes were first introduced by Harold Lloyd). Once Thalberg had edited the picture he almost invariably ordered new scenes to be shot and original ones to be reshot in order to improve it. As a result, Hollywood soon began referring to M-G-M as Retake Alley.

Whatever he did gained attention particularly because, as the *New York Times* editorial had rightly pointed out, he never forgot the box office and—usually, at any rate—judged creativity from the optic of the balance sheet. In the eyes of their peers, Mayer's and Thalberg's greatest achievement was that in the economic climate of the Depression, M-G-M was the only studio consistently to show an annual profit.

Yet Thalberg did anything but cut corners on a movie. He made what he called "quality pictures," defining quality with the equation: star (or stars) plus Broadway hit or popular classic plus high standard of production equals good box office. If this seems obvious now, it was a revolutionary approach in the motion picture industry, which had always believed that the success of a film depended on star power, regardless of story or production.

When the other studios followed suit, Thalberg began to pair two major stars in the same picture (Garbo and John Gilbert in *Love,* for example), a practice that had always been considered a waste of resources. Then he went further and introduced the all-star picture with *Grand Hotel,* which had a cast of five top box office stars—Garbo, Joan Crawford, John Barrymore, Lionel Barrymore, and Wallace Beery.

Place his achievements against the background of a lifelong struggle with a wasting heart disease that he knew would cause his premature death, and you have a portrait of a driven man, a genius in his own way, desperately racing against time with two objectives—to leave his imprint on a world of fantasies, dreams, and American folklore and to make as much money as possible. Thalberg's enormous appetite for cash was one reason behind his unrelenting drive. When he came to Hollywood he was earning $60 a week.

When he died nineteen years later he left $4,490,000 before tax. In his second objective, then, he would generally be considered successful, although he himself always felt that he deserved more.

But what about the first objective? Judged on the durability of his pictures alone, his legacy is a mixed one. One reason his images and ideas don't always stand the test of time was what amounted to an obsession with bringing Broadway to the screen. All too often his film versions of successful plays by the likes of Coward and O'Neill, which he called "prestige" films because he knew they would never make serious money, look studied and stagy to modern audiences. It went beyond the prevailing Hollywood policy of favoring presold properties—successful plays and best-selling novels. Thalberg felt that the movies' link with theater enhanced the status of the new form of entertainment that had its origins in fairgrounds, amusement parks, and vaudeville shows.

His other problem was an even greater obsession with establishing Norma Shearer as the First Lady of the screen. This resulted in some of his more overblown and overglamorized productions. It is unquestionably true that Thalberg's more lasting films are the ones that do not star Norma Shearer.

He did not have the good fortune to connect with a *Gone With the Wind*—with a landmark movie with which to be eternally identified. A movie that after repeated viewings still comes from behind its familiarity and surprises you. There was, after all, so little time. Had Thalberg lived longer, he might also have worried less about Norma's screen career and broadened his choice of stories, perhaps even found that blockbuster. At M-G-M, Thalberg supervised the making of over four hundred movies, and it would have been to his further credit if at least a tenth of them had been wholly original stories.

But Thalberg deserves a full biography for what he did, not what he might have done. His work at Metro was perhaps the best of what Hollywood did best. Partly, what was so arresting about him and what created an instant mystique was his age. Anyone so young was bound to attract attention in a community as insular as Hollywood in the 1920s and early 1930s. It was a young man's business, but Thalberg was younger still. As a point of comparison, when Thalberg and Mayer formed their studio in 1923, Mayer was forty, Sam Goldwyn was forty-one, and the director D. W. Griffith a veteran at forty-eight. But Thalberg was twenty-four. It had long been common knowledge that he was not expected to live much past thirty, so that even while he was alive there had always been a hint of tragedy about him. He was the doomed prince of the movies.

Also arresting was the sheer scope of his involvement and the extent to which M-G-M movies were his images and his ideas. Warner Brothers Studios released an average of thirty-five films a year, Paramount about twenty, but Metro-Goldwyn-Mayer released fifty. Under Thalberg an M-G-M movie was unmistakable in all its components—the stars, the look of the picture, and the story. M-G-M leading women from Garbo to Myrna Loy, from Shearer to Crawford, were cool, classy, made to look beautiful, and out of the place in the kitchen (there was, in any case, a notable absence of kitchens in M-G-M movies).

M-G-M men tended to be worldly and in control and—like Thalberg himself—went to good tailors. When John Barrymore signed a Metro-Goldwyn-Mayer contract, Thalberg told him that if his wardrobe did not include white tie and tails, he had better acquire them because "that's what you're going to wear from now on." He wasn't speaking symbolically, either. Warner Brothers specialized in antiheroes with designer stubble on their chins à la Humphrey Bogart who ate at roadside diners. M-G-M men dressed for dinner.

"Streamlined" was a word that first appeared in the 1930s in connection with automobiles. It applies equally to Thalberg pictures, as do "glossy," "luxurious," and "technically flawless." Cedric Gibbons, M-G-M's legendary art director, created stylized sets famous for their clean, uncluttered line and oversize proportions—living rooms the size of tennis courts, soaring palace gates that dwarfed the actors. And what Gibbons didn't visualize, studio dress designer Adrian would, gowning the women spectacularly, the fluid lines of his creations caressing the figure in all the right places and managing that peculiar M-G-M combination of distance and sexuality.

Because Thalberg was chronically opposed to location work in foreign countries, where the production would be out of his direct control, virtually every setting from the fifteenth-century Verona of *Romeo and Juliet* to the contemporary Hong Kong of *China Seas* was built on M-G-M's huge back lot. The result on the screen frequently has the unrealistic look of a theatrical set. But Thalberg was not in the business of replicating reality. He was more interested in creating distractions. His art didn't imitate life; it detoured around life to a fantastic world he fashioned for the movie-going public.

His staff lobbied for more realism, but he was not as flexible or receptive to argument as the legend claims. Compared with his fellow moguls, of course, he was the soul of reason. He encouraged his collaborators to express their views, but he was so certain of his own judgment that it hardly ever occurred to him, once he had made up his mind, that he might be wrong. He listened carefully to their opinions, but there was never any question about whose decision was final.

Cedric Gibbons once complained to him that the script of the 1935 musical *Paris* included a love scene in that city with a moonlit ocean in the background. You had to be well armed if you hoped to make a dent in Thalberg's thinking, so Gibbons showed him maps and photographs to prove that there was no ocean close to Paris.

Thalberg wouldn't budge. "You can't cater to a handful of people who know Paris," he told the art director. "Audiences only see about ten percent of what's on the screen anyway, and if they're watching your background instead of my actors, the scene will be a failure. Whatever you put there, they'll believe that's how it is."

Gibbons built the set under protest. After *Paris* was released, Thalberg, who always remembered everything, asked him how many letters the studio had received pointing out the mistake, and Gibbons had to admit that there were none. "That proves I'm right," said Thalberg. Then he added: "But it doesn't prove you're wrong."

Such disarming admissions helped to tone down his quiet arrogance. "L. B. Mayer wanted to be liked, but Irving never tried to be popular," one of his favorite writers, Donald Ogden Stewart, wrote to a friend years later. "He was too busy getting his way." Thalberg's determination could be daunting when he wanted something. When he was trying to persuade a very reluctant Edward G. Robinson that he should sign an M-G-M long-term contract, the actor was so shaken by his relentless persistence that he ran out of his office and threw up.

This single-minded pursuit of a sole objective comes out clearly in existing Thalberg documents. Having not only finished high school but also attended business courses, Thalberg had none of the inhibitions of his less educated contemporary studio bosses about writing letters, telegrams, and memos. As a result, there are generous and revealing helpings of Thalberg material in the University of California Cinema Television Library, the Atlanta archives of Turner Entertainment, which acquired Metro-Goldwyn-Mayer Studios in 1989, and the archives of Universal Studios, most of which has never before been examined.

The documents ranged from a record of his battle with the Hays Office, the movie industry's own censorship system, over how many times he could use the word *impotent* with reference to King Louis XVI in *Marie Antoinette* (the Hays Office was insisting that it should be only one time, Thalberg's script included five) to a memo casting Clark Gable as the Baron in *Grand Hotel,* a role eventually played by John Barrymore. Verbatim reports of endless script and editing conferences, now kept at USC, show clearly the close attention he lavished on even minor M-G-M productions— long forgotten films like *Frisco Sally Levy* and *When a Feller Needs a Friend,* the latter film, incidentally, co-written by his sister, Sylvia Thalberg.

It was true that Thalberg's movies often came out of his head: he would describe scenes, many times complete with improvised dialogue in a stream-of-consciousness monologue with the director and the writers feverishly scribbling notes. Here is Thalberg discussing a scene in an early script conference for the picture *China Seas*: "I'd like to open this sequence on a roaring gale at sea. . . . I think it might be better to open just prior to the storm—that awful calm before the storm . . . and the typhoon hits and they go through all that hell, and the terrific tiredness after the fight is over—the weariness of Gaskell [Clark Gable], and from behind him this China woman comes and their affair [begins]." The typhoon scene was included in the picture, as Thalberg's scenes usually were.

It so happens that the *China Seas* file provides a further insight into the way Thalberg worked. The original script he developed for the picture was a powerful melodrama in which sea captain Clark Gable falls under the spell of the beautiful daughter of a powerful Chinese merchant. There is an affair on his ship, and then a child, and the two marry. To prevent Gable from going to sea again, the woman discredits him with his bosses in the shipping company, and he is dismissed. Finally, in a desperate bid to free himself from the clutches of his possessive wife and her family, Gable kills his wife. "We see him degenerate," Thalberg explained to his writing team, "the man who was master of himself, of his ship, is finally beaten to a pulp by this woman, but finally rises up with sufficient strength to kill her at the finish even though he does love her. You've got a great story!"

A great story, perhaps, but a controversial one. The studio's senior management—the front office—was not enthusiastic about Gable killing a Chinese woman, or any woman, for that matter; and Thalberg himself could never come up with a motive for the killing that would not reflect badly on the hero.

Then he had second thoughts about public reaction to what he called "the color line," the interracial romance. At about the same time, *Red Dust* was released and became an instant box office hit thanks to its starring pair, Gable and M-G-M's blond sensation Jean Harlow, who was neither Chinese nor subtle, and theater managers were asking for more Gable-Harlow pictures. So an unusual and exotic picture was reworked into a frothy adventure, and Yu-Lan, the Chinese siren, became blond China Doll, "the swellest gal in the Archipelago."

What of the private Thalberg, the family man with a wife, small son, baby daughter, and formidable mother? Most of his life in Hollywood, his working day was from ten in the morning until two the following morning. At weekends at home he viewed rough cuts and rushes—the day's film footage. Social occasions were movie-oriented. The movies clearly came first. Howard Dietz, the New York–based head of corporate publicity at M-G-M, didn't remember ever having a conversation with Thalberg that wasn't about movies. Norma Shearer said simply, "Movies were his life."

The remark was made at a party in Beverly Hills in which guests had gathered to watch the Oscar presentations on television. Norma had arrived three-quarters of the way through the evening and made a star entrance, pausing for effect at the door and then sailing grandly into the room with a ripple of silk and black sequins. Marti Arrouge followed two respectful steps behind, and because she was small and he very tall, their arrival reminded me of Queen Elizabeth II and Prince Philip. She was then sixty-four or so, yet from a distance she seemed unchanged from her last screen appearances in the early 1940s: the same smile, the same narrowing of the eyes, the same tilt of the head, the pointed chin. Close up, though, it was obvious that the effects of time had not been stopped, merely blurred through generous application of her characteristic white makeup.

When the presentation of the Irving Thalberg Award was announced, Norma broke off in midsentence and looked at the television screen with great anticipation, as though expecting Thalberg himself to appear. Then, as filmdom's tribute to her dead husband was presented, Norma said: "Irving wouldn't have liked that award. He hated that kind of publicity. I told them so at the time."

A few days later I found myself, by coincidence, standing behind Norma Shearer and Arrouge at the checkout counter of a Beverly Hills supermarket, which, to adapt the famous M-G-M slogan, had more stars in its aisles than there were in heaven. Her full, pleated gray slacks were a little island of style in an ocean of trendy, hip-hugging bell-bottoms and imported Indian shirts. When Arrouge explained where we had met, she said brightly, "Of course, Irving's award. That was such a fun evening!" Even though he would not have approved, it was still, in her mind, Irving's award.

1

IN THE
OLD COUNTRY

The founders of the American film industry were mainly immigrants or the sons of immigrants who arrived in America from Russia and Eastern Europe during the mass immigration of the late nineteenth century. Louis B. Mayer would later claim not to remember the date of his birth, but he could vividly describe his arrival at New York's Castle Garden immigration station as a small child; Hungarian-born Adolph Zukor came "as an orphan boy of sixteen with a few dollars sewn inside my vest"; Harry Warner was born in Poland, but his three younger brothers were born in different American towns as their father traveled as a peddler. Of the eight major studios, six were started by these pioneers of Orthodox Jewish parentage. Few movie tycoons continued to follow the Orthodox practices, but Mayer's father was a Hebraic scholar and his wife the daughter of a rabbi. Zukor's mother was also a rabbi's daughter, and his brother became a distinguished rabbi in Germany.

They came to America in search of opportunity, to escape the poverty endured by their families, to flee the oppressive life of the ghetto. Not that life in their new country was entirely free from exclusion and antagonism. But to the "poor, huddled masses yearning to breathe free" of Jewish poet Emma Lazarus's verses, America was still preferable to the deprivation and uncertainties of turn-of-the-century central Europe. Curiously, the film industry has never successfully attempted a major picture about the remarkable story of its own emergence. The epic saga of the movie moguls begins with each of them working in another occupation, usually with a good share of failure and frustration: Louis Mayer in the scrap iron business, Sam Goldwyn—who had changed his name from Goldfish—selling gloves. Then the movies provide them with the opportunity they all seemed to have been waiting for.

Irving Thalberg belonged to the second generation of major Hollywood figures, those who moved immediately into the upper echelons of an emerging industry. There were other ways in which he differed from the former fur salesmen, boilermakers, waiters, and pants pressers of the older generation of moguls. For one thing, as I mentioned earlier, he had had an education. He came from a German Jewish family, which in the pecking order of Jewish society made him the social superior of the movie community's Eastern European Jews. Moreover he was born in America, in stable middle-class surroundings.

Thalberg neither changed his name nor fictionalized his origins. The Thalbergs came from Wetzlar, a Rhineland town a dozen miles north of Koblenz. A plaque outside the family home read "In this house lived Johann Wolfgang von Goethe." Not that the Thalbergs claimed any family relationship with the great German writer. They had simply acquired the house. But the family did sometimes speak of Sigismond Thalberg, a minor nineteenth-century composer and pianist who enjoyed a brief, dazzling career both astonishing and touching crowded audiences all over Europe and

North and South America. His compositions for his instrument included a well-known set of variations on the British national anthem, "God Save the Queen." Sigismond's musical gifts were not passed on to Irving, for it was well known at M-G-M that music was his blind spot. He had no musical knowledge or appreciation, and some maintained that he was tone deaf.

Fabric, not music, provided the Thalbergs' living. Some time in the middle of the century Jakob Thalberg, Irving's paternal great-grandfather, had opened a lace and fabric store in nearby Andernach. It was a thriving business, but not large enough to support all three sons of Jakob's eldest son. So in the 1880s the youngest of those sons, Wilhelm, took the well-trodden path of emigration to the United States. He settled in Brooklyn, where through family connections he set himself up as an importer, mainly of lace.

In America, Wilhelm became William, but he did not become rich. He was an immigrant without the immigrant's historic inner drive for self-improvement. From descriptions of him he emerges as a bland man, hardworking but unambitious—in fact, somewhat defeatist. He earned what he considered a reasonable living and thought it unlikely that his capabilities would carry him much farther. Ironically, the woman he sought to marry had the opposite character. Henrietta Heyman was the daughter of another family of German Jewish immigrants who had come to the New World, not to escape from the old one, but rather out of a sense of adventure to expand their modest-size empire.

The Heymans owned a large clothing store in their native Hamburg and in the 1860s decided to open a similar one in Brooklyn; this was later expanded into a department store. Like William, Henrietta was also born in Germany— but only just. Her father was sent to run the Brooklyn store, Heyman & Sons, but the family postponed their departure until after Henrietta's birth.

For a long time she had been an only child, and her father, anticipating that she would one day take over the store, had involved her in the business as he would have done a son. Then the Heymans had a son, and Henrietta found herself relegated to a secondary position. Irene Selznick, the eldest of Louis B. Mayer's two daughters and the wife of David O. Selznick, remembered her in later life as plain, strong-willed, and hyperactive, with "very dark and menacing eyes." And Norma Shearer once mentioned to Eddie Lawrence, an M-G-M publicity man who was her occasional confidant, that Henrietta Heyman married William Thalberg on the rebound—not from another man, but from the rejection she felt when her younger brother was born. It was, Norma had said, the only way to explain the mismatch between the ambitious, forceful woman and her unprepossessing husband who was her social inferior.

When William showed no sign of falling in with her determination to be somebody, it added up to a sum of almost inhuman frustration. So energetic and driven was she that the more detached he remained, the more aggressive she became. In short, Henrietta Thalberg had the pushiness, stamina, persistence, and strength of will of a classic stage mother.

On May 30, 1899, she gave birth to a son in one of the small rooms in William's dim but comfortable attic at 19 Woodbine Street. The Thalbergs called their firstborn Irving, and Grant after Ulysses S. Grant because it made him sound more American. But the Thalbergs' joy was darkened by the condition of the baby's health. He was frail, with arms and legs like matchsticks. Worse, he had the slightly bluish complexion that indicates cyanosis, a lack of oxygen in the blood. When the doctors told the Thalbergs their son had a congenitally defective heart, they both reacted in character to the shock—William fatalistically, Henrietta by refusing to accept that her son's condition would shorten his life and be an impediment to his distinguishing himself. In time she came to regard him as in some way chosen, and although he might not live very long, she was determined to help him be remembered for much longer.

With a delicate baby to care for, Henrietta felt that a move to a larger home was imperative, and William obliged by renting an apartment on Madison Street, where their second child, Sylvia, was born. But what Henrietta wanted was her own house, and by the turn of the century the Thalbergs had purchased a greystone front at 1303 Bushwick Avenue, a more prosperous middle-class neighborhood.

Despite the arrival of a baby daughter, Irving remained the focus of his mother's attention and the center of her hopes and dreams. As a small boy he was prone to chest pains. Henrietta nursed him vigilantly and unceasingly. She administered analgesics to combat the pain and gave him massages to improve his circulation, rubbing the thin body and at the same time distracting him with fairy tales and nursery rhymes. Because cyanotics are prone to bronchitis, she always put a hot-water bottle in his bed in winter. And she slept in a small room next to his, to be close at hand if he had a bad night.

Yet when the doctors warned her that if her son was going to survive he would have to be treated as a semi-invalid, Henrietta dug in her heels and determined to prove them wrong. Her mind was fixed on his leading as normal a life as possible to fulfill his special destiny. She willed him to go to school, and at P.S. 85 he quickly showed himself to be a natural student, alert, inquisitive, and capable of remarkable concentration. At the end of his first year he was the top of his class.

Henrietta's determination may have reflected her refusal to accept the fact that she had given birth to a son with a heart condition in the first place. It is an intriguing question to which there is no available answer. Nothing in the portrait that emerges of her suggests that she in any way blamed herself. She could have somehow held William responsible, which would help explain the low regard she appeared to have for her husband throughout his life. Whatever her feelings about Irving's illness, she occasionally pushed the fiction that he could lead a normal life to dangerous levels. She let him play street stickball and other games, even though he occasionally played almost until he dropped. At such times he was forced to spend days in bed to recover from overtaxing his limited physical resources. His mother finally banned such exertions altogether.

He was a year older than the other boys in his class, and he pushed himself hard, hoping to skip a grade and catch up to his own age group. He never did. When he was in sixth grade he contracted a bronchial infection and was confined to his bed for a long period. Henrietta persuaded his teachers to come to the house and tutor him privately so as not to interrupt his schooling, and he was able to graduate from P.S. 85 and enroll at Bushwick High.

Then in February 1913 he was stricken with diphtheria. A specialist thought he might resume school in a year, but the family doctor's more pessimistic view was that Irving would be bedridden for the rest of his life.

Irving spent the next year and the first two years of his teens in bed. He accepted his illness without protest, partly because he was not by nature a complainer, but also because being ill opened up for him the excitement of reading. It was his mother who kept him supplied with books from the public library. But Henrietta was doing more than stimulating a youth's interest in books: she was also helping him create a fantasy world to replace the real one of which he could never fully be a part. By the age of fourteen Thalberg had fought alongside the Three Musketeers, mounted the steps to the guillotine with Sidney Carton, and been moved by La Dame aux Camélias. He had ridden with Napoleon across the frozen Russian wastes, brooded with Hamlet, and climbed balconies with Romeo (a copy of Shakespeare's collected plays given to him by Grandfather Heyman was still in Thalberg's library when he died). These were the companions of a bedridden boyhood, a boyhood isolated from other children, watched over constantly by a vigilant mother and from a distance, perhaps longingly, by an affectionate father who throughout Thalberg's life remained an inconspicuous shadow in the wings.

When he became curious about philosophy, his mother

obediently took herself to the library and asked the librarian for nothing but the best, coming back with armfuls of Kant and Nietzsche. But it was the more readable William James, brother of the novelist Henry, who impressed Irving most and shaped his beliefs. James, who had coincidentally just died of a heart condition, had helped popularize philosophy through his books, notably his brilliant and epoch-making *Principles of Psychology, Pragmatism,* and *The Meaning of Truth.*

By now Thalberg was almost sixteen and ripe for guidance. James's fascinating style and his broad culture made him the most influential thinker of his day. Neither William nor Henrietta was particularly religious, and Irving adopted James's view of human will and interest as the primary human factors, his pragmatic approach to truth as only "the expedient in our way of thinking" of knowledge as something not "pure" but applied—a collection of ideas that survive through their effect on history. James is widely thought to have originated the term "pragmatism," but it had previously been used by another philosopher, Charles S. Pierce.

How much he actually absorbed at the time is hard to say, but it stirred an interest in philosophy that lasted throughout his life. James's theories on human will may well have helped when his mother dragooned him into leaving his bed and returning to normal life. Watching her son propped up in a semireclining position day after day filled Henrietta with compassion and frustration—compassion for Irving and frustration that her plans for him seemed destined to come to nothing. Without the doctor's knowledge, she would periodically make Irving pace up and down the room to ensure that he didn't forget how to walk. Then one morning she took a bold and potentially risky decision and talked him into going back to school. "You've been sick long enough," she said to her son. "I want you to make something of yourself." She spent an anxious day worrying about how the exertion might affect his condition, and she was waiting outside the school long before the bell rang in the afternoon. To her intense relief, she saw Thalberg walking out of school apparently none the worse.

He did not return to his bedridden state after that but resumed his education. He was predictably small for his age but quietly assertive and sure of himself: an articulate, bookish youth ready to debate on any subject and dreaming vague dreams of becoming a lawyer. He managed to graduate from high school despite his illness, but hopes of a legal career were dashed when Henrietta took him for a medical check-up. His heart was so severely damaged that he lacked the physical stamina for the pressures of law school.

Keenly aware from his teens that, short of a miracle, his life was likely to be short, Thalberg decided to forgo college altogether and instead took a business course at New York University, along with night courses in Spanish (he already spoke good German) and shorthand at a Brooklyn business school. Rachel Laemmle, a German immigrant friend of Henrietta's, suggested a career in the movie industry and offered to introduce Irving to her husband, Carl Laemmle, head of the Universal Film Manufacturing Company. But in 1916 the movies were still largely considered a fly-by-night operation. Henrietta was sure her son could do better than a job in Carl Laemmle's office, and Thalberg himself was content to follow his mother's advice.

He had seen a few movies, but like Henrietta, he regarded them merely as a curiosity. The theater, on the other hand, fascinated him. His mother had occasionally taken him to see a Broadway production. He found the atmosphere exciting and watching a play even more absorbing than reading. At school he had auditioned for the part of Marc Antony in a production of Shakespeare's *Julius Caesar*, but physically he was too small and his voice too light for a leading character, so he had to be content with carrying a spear. The setback convinced him the stage was not for him. But within five years he was to become a key figure in the new form of entertainment destined to dwarf the theater in its vast popular appeal.

2

THE
LITTLE FELLOW
AT UNIVERSAL

ITUATION WANTED: Secre-
tary, stenographer, Spanish,
English, high school school
education, inexperienced; $15." Thalberg's advertisement in
the *New York Journal of Commerce* appeared while he was tem-
porarily working in his grandfather's department store, writing ads. It produced a number of responses, and Thalberg
chose to go to work for the Hudson Trading Company
handling general business correspondence. The small
Manhattan firm imported rice from the Orient. He quickly
decided the job was a dead end and moved to another import-export firm from his original list of job offers. Here,
the young new stenographer immediately caught the attention of the firm's owner by bombarding him with sound
suggestions for making the company more cost effective,
and within a year Thalberg had risen to assistant manager
at thirty dollars a week.

But the work was tedious, and there was no immediate

prospect of further advancement. To an ambitious young man in a hurry, it must have seemed that he was slipping into a rut: that he couldn't get where he wanted to go from here.

Yet where was he going? Barred from a law career, Thalberg seemed uncertain which direction to take. With World War I just over, his Thalberg uncles had invited him to visit Germany. The family had lost two sons in the Kaiser's army and had no male members to carry on the business. Irving might step into the breach and, one day, take over. But Irving declined the invitation to go to Andernach to run the family firm. He had no interest either in leaving America or in his father's business, which had at best provided no more than a modest living, and he was influenced by Henrietta, who had set her sights much higher for her son—although neither was quite sure on what. Had he decided to go to Germany, of course, Hollywood would have lost one of the seminal figures of its golden years.

His mother introduced him to politics: if not a famous attorney, then perhaps a senator. She was herself a Socialist party activist, and she arranged for her son to meet a politician who was running for mayor of New York on the party ticket. Typically, Thalberg prepared for the meeting by reading Bernard Shaw's *Guide to Socialism,* and the candidate, Morris Hillquit, was impressed with the quiet, articulate young man who was then not yet eighteen. Thalberg was hired as Hillquit's campaign speech writer at ten dollars a week.

Politics brought out Thalberg's capacity for total absorption and single-minded determination. Besides writing Hillquit's speeches, he also made campaign speeches himself in Union Square, a tough, economically depressed neighborhood. He was no orator, but his speeches were carefully prepared—rehearsed in front of a mirror or tried out on his mother—and his arguments quietly persuasive. He was too self-confident to be shy, but he was not gregarious or outgoing, either, and he was conscious of his shortcomings as a public speaker. The presence at his meetings of Tammany Hall thugs who shouted him down or frightened the crowd away added an element of danger that the imaginative young political activist may well have romanticized. He was Lenin rousing the masses, being attacked by the czar's police. The Russian revolution was then in full ferment.

Thalberg would later claim credit for winning Hillquit the local vote, but the candidate fared badly in more affluent areas and was defeated. It was an experience that put Thalberg off politics for the rest of his life, leaving him a political cynic. In later years he would cite it as an example of how the end in politics justified any means, however devious. "We could sit down here and figure out dirty tricks all night," he once told actor Fredric March, "and every one of them would be all right in a political campaign."

For Thalberg there must have been something of the famous Atlas body-building advertisement about the Hillquit experience. It convinced him of the importance of building up financial muscle. Concluding that money controlled politics and that real power came with wealth, the student of William James forsook socialism for capitalism and decided that rather than become a politician, he would concentrate on becoming rich. Being an assistant manager in a small import-export firm hardly seemed the quickest route to this objective, so Thalberg resigned and decided to take a vacation and rethink his career strategy.

Part of this time he spent with his maternal grandmother, who owned a cottage out in Edgemere on Long Island. Carl Laemmle of Universal, who was a neighbor, provided evening entertainment for the area residents by stringing a sheet across the front porch and project movies for his family and neighbors, taking note of their reactions and comments. He was continually impressed by Thalberg's astute remarks and at the end of the summer offered the young man a job as secretary to D. B. Lederman, a senior executive in Universal's New York office. Thalberg was undecided, but Henrietta, who had meanwhile seen Rachel Laemmle riding around in her new limousine and had revised her opinion of the movie business, urged him to accept.

Years later, Thalberg's official M-G-M biography provided a different account of his entry into pictures. In the M-G-M account, which Thalberg will have approved, he rejects Laemmle's initial offer, only to get himself hired by Universal under his own steam without Laemmle's knowledge or assistance. It did not do to attribute this important first step to family connections!

The president of Universal was an impulsive, excitable, and sometimes giddy operator. He was five feet two inches tall and a paranoid who was convinced that everyone was out to cheat him—from business associates to the waiter who brought his check at a restaurant. He worked in a state of perpetual crisis, firing off telegrams of complaint and constantly dashing back and forth between his office in New York and Universal City, his sprawling studios on the fringes of Los Angeles and his native Germany. In an industry notorious for its nepotism, he set records for the number of useless relations on the payroll—a trait lampooned by the verse satirist Ogden Nash in the line "Uncle Carl Laemmle has a very large faemmle."

Even from a distance it did not take long for Thalberg to see that the company he had just joined was a chaotic place. Fifty-one-year-old Uncle Carl, as he was universally known throughout the industry, hired people without specifying their exact jobs, and the result was a constant squabbling over areas of responsibility. This was partly Laemmle's tactic to ensure that no executive became powerful enough to challenge his own authority, but years of internal tension had corroded the studio's productivity, and when Thalberg came on the scene Laemmle's film factory was in decline.

Nominally in charge of the bureaucratic maze at the studio, which Laemmle referred to as the Bottomless Pit, was Laemmle's brother-in-law Isadore Bernstein. He was Universal's West Coast manager, but he competed for authority with two other executives, one of whom was a Laemmle cousin who was after Bernstein's job.

Under this squabbling triumvirate, the studio produced movies of fluctuating quality and appeal. It concentrated on quantity—westerns, spy melodramas, sentimental love stories—and was a seething mass of almost uncontrolled activity. Its most consistent success was Laemmle's own brainchild, the Universal tour. At twenty-five cents a head, including a boxed lunch, it attracted an average of five hundred visitors a day. They toured the back lot with its various stages, then sat on bleachers to watch filming in progress. (The Universal tour was discontinued in the 1930s, then successfully revived in 1964.)

Universal had recently lost Mae Murray and Rudolph Valentino as a result of unhappiness with what Laemmle was paying them. It had a promising actor in Lon Chaney, not yet developed as a star, and the directors Tod Browning, Erich von Stroheim, and John Ford. But its main female star, Louise Lovely, had begun to lose her allure through overexposure. Thalberg, efficient and conscientious, screened Universal's current pictures, studied the profit-and-loss records, read the scenarios of upcoming productions, pored over Laemmle's communications with his West Coast executives, and in the process became fascinated with the business and the intricacies of running a huge motion picture concern.

Inevitably he began transmitting the same ideas to Laemmle himself. As a result of his business training, Thalberg was quite at home with written communication. In later life this was to be another difference from other, barely literate movie moguls like Louis Mayer, both incapable and suspicious of committing themselves to paper.

What Thalberg told Laemmle in his functional and rather long-winded style, tactfully skirting the subject of relations, was that he needed to delegate authority more clearly and give the studio a distinctive profile by raising its overall standard of production. To do this the studio needed to stop the defection of top talent by offering them attractive contracts. First startled and then grateful, Laemmle came to realize that he had a phenomenon on his hands, calm, shrewd, analytical, and just twenty. He appointed Thalberg his executive secretary.

Sam Marx, then a young employee in the same office and years later M-G-M's story editor under Thalberg, remembered the new arrival as tireless despite his obvious frailty. Everything in his life seemed to move with a rush. He was always the first in and "stayed on after all the others had gone home," lingering to talk to Marx about what he would do if he were in charge of a studio.

In July 1919 Uncle Carl made a hastily arranged trip to Universal City, taking his secretary with him. Henrietta rushed from Brooklyn to Grand Central Station with a suitcase for Thalberg packed with clothing, medicines, and a hot-water bottle and then cried at the prospect of their first separation. At Universal City Thalberg trailed dutifully behind his diminutive boss, touring the studio, attending meetings, and taking in the situation. What he saw at first hand confirmed the impression he had already formed from a distance: the root cause of Universal's problems was bad management.

Confronted by Laemmle, the executive trio blamed each other for Universal's many failures and claimed sole credit for its fewer successes. His complaints that they had not carried out his instructions sent from New York were met with claims that the telegram in question was never received. Eventually Laemmle prepared to depart on one of his periodic trips to Europe, frustrated and with nothing accomplished.

Then he had a sudden brainwave. He expanded his trio to a quartet making Thalberg the fourth member with a salary of sixty dollars a week. Thalberg would always remember the date of Laemmle's departure—July 6, 1919.

Thirty-seven days after his twentieth birthday, California became his home for the rest of his life.

It was typical of Laemmle that he failed to spell out for his studio executives exactly what Thalberg was supposed to do. Clearly the young newcomer was to be his master's eyes and ears in Hollywood, but beyond that Thalberg had no specific brief. His three colleagues paid little heed to the young man Laemmle had wished upon them. But like the good strategist that he was, Thalberg dug himself in and began to study the world that was to become more real to him than any other. He took a room in a hotel in downtown Los Angeles near the Western Union office, from where he cabled Laemmle at night and picked up his employer's replies in the morning, away from the prying eyes of the office staff. Casting around for allies, he became friendly with Edwin Loeb, Laemmle's diminutive attorney in Los Angeles, who would eventually become his own adviser and lawyer. With his equally diminutive brother, Joseph, Edwin founded the law firm of Loeb and Loeb, which represented most of the big studios.

Universal was founded in 1912, but Universal City had been operating for only four years. Unlike other Hollywood studios, it was not a series of buildings but a ranch that sprawled over some four hundred acres of terrain in the San Fernando Valley, ideal for scenery but difficult to manage. Trying to control it was like trying to control a game reserve. Jackrabbits and mountain lions still roamed it. Tracking down a company and rounding up stray extras was like being on safari or perhaps like rounding up stray cattle on the range.

Thalberg's ascendancy at Universal was as swift as it was unlikely. By the time Laemmle returned from his trip, Thalberg had prepared a detailed report of the situation, focusing on the lack of central control, the corporate infighting, the erratic accounting methods, and the overreliance on formula movies, and ending with the recommendation that a supervisor should be appointed, directly responsible to Laemmle himself—not necessarily to manage the studio, but to coordinate production there. Laemmle agreed and appointed Thalberg. Within six months Thalberg had hacked his way through the thicket of chaos and intrigue and emerged as general manager—the effective head of the California operation.

Two of his rivals were encouraged by Laemmle to resign, and the third was demoted to a figurehead position. The management quartet was now a solo performer.

Thalberg may have inherited an outfit in need of reorganization, but it was also profitable. At the end of 1920, despite its disarray, Universal posted a profit of $2,310,000. Good as this was, it fell short of the performance of other major studios. Silent movies were then reaching their peak; Hollywood was in the middle of a box office boom, and Thalberg was determined to bring Universal's revenue closer to that of the leading studios, notably Paramount, which was then number one. It was the business side of movie production that drew Thalberg, as he told his friend Loeb at the time of his appointment. His interest in the creative aspect came second. The sheer size of the investment, to say nothing of the profit potential, made each production a new challenge. It was a business in which a man could get rich.

But in the early twenties, picture making was still relatively simple and the motion picture business very fluid. By the end of the decade the technology had been greatly complicated by the introduction of sound and the financial side by the sizable cash flow required to service the increasing demand for "product." By the thirties the major studios had emerged as such complex structures that Thalberg's spectacular single leap from the bottom rung of the career ladder to the top at Universal would have been much harder, if not impossible, even at the express wish of the owner of the studio.

Not that operating Laemmle's company seemed simple to its young new general manager. To offset its factory reputation, Universal periodically splurged on more ambitious productions, which were promoted as "Laemmle's Jewels." When Thalberg first made his entrance at Universal, Laemmle's most expensive Jewel ever was in production, and it turned out to be the first test of Thalberg's mettle.

The film was *Foolish Wives,* the last of a trilogy of erotic films starring the extraordinarily gifted and reckless Erich von Stroheim, who also directed the picture. Stroheim's two earlier movies, *Blind Husbands* and *The Devil's Pass Key,* had each been a tremendous popular success, bringing Universal wide prestige, and as a result Laemmle had given von Stroheim carte blanche for his next production. It was all the encouragement the director needed to indulge his reputation for extravagant spending. Laemmle's generous budget of a million dollars for the production was quickly swallowed up in lavish sets, props, and costumes. Months after his scheduled deadline, von Stroheim was still shooting and costs still escalating. Reels and reels of footage had been filmed, and still there seemed to be no end in sight. It fell to Thalberg, as the new general manager, to try to bring the production to an orderly halt before it swallowed up all the studio's working capital.

On the surface, *Foolish Wives* was a nasty, melodramatic tale of a depraved Russian "count," Sergius Karazmin, who made a living seducing and blackmailing rich American women tourists. What gave the picture its force was the powerful backdrop of misery and decadence in Europe after World War I. The setting was Monte Carlo, and the director had built a sizable portion of the famous resort at Universal dominated by the facade of the Monte Carlo Casino.

The cost of that set alone had staggered Thalberg when he learned of it, but it was von Stroheim's obsessive spending on unnecessary detail that finally led to Thalberg's confrontation with the formidable director. On October 19, shortly after taking over, Thalberg learned that a big, expensive banquet sequence was held up for a whole day because von Stroheim had ordered hundreds of champagne glasses with half-inch gold rims, and glasses with only a quarter inch of gold were delivered instead. Von Stroheim had refused to shoot the scene until the right glasses were sent to the set, and the production wrapped for the day without any footage at all.

Thalberg called von Stroheim to his office, and the director marched into the room in the full uniform of an officer of the Russian Imperial Guard, which he wore in the picture, and escorted by loyalists from his production team. Von Stroheim had seen studio heads come and go at Universal, and none of them had dared question his spend-thrift working habits. Important directors were, in any case, a law unto themselves. Few were troubled by interference from the front office, the studio business executives, because (1) it was a seller's market for top filmmakers, and (2) the front office knew little about production methods.

So von Stroheim took stock of the young man facing him across the desk and decided that he represented no threat. Thalberg was about five feet six inches tall and weighed less than a hundred and twenty pounds. His dark features were delicate—almost feminine—with a high fore-head, large, dark brooding eyes, long, fine nose, and a wide, fleshy mouth. He had a well-developed chest, but his arms and legs were sticks: one woman friend recalled that she never thought about Irving's "condition" until she saw him in a bathing suit.

But von Stroheim was not to know that the young whippersnapper's appearance concealed an iron will. Von Stroheim was also short but seemed taller because of his powerful build and the fact that he wore built-up shoes to add to his height. With his military swagger, cropped hair, monocle, and deep, commanding, heavily accented voice, he easily passed for the former officer in the Austro-Hungarian army he claimed to be. Thalberg, however, would have made it his business to learn as much as possible about the director before confronting him and would have known von Stroheim was the Vienna-born son of a Jewish hat manufacturer.

Thalberg quietly spelled out the situation. Von Stroheim

must start winding down the picture. Although he may have stopped short of threatening to dismiss the director from the picture, he implied it. Von Stroheim's dismissive reply was: "Remove me as director and you remove me as star, and you don't have a picture." With that, he went back to the set.

Thalberg had lost the first round. Von Stroheim had already appeared in too many key scenes for any threat of replacement to be taken seriously. Unable—for the moment—to stem the rising costs, Thalberg tried to turn the crisis to advantage by exploiting the publicity angle. Throughout the spring of 1921, stretched over the height of three floors of New York's Astor Hotel at Broadway and Forty-fifth Street, a giant electric sign boasted: THE COST OF FOOLISH WIVES UP TO THIS WEEK, with the dollar figure changed weekly by the studio's publicity department.

But, following the champagne glass incident, Thalberg was keeping a close watch on von Stroheim's daily footage. As soon as he judged that there was sufficient film to put together a coherent narrative, he made his move. One night von Stroheim's cameras were carted away, and shooting ceased.

When von Stroheim edited *Foolish Wives*, his version of the picture ran twenty-five reels (approximately five and a quarter hours), and he planned to release it in two parts. A top director's final cut was sacrosanct, but Thalberg committed the sacrilegious act of giving the film to a studio editor, Arthur Ripley, with instructions to reduce it further. Ripley pared down von Stroheim's picture to fourteen reels (about three hours), and von Stroheim called the film released by Universal "the skeleton of my dead child." Since the unused material was scrapped, it would be hard to assess the damage done. But even in its trimmed-down version, *Foolish Wives* remains a brilliant, brutal film, with von Stroheim himself giving an electrifying performance as the sexually obsessed Karazmin. What must have been doubly frustrating to Thalberg was the fact that despite its huge popular and critical success, von Stroheim's picture just barely broke even. A potential money-maker had been undermined by its extravagant cost.

It was easy to see the dispute as another battle between art and commerce, but there was more to it than that. Thalberg did not necessarily admire von Stroheim, but he was impressed by the scale of the director's thinking and fascinated by his approach to sexuality. *Foolish Wives* appealed to Thalberg's own interest in sexual perversion. Not, as we shall see, to practice, but to talk about with his wife and friends or to watch in pornographic movies. But he was committed to restoring order to Universal Studios, and he must have realized that bringing von Stroheim under control would be a useful shortcut in asserting his authority. On a personal level, one kind of autocrat met his match in another. Their fighting styles reflected their opposite personalities. Von Stroheim slashed and hacked with a broad, heavy sword—a cavalryman's saber—and Thalberg parried and thrust with a thin, supple fencing foil, and Thalberg had drawn first blood. But the duel was not yet over.

By the time *Foolish Wives* was released the Thalberg–von Stroheim feud had become the talk of Hollywood. It was well known that the young general manager and the director were fencing once more over the script of the latter's next picture, *Merry-Go-Round.*

Set in prewar Vienna, the film was intended as the first in another erotic trilogy unfolding against the background of the decline of the Hapsburg empire. The central character was—inevitably—a count, a man at odds with a world in the process of dramatic change between the rigid, mannered society he had known and the unfamiliar new order that had made him a stranger in his own country. Thalberg rejected von Stroheim's script and prepared a version of his own, which the director angrily refused to accept. Next, Thalberg assigned another writer to work on a third draft—which nobody liked. Finally, Thalberg and von Stroheim—who had never before agreed to work with a collaborator—worked together on a script, arguing over it line by line.

Von Stroheim tailored the role of the count for himself, but Thalberg had learned a bitter lesson from *Foolish Wives* and refused to allow the director to appear in the movie. Von Stroheim accepted this stipulation, but the inference was clear: he could more easily be removed if Thalberg deemed it necessary. Moreover, Thalberg extracted a promise from von Stroheim that he would behave and, as insurance, imposed a unit production manager named James Winnard Hum to oversee the production and control spending. Hum, Thalberg told von Stroheim, had full veto powers.

Merry-Go-Round went into production in August 1922. Von Stroheim set to work in his usual extravagant style, without regard to costs and shooting schedules. He had built a massive reproduction of the landmark amusement center in Prater, Vienna, and its famed attraction the merry-go-round, which was to be the central image of the movie, and he had imported Emperor Franz Josef's carriage from the Austrian capital to add realism to the picture.

His promise to Thalberg that he would stick to the agreed script also went by the board: more and more new material was added until the scenario had grown to 1,500 scenes, or over twice its original length. His quest for microscopic detail continued to halt progress. One day he stormed around the set, cursing the art director and threatening to call Thalberg because the grass on a bridle path was not what he deemed the proper shade of green (this was a black-and-white film, of course). A fanatic about military matters, he spent three days drilling a group of extras who were playing Imperial Dragoons in the correct way to give the regimental salute—for a shot that would take seconds on the screen.

Given his earlier problems with Thalberg, the director's behavior seemed suicidal. It's possible, however, that the idea of dismissal was simply unthinkable to him or that he felt he could go over Thalberg's head to Laemmle, and the studio boss would surely want to keep his most prestigious director happy.

Meanwhile, Thalberg was receiving detailed reports from Hum, and on October 6, six weeks after shooting began and with only 25 percent of the picture completed, von Stroheim's hitherto irresistible force met its immovable object. When he arrived on the set he was called directly to Thalberg's office and fired.

With Edwin Loeb at his side, Thalberg handed von Stroheim a letter signed by himself. It contained a catalog of the director's misdeeds. Thalberg cited "totally inexcusable and repeated acts of insubordination . . . extravagant ideas which you have been unwilling to sacrifice in the slightest particular, repeated and unnecessary delays occasioned by your attitude in arguing against practically every instruction that had been given to you in good faith, and your apparent idea that you are greater and more powerful than the organization that employs you . . . [attempting] to create an organization loyal to yourself, rather than the company you were employed to serve."

Among other difficulties, the letter went on, "has been your flagrant disregard of the principles of censorship, and your repeated and insistent attempts to include . . . situations and incidents so reprehensible that they could not by any reasonable possibility be expected to meet with the approval of the Board of Censorship."

Without a word, von Stroheim walked quickly back to the set and informed his people, then he left the studio. Thalberg made his own announcement to the company, explained the decision, and introduced von Stroheim's replacement, a little-known director named Rupert Julian. Von Stroheim raced to New York to put his case before Carl Laemmle. But the studio boss backed his general manager's decision. It was Thalberg who was irreplaceable.

Why Thalberg chose Julian is uncertain. At the time it was widely seen as a deliberate coup de grace, the ultimate humiliation, because during World War I Julian had been von Stroheim's chief rival in Prussian character parts in war epics. In 1918 he had directed and starred in Universal's successful *The Kaiser—Beast of Berlin*. Since that time, however, he had made only one insignificant western. By no stretch of the imagination could he be regarded as a filmmaker of von Stroheim's caliber.

David Selznick once suggested that Thalberg's choice had been determined by who could be found to take over on such short notice. Thalberg "was faced with the problem of who was available, who will step in on something they haven't prepared," Selznick said. Whatever Thalberg's reasons, the perception at the time was that he had replaced a giant with a garden gnome, and that gnome was clearly there to do his bidding.

His dismissal of von Stroheim was an earthquake in movie circles. "It took great guts and courage," David Selznick observed. "Thalberg was only twenty-two. A matter of hundreds of thousands of dollars in those days could wreck a company which was not strong. Von Stroheim was utterly indifferent over money and could have gone on and spent millions, with nobody to stop him." With one bold stroke "the little fellow at Universal"—as director Rouben Mamoulian called him—had asserted the primacy of the studio over any director and altered forever the balance of power in the movies. "That was the beginning of the storm and the end of the reign of the director, the mighty oak," was how Mamoulian would characterize Thalberg's action years later. "The storm grew fiercer. Following the birth of the first producer, Irving Thalberg, came others, each adding to the ferocity of the storm, each outdoing the others in establishing absolute power, and when the storm subsided there was no D. W. Griffith, no von Stroheim, no Rex Ingram. . . . These men knew only one way of working . . . select the story, have a hand in the writing of the story, cast it, cut it, etc. Deprived of that method, they couldn't function."

Irving Thalberg was now a name everyone knew and a

man everyone wanted to know more about. So the Thalberg stories began. The story of waiting to see Irving, for example, dates from this period. Every producer's day is a maelstrom of conferences and consultations. Thalberg's was doubly so because of his perfectionist's insistence on being involved personally in even the most minute aspect of the production. It had started at Universal in the days when he trusted no one and subsequently became a habit. The room outside his office was perpetually filled with waiting people, and sometimes it took days to gain admission to him. His secretary, Dorothy Howell, who eventually followed him to M-G-M, became very creative in making excuses on his behalf.

His youth was a constant fascination, and there were endless anecdotes about how he was mistaken for a junior employee. Invited to meet him, columnist Louella Parsons arrived for her appointment to be greeted by Thalberg himself. "What's the joke?" she asked. "Where is the new general manager?" Thalberg replied quietly, "I am the general manager." Five minutes of conversation with Universal's Boy Wonder, Parsons wrote, was enough to convince her of his worth. "He might be a boy in looks and age, but it was no child's mind that was being asked to cope with the intricate politics of Universal City."

He could be very touchy about his age and never forgot a slight, as the silent star Nazimova, among others, learned to her cost. Nazimova once snubbed him at a party, mistaking the young head of Universal for a junior member of the staff. Years later, her film career in shambles, she applied to M-G-M for a contract, and there was Thalberg. Nazimova didn't remember the earlier meeting; but Thalberg had not forgotten. "Never, madam," he is reported to have told her with an icy smile. "Not as long as I'm here." One might charitably add that his youth was to blame for his lack of sensitivity about other people's problems. On one occasion, when Curly Stecker, Universal's animal trainer, was mauled by a lion in the studio zoo, Thalberg went to the hospital and lectured Stecker on the proper way to take care of wild animals.

Yet his touchiness about his position was balanced by a refreshing lack of ostentation or self-aggrandizement. He lived in a succession of Los Angeles hotels, never straying very far from his private line of communication to Laemmle, the Western Union office. But in the summer of 1921 one of his telegrams was to Henrietta and William. He told them Laemmle had raised his salary to $400 a week and invited them to come out to live in California. Henrietta arrived within a week.

In a sense, Thalberg's dismissal of von Stroheim had accelerated the inevitable. Market forces—rising demand for movies, more sophisticated audiences—were changing the way the studios deployed their financial and human resources. The need for a more regular flow of what was beginning to be called "product," combined with rising production costs, required better organization and tighter management control. So by asserting the primacy of the studio over any director, Thalberg had spearheaded a change that was eventually to lead to the decline of the independent director. D. W. Griffith saw it coming in the early 1920s: "Rex, you and I are building on sand," he said to fellow director Rex Ingram. A few got out, including Ingram, who for a while made films in the south of France, financed by Marcus Loew, owner of the biggest chain of movie houses in America. Ironically, though, within three months of his clash with Thalberg, von Stroheim resurfaced at the Goldwyn Studios filming Frank Norris's novel *McTeague,* an undertaking that would eventually bring him once more into conflict with his young nemesis at Universal.

In later years, Thalberg himself would describe the von Stroheim debacle as part of the learning experience. Laemmle had pitchforked him into a senior studio post without preparation, and his early years in Hollywood amounted to a crash course in the complex business of film production. His years at Universal were his "freshman years." From the age of twenty his days were filled with rushes, scripts, contracts, rough cuts, and all the ingredients that were to occupy most of his waking hours until the end of his life.

Next to the business side of movies, he was most interested in the writing. Writers intrigued him. He had quickly come to the conclusion that a good story was pivotal to the success of a picture, but he also found the writers themselves more interesting companions than actors, directors, or other film folk. It was perhaps to understand the creative process better that he wrote an original scenario, working nights in the study of Loeb's home. It was a frothy story called *The Dangerous Little Demon*. He put it into production starring Universal's doll-like bathing beauty, Marie Prevost, and gave himself a writer's credit under the name I. R. Irving.

The end result was no better than passable in spite of the attention he lavished on it, and it's not known what lessons he learned from the writing experience. The name I. R. Irving never again appeared on the screen, but Thalberg subsequently made it a practice to work closely with the writers on most of his pictures. He may also have been the only writer he had allowed to work alone on a script, for it was Thalberg who developed the practice of having several writers working on the same screenplay, sometimes in succession and sometimes even simultaneously, unknown to each other. Moreover, *The Dangerous Little Demon* is one of Thalberg's very few films to be based on an original story. His hallmark, as we have said, was the best-selling novel or successful Broadway hit.

His first real test as a producer was *Reputation*, a Laemmle Jewel and therefore an important production. When the melodrama starring Priscilla Bain was close to completion, Laemmle agreed to make a special trip from New York to see what his young discovery could do. When Laemmle arrived with his daughter, Rosabelle, Thalberg was in the cutting room still fussing over the last refinements. He wanted the film to mount to an emotional climax, and to achieve this he spent hours working with the film editor. As he switched and reswitched scenes, the screening was postponed hour after hour, and then to the next day, and then to the day after that.

Two days was all Laemmle was willing to devote to watching a movie, and he announced that he would return to New York the following morning. After some frantic last minute touches, Thalberg reluctantly agreed to screen the picture for Laemmle and his daughter, and *Reputation* endured a difficult late night baptism. When the film was finally over and the lights came on in the projection room, Laemmle was slumped on his seat. He got up, shook himself, and walked out without a word. Thalberg was stunned. "Your father was asleep," he said to Rosabelle. She replied, "He always pretends to be asleep when he cries at a movie." Thalberg spent a miserable night brooding in his office. But in the morning he received a consoling telegram: PLEASE THANK ALL CONNECTED WITH THE FINEST PICTURE EVER TO CARRY MY NAME. It was signed "Carl Laemmle."

Thalberg was on surer ground with *The Hunchback of Notre Dame*. He had read Victor Hugo's novel while suffering from rheumatic fever. His no-expense-spared reproduction of the facade of the Cathedral of Notre Dame and its fifteenth-century environs could not have been larger and more lavish if it had been ordered by von Stroheim himself. Thalberg may have learned something from the director's extravagant style after all, but the other traits in the picture were exclusively his own—a story with good literary pedigree, dramatic star parts, sublimated romance, and a completely neutral director—in this instance Wallace Worsley—to transmit his own vision to the screen.

He had taken to carrying a small notebook in his pocket in which he made notes while watching movies. One entry in 1922 read: *"Oliver Twist,"* followed by the notation "Lon Chaney." The relatively unknown young actor who played Fagin had impressed him and he cast him as the hunchback bell ringer Quasimodo. An expert with makeup, Chaney attached a seventy-pound hump to his back and wore a leather harness to make it impossible to stand up straight. His face was disfigured with mortician's wax in his mouth and a bulging false eye. If his suffering seems heartfelt, much of it was genuine. Thalberg's version of the story toned down Victor Hugo's anti-clericalism, made the archdeacon of Paris's brother Jehan the villain, and supplied a happy ending in which Esmeralda was reunited with her captain after Quasimodo's death. When Thalberg saw the assembled footage, he was excited by Chaney's performance but felt the movie needed more spectacle. To widen its scope, he ordered the film back into production—at the time, something quite novel in the industry. The new scenes were crowd night shoots requiring hundreds of extras. Every available arc light in Hollywood had to be rented or borrowed.

News eventually reached Laemmle that his supposedly economy minded protégé was reshooting scenes from *The Hunchback of Notre Dame* at an additional overbudget cost of $150,000. But Laemmle was on one of his periodic trips to Germany and therefore unable to intervene. Upon returning to the United States, he demanded an explanation. Thalberg assured him that the gamble was worth it. *The Hunchback of Notre Dame* was given an expensive launching and made Lon Chaney a major star. Released in 1923, after Thalberg had left the studio, it remained Universal's most celebrated silent production.

Years later, Laemmle's New York partner Robert Cochrane would remember asking Laemmle how his former secretary "was able to acquire such amazing insight into the business at such an early age." Laemmle didn't know. "Irving was that way from the first," he said. That was, of course, the question at the heart of Thalberg's story. When it came to absorbing information, he was a sponge. Because he had a retentive memory for everything he read or was told, a few months of intensive work at Universal had more than average effect. But what made the difference was his supreme self-confidence. You sift through the available information for a flicker of self-doubt without finding one. When he stood up to von Stroheim, it was without any kind of hesitation. To the editor who was having trouble cutting *The Flirt,* he said, "Cut it all from the point of view of the father, and it will come down to the proper length." When the editor later reported, "It worked!" Thalberg said, "What did you expect it to do?" When Laemmle failed to praise his picture, it diminished his belief not in his picture, but in Laemmle.

3

FATHER
AND SON

By the end of 1922 Thalberg had supervised the production of well over one hundred movies, reorganized Universal from top to bottom, including the studio zoo, centralized managerial control with himself at the center, stopped the defection of the studio's leading stars by offering them better contracts, boosted the studio's prestige by making more of Laemmle's "Jewels," sustained a level of profitability, and was having an affair of sorts with the boss's attractive daughter, Rosabelle.

He had long been infatuated with her from a distance. Sam Marx remembered that his conversations with Thalberg in his early days in New York always seemed to get around to the subject of Rosabelle Laemmle. But by the time Rosabelle was returning his interest, Thalberg had made his mark in Hollywood and was no longer certain of his feelings. He was no longer Laemmle's reserved, youthful secretary. In Hollywood he had become somebody. His combination of youth, power, and ability, plus the story of his illness, which was now common knowledge, had a powerful magnetism for women, and few men in the movie community were more ardently pursued. Also, at closer range, Rosabelle's character both fascinated him and caused him to hesitate, and the relationship was a blustery one. Laemmle's daughter was an extremely willful, headstrong woman who continually tried his patience; and their arguments, like their romance, were welcome fodder for the town's gossip mongers.

Bright, expensively educated in Europe, Rosabelle adopted a rather superior attitude toward Hollywood. She wanted Thalberg to spend more time in New York, and she talked about traveling to Europe, particularly to France and Germany. She herself spoke fluent German (a prerequisite in the Laemmle family) and French. But Hollywood was proving to be Thalberg's promised land, and her criticism of it irritated him.

Henrietta's reaction to her son's first serious romantic attachment may have been a factor. Thalberg's mother was barely civil to Rosabelle in person and openly hostile toward her behind her back. At the time, Henrietta and William lived with Thalberg in a house he had rented on La Cienega Boulevard, where Henrietta watched over him with the same vigilance she had exercised in New York. When he worked late at the studio, he received a telephone summons to come home; when he returned from a social engagement or a date, she was waiting with medicines and complaints that the damp evening air was bad for his condition.

Rosabelle was a girl most mothers would have considered a good catch, but the prospect of an independent-minded daughter-in-law did not appeal to Henrietta, who saw her as both a threat and a hazard. The threat was to her own position as the dominant influence in her son's life and to the task to which she had dedicated her existence, which was to prolonging his. The hazard was to Irving himself, should he be cut off from Henrietta's ministrations. So the woman Irene Selznick once described as "shrewd and inclined to be harsh" made no secret of the fact that, to her, Rosabelle Laemmle was bad news.

Thalberg's relationship with Rosabelle inevitably had repercussions for his position at Universal and was ultimately the cause—or at least one cause—of his leaving the studio. The Laemmles prayed that Irving would marry Rosabelle. Uncle Carl did not relish having the formidable Henrietta as a relation by marriage, but as a group the Hollywood moguls clung to the old world values. They wanted their sons to be educated and their daughters to marry nice Jewish boys. ("What do I have to do?" Louis B. Mayer complained as his eldest daughter, Edith, entered her twenties with no husband in sight. "It isn't enough that I'm L. B. Mayer.")

But although Rosabelle was now actively pursuing Thalberg, accompanying her father to California to see him and monopolizing him on his regular trips to Universal's New York office at 1600 Broadway, Thalberg responded with a noticeable lack of enthusiasm. According to the most reliable accounts, his signals that he was not eager to become Carl Laemmle's son-in-law coincided with Laemmle's own shifting attitude toward his general manager. The reason was not so much the implied slight to Rosabelle, although that was probably a factor. The main problem was that Thalberg had succeeded too well in carrying out his brief to reorganize the studio, and Laemmle was becoming paranoid over Thalberg's control.

Suddenly Thalberg's health became a concern. Laemmle told Loeb he was worried that Universal's operations should be wholly dependent on someone with a serious heart condition. Loeb took this to mean that Laemmle would not have been unhappy to see Thalberg leave the studio. When Thalberg asked for a salary increase, Laemmle, who was notoriously tight-fisted, gave him a fifty-dollar-a-week raise. Thalberg believed his record of profitable pictures merited better recognition. After just two years in Hollywood, he was a marketable talent, and he knew it. He requested more, and faced with a flat refusal from Laemmle he decided that it was time to test his real worth. He told Edwin Loeb to quietly spread the word that he would entertain offers from other studios.

There was an initial flicker of interest from Cecil B. De Mille, who, however, failed to convince his partner, Jesse Lasky. "The boy is a genius," De Mille told Lasky when he learned Thalberg was available. "I can see it. I know it." Lasky wasn't impressed. "Geniuses we have all we need," was his reply. Thalberg did receive an offer from Hal Roach, whose studio specialized in slapstick comedy featuring such comics as Charlie Chase, Stan Laurel, and Oliver Hardy (then not yet working together). Roach needed a head of production and was prepared to pay $550 a week. Thalberg had a good track record, but one blind spot: no experience in comedy production. So at the last minute Roach hired instead a producer who had worked with Mack Sennett. Then, late in 1922, Thalberg met Louis B. Mayer at Loeb's home.

Thalberg felt very tired that evening, but he made a deep, immediate impression on Mayer. Both men were aware that this was a kind of audition, and there was nervous expectation as Mayer sought the younger man's views on a particular production problem. Mayer's studio had made a picture, *Pleasure Mad,* which Mayer found embarrassingly risqué. But the film was already presold to exhibitors. Mayer wanted to know whether he could still dump the picture. Thalberg replied that he would. It was up to the producer to make the decision because he was the ultimate authority at the studio.

Mayer was impressed. He was further taken with Thalberg's explanation of how much he owed to his mother and by his shrewd knowledge of the business. He talked as if he had been a producer for decades instead of only a few years. As Loeb saw him to the door that night, Mayer said, "Tell him if he comes to work for me, I'll look after him as though he were my son."

But Mayer and Thalberg did not join forces immediately. Throughout the remainder of that year they edged toward agreement on a working relationship, so that when it happened on February 15, 1923, it seemed as inevitable as spring following summer. But meantime they had talked movies, finding themselves in agreement—for example— that even a great star needed the backing of a good story. They had sized up one another's characters and come to the conclusion that their opposite natures formed a complementary pairing.

Mayer looked older than his thirty-eight years, Thalberg much younger than twenty-three. Thalberg was painfully frail to look at. Mayer, despite his hypochondria, was robust and powerfully built, with a barrel chest so well muscled that he gave the impression of being stout when he was anything but. Mayer was a strong, ebullient personality who could simulate rage, tears, and even a fainting fit to gain a point. Thalberg was so low key that, as Irene Selznick observed, "it was hard to believe anyone that boyish could be so important."

In his new post of vice president in charge of production at Louis B. Mayer Productions, Thalberg's salary was $600 a week. On the face of it, the move was a step down. Universal was a major studio, Mayer a one-man show. But Mayer had talked of an eventual partnership, a share in the profits, a chance to begin making serious money. Mayer's films were undistinguished, albeit profitable, and as Thalberg noted on a visit to the studios on Mission Road in Los Angeles, economically and efficiently made. Mayer was clearly a capable administrator, with an astute business sense: what he lacked was Thalberg's almost unerring ability to combine quality with commercial success, to bring artistic aspiration in line with the demands of the box office.

Like Thalberg, though, Mayer had no life outside picture production and talked enthusiastically of his plans for improvement and expansion. Laemmle, on the other hand, was an absentee landlord who ran his studio by memo and telegram, devoting a great deal of his time to postwar relief work in Germany. Thalberg disapproved of this approach, believing that Laemmle was neglecting his responsibilities. When, years later, Mayer became active in Republican politics and developed other interests outside moviemaking, such as horse racing, Thalberg acted like Mother Superior toward a nun who had deserted the cloister, accusing him of betraying his vows toward motion pictures and his commitment to the common purpose they had both pursued for decades.

There was also a secret side to the new partnership involving not motion pictures, but real estate. In the twenties, land in southern California was there for the asking, and in January 1923 Louis B. Mayer formed a real estate company in partnership with Irving and William Thalberg (the latter brought in by his son) and the businessmen Melvil Hall, A. B. McGrillis, and J. B. Rhodes. Their first venture was the purchase of 625 valuable acres of land north of Cumberland Drive and west of the Baldy Mountains in Valinda, near West Covina.

The hidden partnership would continue for years, giving a special complexion to Thalberg's relationship with Mayer. It was, too, the one investment that consistently produced a profit for Thalberg. Mayer was to concentrate on property development, and this insulated him from the worst effects of the Depression. Thalberg, on the other hand, would diversify his investments and suffer heavy losses.

But for the moment, as Irene Selznick recalled, Mayer had "found a son without having to raise one" and Thalberg a father to fill the void left by his real one. Mayer had allayed Henrietta's suspicions by promising he would join forces with her in seeing that her son was not overworked and his health protected. Henrietta, of course, had her own reasons for backing Thalberg's change of employment. She hoped that leaving Universal would put distance between him and Rosabelle.

Mayer, on the other hand, was keenly aware that Thalberg would come into contact with his two daughters.

A nice Jewish boy he might be, but apparently a dying one. Before Thalberg's introductory dinner at the Mayer house, the studio head warned his two daughters. "He's attractive. I don't want you girls getting any ideas in your heads, ever." He told them he had almost changed his mind about hiring the young man because of the risk that one of them might take it into her head to want to marry him. While they remained unmarried, every visit by Thalberg was preceded by the same grim reminder: "I don't want to have a young widow on my hands."

Thalberg liked the company of Mayer's daughters, but he too had been warned by Mayer to avoid any romance with either. So he was even-handed in his attentions. At parties and night clubs, he would dance first with one and then the other, and the girls had instructions from Henrietta to pretend to be tired and ask to sit down any time her son became flushed from dancing too energetically. They were also supposed to discourage him from playing tennis and to telephone her immediately if he still insisted on doing so. Henrietta would appear, march onto the court, and snatch away his racket, leaving him looking defiant.

Mayer saw nothing incongruous in the head of production of his studio being publicly embarrassed in this manner. To him mothers were the ultimate authority. He was the archetypal Hollywood pioneer, brought up by a stern, autocratic father against whom he rebelled and a mother to whom he remained devoted all of his life. Born Lazar Meir, he used to say that he had forgotten exactly where in Russia he came from and his date of birth, and had thus appropriated the Fourth of July for his birthday. He had settled with his parents in maritime Canada, where his father built up a junkyard business and salvage operation. By his teens Lazar—now Louis—had broken with his father and moved to Boston, where he began to salvage junk from Boston Harbor. A restless, determined man, he liked to show off his strength by moving heavy objects himself, which helped build up his powerful arm muscles. He would also don diving equipment and survey submerged wrecks in the harbor.

In the spring of 1904 he married Margaret Shenberg, daughter of a cantor in a Boston synagogue. A year later Mayer went into the movie business, leasing a theater in the Haverhill district of Boston. Very successful as a theater operator, he moved into film distribution and then, as the demand for motion pictures increased, set up Louis B. Mayer Productions, first in Brooklyn and—by 1915—on Mission Road in Los Angeles, where he acquired a solid reputation for turning out marketable, medium-budget productions. With Thalberg in charge of moviemaking, Mayer was hoping for a leap in both quality and output that would give the studio a boost in status and profits.

But what vaulted Mayer and Thalberg into the front ranks was a serendipitous sequence of events set in motion by Marcus Loew, the son of a New York waiter, who had progressed from working as a salesman for a garment manufacturing company to operating vaudeville theaters and later, a large and still growing nationwide chain of movie theaters. In his ongoing effort to keep his theaters supplied with pictures, Loew had bought Metro Pictures but was extremely dissatisfied with both that studio's output and its management. While on vacation in Palm Beach he told Lee Shubert, the Broadway stage producer, that he planned to sell Metro. But Shubert, who owned a share in the Goldwyn Pictures Corporation—a studio Sam Goldwyn founded but no longer owned—had another idea. He persuaded Loew not to sell Metro, but to buy Goldwyn Studios instead and merge the two companies. The Goldwyn establishment, though in debt at the time, had a lavishly equipped plant in Culver City. Loew considered the proposal worth investigating. He was then fifty-three but in poor health, so the Loew's merger team consisted of his second-in-command, Nicholas Schenck, and Metro's legal counsel, J. Robert Rubin.

The merger was quickly completed, but that still left the question of who would head the new concern, since on the basis of past performance, neither the executives at Metro nor those at Goldwyn could be regarded as suitable. Rubin, a cultured, well-educated, well-bred lawyer who had been a district attorney in upstate New York before becoming a film attorney, happened also to be L. B. Mayer's counsel and a partner in the latter's studio. In 1923 Loew visited California, and Rubin took him to visit Mayer's studio. They watched the filming of two productions, *Thy Name Is Woman,* and *Women Who Give,* and met Mayer and Thalberg. Loew was favorably impressed by what he saw, as Rubin must have felt that he would be, and Mayer was invited to New York to discuss the possibility of taking over as manager of the new operation.

Mayer and Thalberg went to New York and checked into the Waldorf-Astoria. Several days of complex haggling followed, with Rubin as the intermediary shuttling back and forth between Loew's headquarters and the Waldorf. In due course an agreement was reached whereby Loew's Inc. bought Mayer's studio for $76,000, including its stars, directors, and staff, and Mayer himself was named West Coast head of the new company—the triple merger of a long established but inefficient studio, a financially ailing one, and Mayer's smaller but thriving outfit.

In a secret profit-sharing deal, Mayer, Thalberg, and Rubin were to receive 20 percent of the new company's profits after an annual dividend of two dollars per share had been paid to holders of common stock. Mayer was to decide whether a film would be released with the trademark Metro-Goldwyn or Metro-Goldwyn-Mayer, but in the former instance the film credits would include a title that read "Produced and Presented by Louis B. Mayer." After 1925, however, this provision fell by the wayside because the studio became permanently known as Metro-Goldwyn-Mayer.

The new company's raison d'être was to provide suitable "product" for Loew's 111 movie theaters (including the State and the Academy of Music in New York), with an estimated seating capacity of 150,000. There were at the time twelve more Loew's houses under construction, plus a small theater chain acquired along with the Goldwyn Pictures Corporation, including half an interest in the New York Capitol, then the largest and most luxurious movie palace in America.

Though the signatory of the main agreement was Louis Mayer, the fact that Thalberg was included in the profit-sharing deal indicated that his worth to the new company had been fully recognized. Following the merger, Mayer boasted publicly that the new studio would produce fifty-two pictures a year. He was really committing Thalberg to deliver on that figure, which was unrealistic—at least for the time being. Fortunately for Thalberg, the agreement stipulated a more modest minimum target of fifteen pictures in the first year in order to avoid cancellation, and that was within his scope.

The merger had cost them both something. For the first time, Mayer was no longer his own master. In the new organization, he reported to Marcus Loew and Nick Schenck. As for Thalberg, fifteen films a year or fifty, he faced a formidable task not calculated to improve his delicate condition. Both Mayer and Thalberg knew the merger amounted to a tremendous opportunity: the chance to form a major production company, to become key players in their industry. But first they would have to weld three disparate organizations into a cohesive studio, with its own distinctive style and common identity. Both must have known who would carry the main burden for giving form and substance to their ambitious venture.

On April 26, 1924—one of the most important days in movie history—they stood side by side on a wooden platform on the lawn outside Goldwyn Studios at Culver City, a locality on the southern edge of Los Angeles that that afternoon became a fixed point in world geography, and inaugurated Metro-Goldwyn-Mayer. Thalberg was a month away from his twenty-fifth birthday; he had been in

California barely five years, and he watched the opening celebrations not as an employee of the new studio, but as a partner. Seated among the guests were William and Henrietta. For Thalberg's mother it was a moment of triumph perhaps greater than for her own son.

Bunting hung from the platform, in the center of which was a massive portrait of Marcus Loew, father of the triple merger. A navy band played, and employees from Metro, Goldwyn Studios, and Mayer's own company gathered to witness the ceremony and no doubt to ponder their own future in the new corporation.

The impressive array of movie talent included, from the Mayer company, directors Fred Niblo, John Stahl, and Hobart Henley and actors Huntley Gordon, Renée Adorée, Marie Prevost (brought over from Universal by Thalberg), and a new arrival named Norma Shearer; from Metro, Mae Murray, Ramon Novarro, Jackie Coogan, and directors King Vidor, Rex Ingram, and Robert Z. Leonard; and from Goldwyn, Eleanor Boardman, Aileen Pringle, and directors Victor Seastrom, and Thalberg's old enemy Erich von Stroheim. Vice President Mayer made the inaugural speech.

"From the production standpoint," he intoned in the voice he reserved for solemn occasions, "you can count on it that Metro-Goldwyn-Mayer will reach a point of perfection never approached by any other company. If there is one thing I insist upon, it is quality." The new company's motto, Mayer announced, was *Ars Gratia Artis*, "Art for Art's Sake." Next he read out telegrams of congratulation from President Calvin Coolidge and his secretary of commerce, Herbert Hoover, and then Abe Lahr, former head of Goldwyn Pictures Corp., handed him a giant key engraved in gold with the word *SUCCESS*.

As Mayer spoke, there was a stir among the guests: director Marshall Neilan pointedly walked out, blowing a loud raspberry as he went and taking the regular members of his film crew with him. Neilan's protest reflected the deep unease of moviemakers in the Metro and Goldwyn companies over Thalberg's reputation for tight control. Thalberg himself did not speak at the inauguration, although he was introduced as second vice president and supervisor of production (Mayer was the first vice president).

While Mayer conducted a purge of Metro and Goldwyn executives, replacing them with his own team, Thalberg began tackling the work in progress in the three studios, including two inherited problem productions of major proportions, both pressing for immediate attention. The filming on location in Italy of *Ben-Hur* was out of control; closer to home there was *Greed,* a just completed film of massive length based on Frank Norris's novel *McTeague* and directed by Erich von Stroheim at Goldwyn before the merger.

It must have been a shock to von Stroheim to find himself once more under Thalberg's iron fist. As M-G-M came into being, the director had finished editing down his customary mass of footage to a work print consisting of twenty-two reels. *Greed* was a gritty, realistic account of the effects of money on five poor people of below average intelligence. In von Stroheim's hands it became an experiment in dispensing with the accepted convention of adapting a novel for the screen and, instead, filming the narrative almost page by page. Von Stroheim had shot the film on location in San Francisco and in Death Valley, and after weeks of cutting he had reduced the footage to five hours, which he felt was a minimum screen time for a six-hundred-page novel.

Then Thalberg reappeared in his life, hovering above him on the platform outside the Goldwyn Studios like an avenging angel. Von Stroheim had not forgotten how Thalberg had shriveled *Foolish Wives* to the "bones," and he wanted to spare his new picture the same fate. Desperate to avoid a repetition of what he considered philistine butchery, he quickly dispatched an edited print to New York to his friend Rex Ingram, whose work he admired, with an appeal for help: Would Ingram pare down the picture further?

Ingram and his editor worked on *Greed* the whole summer and eventually reduced the twenty-two reels to fifteen. Thalberg viewed the shortened version and then did what von Stroheim had hoped to prevent: he gave the film to a studio editor, who cut it down to ten reels, or less than half its original length. Albert Lewin, Thalberg's new assistant, was one of the few people to have seen von Stroheim's original cut.

"It took me several days to see it," he recalled. "It was superb, jammed full of symbolism. [Von Stroheim] liked symbols very much. I was thrilled!"

As released by M-G-M, *Greed* remained a picture of extraordinary force, but the critics were less thrilled. Thalberg was generally given credit for reducing its length and von Stroheim blamed for making it unreasonably long in the first place. At the time, Robert E. Sherwood's description in *Life* of the director as "a genius . . . in need of a stopwatch" was a view shared by many.

Over the years, the allotment of blame has been reversed. For decades a museum classic, *Greed* is seen as a celebrated victim of the studio system, and more precisely of Thalberg's determination to squeeze every picture into his own concept of an M-G-M production and his own policy of bringing "dignity" and "quality"—two of his favorite words—to the medium.

Some time later Thalberg would, as we shall see, devise the concept of the "prestige picture," a film that might not necessarily do well at the box office yet bring kudos and goodwill to the studio, attracting respectable talent into the company's orbit. But he had a clear, highly subjective idea of what constituted a prestige picture, and *Greed* hardly fitted into that category. From all accounts he felt that audiences would not respond to its unrelenting squalor. In his view audiences did not flock to the movies to see their own and other people's problems replicated on the screen. When he thought of motion pictures as a form of artistic expression, it was not in the shape of a mentally deficient woman traumatized by her husband's brutishness on their wedding night, as in von Stroheim's picture, and thereafter sleeping with a sack of money as her sole bedmate.

In this instance, Thalberg miscalculated public fascination with the bizarre. Despite its poor critical reception, *Greed* netted the studio a quarter of a million dollars in domestic receipts. Von Stroheim, of course, blamed its failure to do even better on botched editing. Years later he asked Al Lewin to find him the discarded footage. As Lewin remembered it, "I had Margaret Booth, the head of the department, go into the vaults, and she made a terrific search: nothing. It had all been scrapped. There wasn't a single thing left but the terribly short version." So at the heart of the discussion about the artistic loss is a five-hour movie almost nobody has ever seen. The *Greed* that shows up on critics' lists of the greatest silent movies is the "uncut" *Greed*, as edited by von Stroheim, its reputation resting on the testimony of a handful of people for whom von Stroheim screened his rough cut in 1924. The amazing if imperfect version distributed by Loew's remains an overwhelming experience at two and a half hours: at five hours it would probably be unbearable.

Despite his resentment, von Stroheim's next picture was . . . for Irving Thalberg. One reason was that the director owed Goldwyn Studios a picture, and all contractual obligations to the three companies had been transferred to Metro-Goldwyn-Mayer. But the deciding factor was that Thalberg had dangled in front of him the irresistible chance of directing a film set in the city and the period he claimed as his own: turn-of-the-century Vienna.

The picture was *The Merry Widow,* naturally minus the music and equally naturally plus von Stroheim's own bent perspective of the sexuality. It is inconceivable that Thalberg expected von Stroheim to portray the operetta's light romanticism, yet he gave the director a free hand to tell the story in his own way. In return, von Stroheim accepted another writer as collaborator to help him shape the script, a Belfast-born Irishman named Benjamin Glazer who had come to Hollywood via journalism in Philadelphia and was an M-G-M contract writer. Thalberg gave von Stroheim the ex-Goldwyn star Mae Murray for the title role and John Gilbert for the prince. Not wanting to tie up a major star like Murray for the long months of a typical von Stroheim picture, Thalberg offered the director a $10,000 bonus if the film was shot in less than six weeks and $7,500 if completed in seven weeks.

L. B. Mayer was aghast at von Stroheim's script, which drooled over the seamy underside of *belle époque* Vienna. Mayer had been expecting glamour and waltzes. What he got was uniforms, sexual perversion, alcoholism, and corruption in high and low places. In the operetta the liaisons take place discreetly off stage; in von Stroheim's film they burgeoned into full-scale orgies. Mayer complained to Thalberg. But if Thalberg had wanted moderation, he would surely not have chosen von Stroheim. He made a number of structural changes but otherwise accepted the director's narrative, high jinks and all, and shooting began on December 1, 1924. Thalberg felt that in *The Merry Widow*, unlike in *Greed*, the basic box office elements were all there—a famous classic, famous stars, spectacle, even a happy ending. Everything else could be controlled.

Besides, Thalberg liked the script's sexual innuendo and was quite prepared to test the limits of censorship. As usual, von Stroheim got carried away and Thalberg frequently had to rein him in. On one occasion the director showed Thalberg a long sequence of the inside of a shoe closet. As shot followed shot of boots, women's high heels, and lace-ups, Thalberg became first impatient and then irritated. "What the hell's all this?" he asked the director.

"I wanted to show the character was a foot fetishist," von Stroheim replied, and in fact, the character actually dies in the shoe closet.

"Well, you're a footage fetishist," Thalberg snapped back.

But the real clash of wills was between the director and

Mae Murray, who fought a losing battle to dominate the production. The diminutive blonde, celebrated for her "bee-stung" lips, arrived with her own hairdresser, makeup man, and cameraman. As the director's regular cameraman was also present, there were two camera crews on the set whenever the star was involved.

From the start she was appalled at the director's bizarre approach to the story. When she found herself taking part in a full-scale orgy, it was too much and she complained to Thalberg.

"This is filth!" she told Thalberg. "Kissing people's bottoms and kissing feet. The old man behaving obscenely with a closet full of shoes."

"The man's a genius. He's giving the picture dimension," Thalberg said, knowing full well that little of the orgy footage would be allowed by the censor.

"Degeneracy is what he's giving it," Murray replied. "And you're letting him."

In retrospect, Mae Murray concocted the absurd theory that Thalberg had cast her in *The Merry Widow* to undermine her position as a star, thus leaving the coast clear for Norma Shearer, in whom—incidentally—Thalberg had shown little interest by that time. When she got no satisfaction from Thalberg, Mae Murray appealed to Mayer, who was more sympathetic. Unlike Thalberg, he was shocked by some of the footage, and when Mae Murray walked off the set following a public clash with von Stroheim in January 1925, Mayer intervened and fired the director. To take von Stroheim's place, Mayer assigned Monta Bell, generally known as a director of light comedies. But the crew and hundreds of extras, among whom was a still unknown young actor named Clark Gable, refused to take direction from Bell and threatened to go on strike if von Stroheim was not reinstated. Mayer held an urgent meeting with von Stroheim and the star and worked out a compromise: von Stroheim was rehired and agreed to apologize—if Mae Murray apologized to him first.

It was left to Mayer to handle the crisis, because on January 23, 1925, Thalberg had suffered a heart attack. He had collapsed at the studio and was taken to the hospital and put on the critical list. All day long and the following night his condition was serious. While his mother kept vigil in the hospital, Mayer gloomily contemplated the prospect of life at M-G-M without Irving, and his recent triumph began to look like a prospective nightmare.

The following morning Thalberg was declared out of danger, but the doctors said the illness had been a warning against overwork. They said he would need to rest in bed for a long period. For the twenty-six-year-old producer the heart attack was a grim reminder of how little time was left and how much he wanted to do. He knew that he had what it took to turn M-G-M into an important, prestigious studio and to reap considerable financial benefit, but it would be a race to achieve his goals. Henrietta hovered around his bed, protesting: Thalberg lay immobile on his back, viewing rushes of *The Merry Widow* and other M-G-M films in production projected on the ceiling of his hospital room. Once he was allowed to sit up, he read scripts late into the night and held bedside story conferences with his associates. Within a month he was on his feet. A fortnight later, brushing aside objections from his mother and doctors, he was back at work at the studio just in time to edit the final print of *The Merry Widow*.

Von Stroheim had finished the picture in thirteen weeks of shooting, which was for him a relatively short time, at a total cost of $600,000. Thalberg ordered some additional scenes of waltzing couples, plus two romantic scenes between Murray and John Gilbert, but none were used in the final version of the picture. Thalberg removed as little as ten minutes out of von Stroheim's rough cut, leaving *The Merry Widow* a long film. It opened on August 25 in New York to rave reviews and ran for months, and it was one of the top grossing pictures of 1925. In accordance with the terms of the merger, Louis B. Mayer was given credit for producing the picture. Of Irving G. Thalberg there was, of course, no mention.

He returned to find that Mayer had not renewed von Stroheim's contract, a decision with which he did not necessarily disagree. When it became clear that no other studio would engage him as a director, von Stroheim moved to Europe and worked mostly as an actor. Seven years later he returned to Hollywood to appear opposite Garbo in *As You Desire Me*. He had been summoned by Irving Thalberg.

4

MORE THAN ALL THE DOCTORS

It is almost beyond my conception that such stuff should have been passed by people of even moderate intelligence . . . that anyone could have tolerated for one single day, the ill-fitting costumes, the incongruous action, the almost silly and typical European movements of the people; not in my wildest imagination could I have pictured anything that broad."

So wrote Irving Thalberg to director Fred Niblo in September 1924 when he first screened footage of *Ben-Hur* sent from Rome. Niblo had just arrived in the Italian capital, heading a rescue mission sent by Mayer and Thalberg. Like *Greed*, *Ben-Hur* was another inherited Goldwyn Studios picture. Based on General Lew Wallace's flamboyant bestseller, it had originally been excluded from the merger deal because Marcus Loew owned it jointly with three others, including Broadway producer Florenz Ziegfeld, Jr., and did not want to further dilute his profits by having to share them with his new M-G-M partners.

Thalberg was relieved not to be involved. Financially the film had been a drain of Goldwyn resources; the quality of the filming was poor, and progress was slow. The tiny but formidable scenarist June Mathis called the shots. Besides writing the *Ben-Hur* script, she had also put together the ingredients of the picture. She had selected her lover, George Walsh, a well-built but untalented actor, for the title role, and Francis X. Bushman to play opposite him. As director she chose a mild, alcoholic Englishman, Charles Brabin, whose chief claim to fame was that he was married to the screen vamp Theda Bara. "The whole company had lost their frame of reference," recalled Irene Selznick, who was to accompany her father to Rome when he took personal charge of the situation. "There was no efficiency. The script wasn't completed . . . the footage was terrible. They'd got huge sets, but you never saw them on film."

Faced with the spiraling costs, Loew soon changed his mind and asked M-G-M to take over the production. Thalberg regarded the entire Italian expedition as sheer folly and wanted to move the production to the M-G-M back lot, but that was not part of their brief from Marcus Loew. He felt that the move would be too expensive and insisted on continuing the picture in Italy. So Thalberg sent out Niblo with writers Bess Meredyth and Carey Wilson to take over the film. Niblo's first wire to Culver City immediately upon his arrival in Rome was hardly encouraging. It began with the apocalyptic announcement: 200 REELS OF FILM WASTED. BAD PHOTOGRAPHY TERRIBLE ACTION.

When Thalberg saw the film he agreed with Niblo's diagnosis. Everything shot to date was scrapped, and Niblo, the solid, dependable filmmaker who specialized in action pictures, started afresh. June Mathis was sent home. Charles Brabin was replaced by Ramon Novarro, a promising Metro star who was being built up at great expense as a box office attraction.

So two months later the movie had a new, powerful, expertly constructed script, a better director, and a more

contemporary leading man, but the problems continued—
slow progress, uneven quality, high costs. One of the obsta-
cles—at least in the visitors' view—was the gap in technical
and professional standards between the visiting American
filmmakers and their Italian counterparts. At the time Italy
had a thriving movie industry, but it was purely for local
consumption, and its craftsmen may indeed have fallen
short of Hollywood's exacting standards. The number of
available Italian actors was small but good, Niblo reported
to Thalberg. But he kept up a stream of requests to the
studio for technical staff—special effects cameramen, optical
effects specialists, model makers, and on one occasion an
entire makeup department.

Thalberg grumbled at the cost but did not hesitate to
send the people. He had spotted the picture's potential to
be the blockbuster the new studio needed to consolidate the
merger and make a name for itself. "We are making great
progress and establishing a wonderful reputation for our
Company in the product we are turning out," he wrote to
Niblo, "and fortunately it is turning out to be not only quality product, but commercially successful. But naturally, *Ben-
Hur,* is the big ace in the hole. It, and you, and all of us
are probably the subject of more conversation in Hollywood
and New York than anything else. Certainly, we have got
to come through with the picture."

A succession of labor disputes further disrupted the production, but there was also bad luck. When Niblo began
shooting the film's centerpiece, the chariot race in the
Circus Maximus, horses were killed, Novarro's chariot ran
out of control, and Francis X. Bushman, who played Messala, crashed into it and rode over the wreckage. Everyone
was convinced Novarro had been killed, but he had miracu-
lously escaped without injury. With bad news flowing in
from Rome, Marcus Loew again capitulated and asked
Louis Mayer to inspect the production personally and, if
necessary, transfer it to Hollywood.

Mayer sailed for Rome in August 1924, accompanied by

his wife and two daughters and by Thalberg's pleas to bring the production home. His departure was an indication of his trust in Thalberg, who was left in sole charge of an increasingly busy studio. Thalberg kept him informed of M-G-M's rapid progress by means of brief, friendly wires. THINGS GOING SPLENDIDLY, he assured Mayer on December 1, 1924. MERRY WIDOW AND SEVEN OTHER PRODUCTIONS SHOOTING WISH YOU WERE BACK HERE LOVE YOURSELF AND FAMILY.

A few weeks in Rome in which he developed a serious infection of the gums, compounded by a dislike for Italian cooking that prompted him to send his wife in search of a good kosher butcher, convinced Mayer that *Ben-Hur* could be saved from disaster only in Culver City. The production was moved in January, hastened by a fire that swept through the property warehouse. The American production unit was convinced it was the work of one or more Italian arsonists.

There was an unexpected bonus from *Ben-Hur*. In Berlin to check out what was happening in the German film industry, Mayer saw a Swedish movie, *The Atonement of Gösta Berling*. Impressed by the film, Mayer offered its director, Mauritz Stiller, an M-G-M contract. But the Swedish filmmaker would accept only on one condition: that M-G-M agree to sign the star of his picture, his protégée, Greta Garbo. Stiller's picture was her first feature film, and Mayer had not been impressed by her performance as an Italian countess married into the Berling family. She was heavily built by Hollywood standards, and her acting was wooden. Still, Mayer finally agreed to sign her to get Stiller: she was given a three-year contract at $250 a week.

On his return Mayer attempted to persuade Thalberg to replace Fred Niblo with another director once *Ben-Hur* was safely in California. From what he had seen in Rome, Mayer felt Niblo was not getting the best out of the actors, nor did he have the stature to make *Ben-Hur* the major movie M-G-M wanted. Mayer even secretly approached

Ernst Lubitsch, who was ready to take over the picture. Thalberg at first agreed to fire Niblo, then decided it would be too time-consuming to switch directors, leaving us with the tantalizing but unfulfilled prospect of Lubitsch directing the famous blockbuster.

The truth was that Niblo was the kind of efficient director Thalberg liked to work with to transmit his own ideas. Once filming began again in Culver City, Thalberg took over direct control, and Niblo's highly professional direction served his purpose better than that of a virtuoso like Lubitsch. As the studio's art director, Cedric Gibbons faced the first of many major challenges designing and building sections of ancient Rome on the M-G-M back lot, including a huge replica of the Circus Maximus. The filming of *Ben-Hur* had focused attention on the new company, and a crowd of celebrities—including Mary Pickford, Douglas Fairbanks, Lillian Gish, and Marion Davies—were on hand at Thalberg's invitation early on the morning of Saturday, October 3, 1925, for the filming of the chariot race. Dozens of cameras were placed strategically around the set, hidden behind statues, buried in sandpits, placed on cars, and positioned among the spectators on the terraces of the vast racing arena built at a cost of $207,000.

Prior to the filming, Thalberg had received a memo from the studio's special effects department giving him details of how each of the three major chariot crashes was to be achieved. In the climactic third crash, Ben-Hur's chariot locks wheels with Messala's, ripping off Messala's wheel. As Messala goes down, another chariot plows into the wreckage. Immediately another chariot comes round the *spina,* or racetrack, tries to leap the wreckage but fails, piling in a heap on top of Messala, his horses, and wrecked chariot.

Messala's wheel was specially sprung to come off when it locked with Ben-Hur's wheel. "Messala's and Ben-Hur's chariots will be connected by an iron bar so that in rounding the corner, they will form an almost perfect arc," the memo stated. Ben-Hur's chariot was to slide along the bar, ripping

Messala's wheel off its axle. "Padded wreckage to take the place of Messala's horses and chariot on the ground . . . second team scrambles through wreckage, finally succeeding in clearing and making exit as other teams pass camera in foreground." Then, said the memo, "We build outline of Messala's and other team on the ground as we bring [a] third team into the scene." This team would attempt to clear the wreckage by squeezing against the wall of the arena, but the team and chariot would overturn onto the wreckage instead.

"This effect is [achieved by constructing a] runway built on level to head of wreckage," the memo explained, "then gradually slope on an angle of 40 degrees, greased midway to cause team to slide onto pile while wires on chariot and outside horse will be pulled causing the complete turnover of team and chariot."

While the sequence was being set up, Thalberg walked to the middle of the arena. Dwarfed by its vastness, he surveyed the crowd. "How many people do you have up there, Joe?" he asked J. J. Cohn, the studio production manager.

Cohn replied, "Thirty-nine hundred." Thalberg told him, "We need more."

Cohn, who was notorious for his cost cutting, protested that it was going to be hard to find more extras at eight o'clock on a Saturday morning.

Thalberg replied, "Pull them in off the street, if necessary."

So Cohn and his assistants fanned out over Culver City and brought in another four hundred extras. Ordinary people taken from the streets, markets, trolleys, buses, and diners found themselves Romans for a day, wearing togas and cheering Ramon Novarro and Francis X. Bushman. When Cohn wanted to call a halt at lunchtime, Thalberg gave instructions to shoot straight through the afternoon. He wanted to finish most of the sequence by the end of the day.

"But these people are hungry, they may riot," Cohn protested.

"Fine," said Thalberg. "That'll add some realism to the scene."

With his doctors and Henrietta protesting that he should be taking things easy, Thalberg continued to force the pace. He was determined to have the picture ready for release at the end of the year, and as usual, he had a hand in every aspect of production from titling to special effects to editing. He bombarded the special effects department with instructions such as "Pick up the shepherds in the distance as they begin to be lighted by an unusual light, a star falling in their direction, in reality coming toward the city of Bethlehem." In the editing, which seemed to go on endlessly, he used about 25 percent of Niblo's Rome footage, including the Joppa Gate sequence in which a tile is dislodged from the roof of Ben-Hur's house and falls on the governor passing by in a parade below.

The New York office requested that he cut the shots of Christ's crucifixion on the grounds that they were too gruesome, suggesting they be replaced by a strong light. Thalberg fired off a long protest to Nicholas Schenck, arguing that "every school child has been trained to see pictures of Christ crucified with blood coming from the nails on the cross and the thorns around his head. . . ." If the shot were removed, he wrote, "the greatness of the great sacrifice of this greatest figure in history has no actual meaning. We do not even feel at the end of the picture that he is dead." Throughout his life Thalberg would occasionally talk of filming the life of Christ, who fascinated him not from a religious point of view, but as a historical figure. Thalberg was not, in fact, religious: that aspect of her son's upbringing had not been high on Henrietta's list of priorities, and when he was filming *Ben-Hur* the M-G-M research department had to tell him when the shofar, the Jewish ram's horn, was sounded, and how many times.

The successful preview in Pasadena on December 20 provided another instance of Thalberg's total involvement in everything to do with the production. "Please see that the organist who played for us during the preview at the Criterion Theatre gets $10.00, if you think that is sufficient," he wrote to Eddie Mannix, M-G-M's general manager. "He did a very good job."

Thalberg was still too unwell to be in New York on December 30 when *Ben-Hur* had its triumphant premiere, but afterward Nick Schenck wired the good news: WELL KID YOU WERE REPAID LAST NIGHT FOR ALL THE HARD WORK YOU PUT IN ON BEN HUR. IT WAS THE MOST MAGNIFICENT OPENING I HAVE EVER WITNESSED. THE ONLY TIME I REMEMBER GETTING AS BIG A THRILL AS I DID DURING THE CHARIOT RACE WAS AT THE DEMPSEY FIRPO FIGHT AND THE ENTIRE AUDIENCE WAS AS EXCITED AS I WAS. THINK OF IT IRVING WE NOW HAVE THREE PICTURES RUNNING AT TWO DOLLARS ON BROADWAY TO A SELLOUT BUSINESS. MORE POWER TO YOU. From the start, the picture was both a critical and a box office triumph.

I CANNOT TELL YOU HOW HAPPY I AM OVER OUR SUCCESS, Thalberg wired Fred Niblo, who was also in New York for the premiere. IT HAS DONE MORE THAN ALL THE DOCTORS TO MAKE ME FEEL BETTER. This cycle of draining energy on a production and then getting a charge from its success was a pattern for Thalberg. And given its past history, *Ben-Hur* was an outstanding success, even though, despite the $7 million it grossed in its first year, it did little more than cover its huge cost to the studio. But it played an important role in establishing Metro-Goldwyn-Mayer's reputation as an important studio. It also helped establish a rule, from which the studio rarely deviated, that no film would be made in a foreign country, and for more than two decades afterward M-G-M location units rarely strayed farther than the San Fernando Valley.

The rescue of *Ben-Hur* from disaster was another chapter in the legend of Irving Thalberg, a legend that took no account of the physical toll involved but portrayed him as Hollywood's miracle worker. Thalberg himself regarded *Ben-Hur* as one of his outstanding achievements, and a

Ramon Novarro *Ben-Hur* poster hung on the wall of his famous outer office, where stars, executives, and writers waited to be admitted to his presence.

M-G-M had proved its worth by turning other people's base metal into box office gold, but the studio had yet to mount a major production of its own. Its very first movie released as a Metro-Goldwyn-Mayer picture was *Sinners in Silk,* "a picturization of the activities of the new generation whose hymn is jazz, whose slogan is speed." It was a trendy movie, but not an important production. That distinction went to *The Big Parade,* which started life as a John Gilbert vehicle but grew in scope and importance when Thalberg realized its potential.

Thalberg had asked King Vidor, "What kind of material appeals to you? Tell me the subjects that interest you."

A man of few words, Vidor replied, "Wheat, steel, and war." It was Vidor's way of expressing his interest in large social themes and their effect on "Mr. Anybody," as he sometimes used to call the central character in his movies.

But populism didn't appeal to Thalberg: he believed Mr. Anybody's place was not on the screen, but in the audience. Nor was he too keen on wheat or steel: agriculture and industry were to figure marginally in M-G-M movies. War, however, had possibilities. There had not been a powerful war film with the possible exception of D. W. Griffith's *Hearts of the World,* and that had been seven years earlier.

He tried to buy the film rights to *What Price Glory?*, the Broadway war comedy by Maxwell Anderson and Laurence Stallings, but the Fox Film Corporation beat him to it. Thalberg, who found it hard to abandon an idea once it had taken hold, then tried to persuade Fox to sell him the rights, but he was turned down. If anything, such setbacks only deepened his resolve. In this instance his solution was to persuade Stallings, who had lost a leg fighting in France in World War I, to write an original screenplay. Traveling west together from New York on the train, they worked on the outline of *The Big Parade.*

The film started out as a John Gilbert picture with a budget of $200,000. Allowed considerable latitude with Stallings's script, Vidor changed the central character of Johnny Apperson (pun intended) from a star role to a human characterization—in fact, Gilbert's finest performance—and the picture from a star vehicle to an antiwar epic. As he viewed the dailies, Thalberg began to realize that the picture had the potential to be something more important than what it had originally set out to be. He decided to enlarge the scope of the production so that *The Big Parade* would live up to its title.

The production cast early shadows of disagreement over the Thalberg-Mayer relationship. When Mayer discovered that John Gilbert was supposed to have a leg shot off in the picture, he was uneasy about a romantic idol being shown with a serious physical handicap, and told Vidor that Gilbert should only limp. But Thalberg went over his head to Nicholas Schenck, who ruled that the script had to be followed to the letter. Mayer was also against the portrayal of John Gilbert as an anti-hero filled with the anguish and self-doubt of the early 1920s. Again, Vidor went to Thalberg; again, Mayer was overruled. Mayer wanted important scenes showing the leading character's mother. Thalberg cut out the sequences. Yet it was Mayer who went to New York to persuade Loew's Inc. to approve an additional $75,000 Thalberg needed to make his expansion plans a reality, returning with the money. Vidor filmed additional battle scenes, including the famous sequence of American infantrymen marching through a sunny forest to almost certain death. In the end the picture cost $382,000 but made a profit of $3.5 million. It was the picture that brought confidence to the new studio, and once again it had everything M-G-M took pride in: story, stars, romance, sentimental ideas, and a vague but assertive air of seriousness.

Critics praised *The Big Parade* as a thrilling spectacle and Vidor as an outstanding director. Vidor did less well financially from it. Years later, he revealed that Thalberg had promised him 25 percent of the profits of the picture but failed to meet his promise. As a result, Vidor lost nearly $800,000. The director and Thalberg also clashed over the editing of the picture. When Thalberg cut the picture without consulting him, Vidor scoured the editing rooms at M-G-M to rescue his lost footage, forcing an irritated Thalberg to accept the director's cut. In spite of all this, Vidor remained a close friend of Thalberg's until the latter's death.

The Big Parade is to Ford Madox Ford's then best-selling novel *No More Parades*—clearly Stallings's inspiration—as water is to champagne. But in 1925, popular culture was the call of demagogues and tycoons alike. To stand in the way of popular culture was unpatriotic, stuffy, stupid, and antiquated. *The Big Parade* was seen by everybody who congratulated themselves on realizing that war was wicked and pointless. It was part of Thalberg's insight that he could foresee such public reaction.

In the fiscal year ending August 31, 1925, its first full year of operation, the studio reported a profit of $4.7 million. Thalberg had supervised the production of forty-six films, had had his first heart attack, and demanded his first raise, thus establishing a pattern that would be in effect for the ensuing decade—overwork, followed by a sharp reminder of his condition, which would in turn dramatically illustrate his importance to the studio and cause him to raise the price of his own worth. Since Thalberg's deal with Loew's was linked to Mayer's and Robert Rubin's, Thalberg's demand for a raise forced Mayer to request a revision of the whole package.

The timing, then, was anything but coincidental. M-G-M was still euphoric over the success of *Ben-Hur*. As Nick Schenck had told Thalberg, M-G-M had three pictures running simultaneously in Broadway movie theaters, and no one was more aware than Thalberg himself who merited the most credit for this remarkable accomplishment. Moreover, no one was more aware that Mayer's five-month trip to Rome from August to December 1924 had clearly shown any remaining skeptics who controlled production at M-G-M.

The negotiations took time because Thalberg was just as determined in his pursuit of money as he was in his pursuit of quality in the movies, and he rejected one offer after another. Then what is it you want? Schenck asked him. Thalberg wanted $2,000 a week, and he got it—an increase of almost 360 percent over his previous pay of $650. Equally important for Thalberg, he now received the same salary as Mayer himself. Mayer had gone from $1,500 to $2,000, Rubin from $600 to $1,000. Additionally, the three M-G-M executives were guaranteed that their annual collective share of the profits would never fall below half a million dollars.

The favorite son's worth was now measured on an equal basis with that of the surrogate father. Moreover, Thalberg was now written about in the extravagant terms hitherto reserved for movie stars. "The more Mr. Thalberg talked, the more intrigued we became," one interviewer wrote in *Motion Picture* magazine in the spring of 1926. "To us, he seemed a combined Horatio Alger hero, Peter Pan, Napoleon, Falstaff, and J. Pierpont Morgan."

The article went on breathlessly to quote the gushing view of scenarist Agnes Christine Johnson that "if he were a politician, he'd be Mussolini; if he were a poet, he'd be Shelley; if he were an actor, he'd be Barrymore! He's so marvellous that no one who doesn't know him can believe it. Seeing him sitting in with all the important people, looking such a boy, and deferred to by everybody, you'd think that either they were crazy or you were. But if you stayed and listened, you'd understand. He has a mind like a whip. Snap! He had an idea—the right idea—the only idea!" Thalberg smiled his boyish smile and took it all in stride. But it would not have escaped Mayer's notice that no one was comparing him with Shelley or Napoleon; no one regarded him as a luminescent new personality. Thus, the first drops of ice water began to trickle onto the warmth of their relationship. Mayer respected Thalberg's ability, his rapidly growing reputation, and the fact that he was becoming something of a cult hero. Yet it was just those things that were making Irving dangerous. Mayer could let himself think of Irving as the son he never had and as a loyal prince. But every king knows that a prince waits to succeed him. So the demonstrations of paternal love were mixed with others of concealed resentment and, eventually, suspicion.

It did not help that Thalberg failed to respond to Mayer's fatherly affection on the same demonstrative level. An effusive performance by Mayer would be rewarded by a boyish smile from Thalberg. Even his low-key working style contrasted sharply with Mayer's: Thalberg walked around the studio alone and usually without fanfare. Mayer moved with a phalanx of aides and a herald sent ahead to announce his coming.

From the start there were Mayer men and there were Thalberg men, and each one was a mirror of his master. E. J. (Eddie) Mannix, the rugged, foul-mouthed Irish general manager who had once managed an amusement park in New Jersey for the Schenck brothers, was a Mayer man. But the quintessential Mayer man was Howard Strickling, M-G-M's publicity director.

Publicity was the fuel that propelled the Hollywood bandwagon; publicity created the stylized theatrical setting in which the star system was able to flourish, and it found its fullest expression at M-G-M. The efficiency and thoroughness of the Metro publicity department was legendary, its power awesomely pervasive. It could create personalities, destroy as well as build up reputations, and keep stars out of jail. By the early 1930s it had a staff of over sixty people, its own three-story building on the lot, and under Strickling was totally committed to L. B. Mayer.

Strickling was a blunt, quick-tempered man who stuttered when he was nervous. He boasted that he rose at five-thirty each morning because Mayer was usually on his feet by six and might need him. For his part, Mayer trusted him and took him everywhere he went, including on his periodic jaunts to Europe.

A former sports reporter, Strickling was one of the two M-G-M employees to whom Mayer left money in his will. This was as much in recognition of what the dear public never learned about Mayer's stars—and for that matter about Mayer himself—as for what they did learn. Mayer's wish was Howard Strickling's command. Mayer's idols were his idols and Mayer's enemies his enemies. Thus he admired Herbert Hoover and hated communists, intellectuals, and homosexuals. Later, when Mayer and Thalberg fell out, Thalberg was added to his list of enemies.

During Strickling's nearly forty years as head of Metro publicity, male stars weren't allowed to appear in fashion layouts or to accept awards for being well dressed because he thought it would make them look effeminate. Strickling's strategy was to concentrate publicity on the stars—especially the women stars—rather than the movies. Directors, writers, and producers were largely ignored, because the aim was to build up a public following that would flock to the movie theaters to see their favorite star, regardless of what the movie was. Loew's exhibitors used to write in asking for "two Gables" or "three Shearers," meaning, of course, two films starring Clark Gable or three with Norma Shearer. It was a seller's market. The demand for exciting news from Hollywood was insatiable: the newspapers, with their large Sunday rotogravure sections, had the space for it, and the public had the appetite. Wire service agencies considered the Hollywood dateline second only to Washington as a source of personality news.

Thalberg no longer had time to take complete charge of every movie production, and he gradually collected a group of associates to work under his general supervision. His closest aides were very different from Mayer's men. All were two to ten years older than him, with one exception well educated, and—whether by accident or design—approximately his height. Mayer found Thalberg's men oversophisticated and kept them at a distance.

Bernie Hyman was Thalberg's production assistant. Gregarious, possessed of a cherubic smile, he was a former film editor who had been Thalberg's editor at Universal and had readily agreed to fill the same role at M-G-M.

Albert Lewin was his resident intellectual. As with all self-educated people, there were gaps in Thalberg's knowledge, and Lewin's function was to fill those gaps. He had a master's degree in English from Harvard and at Columbia had completed everything for a Ph.D. but his doctoral thesis. Thalberg called him the Professor. He was small and scholarly and before moving to Hollywood after World War I had worked as a movie critic for the *Jewish Chronicle.* He was working at Goldwyn Studios in the story department at the time of the merger. Impressed with Lewin's knowledge of literature, Thalberg had appointed him his personal assistant; according to Maurice Rapf, son of Thalberg producer Harry Rapf, Lewin was always "present at conferences where there was need to compare books. After all, they were all doing subjects that had literary antecedents, and . . . Thalberg would have Albert read the books."

While Lewin covered the literary field, Paul Bern influenced Thalberg's choice of material from the theater. Bern had studied at the American Academy of Dramatic Arts and acted and directed on the New York stage before making his way to Hollywood, where he initially worked as a screenwriter. He came into contact with Thalberg after the merger when he, like Lewin, was working on a script at Goldwyn Studios. John Lee Mahin, the M-G-M screenwriter, once told me Bern "tended to see movies as filmed plays. He used to scout the theater for likely properties and then sell the idea to Irving." His input led Thalberg to make some of his most successful movie choices, such as *Grand Hotel* and *Camille,* as well as some of his least effective ones, such as *As You Desire Me,* adapted from a play by Luigi Pirandello.

Because both were German Jewish (Bern had emigrated to the United States when he was nine) and very close, Bern and Thalberg were widely believed to have similar characters. It was true that both were complex figures and ultimately tragic ones, but for different reasons. Bern was broody and erudite, given to extreme changes of mood. Thalberg guarded against emotional upsets and gave the impression of inner control. Bern, a few years older than Thalberg, had no talent for business and seemed to care little about personal wealth. He lived an almost spartan existence, renting a tiny room with a little alcove for his bed high up at the Ambassador Hotel in Los Angeles. Thalberg attached considerable importance to becoming rich and, although not ostentatious, did not hide his affluence.

When it came to romantic attachments, Bern had a talent for becoming deeply involved with exotic problem women: drug addicts, prostitutes, and the like; the more complicated their situation, the deeper his interest. Bern's involvements fascinated Thalberg, but his own relationships—as we shall see—tended to be less committed and his women more robust. Perhaps he had taken a cue from Bern, whose fixations seemed always to end unhappily, sometimes even disastrously. Paul Bern "seemed always to have loved and lost," Irene Selznick once said, but the lure didn't lessen. John Gilbert called it "Paul's Magdalene complex, doing crazy things for whores."

At the time of the M-G-M merger, Bern was squiring Barbara La Marr, who had starred in several pictures at Mayer's studio, and he was trying to help her overcome a serious heroin addiction. Instead she turned Bern onto heroin, and Thalberg had to force him into a clinic until he was cured. Thalberg expended no such effort in helping Barbara La Marr. On his orders she was barred from the studio and, her career shattered, died of an overdose in 1925 at the age of twenty-nine. Mabel Normand was another addict whom Bern tried to help. She sent for him on her deathbed.

If this role of part lover, part social worker, suggested a powerful sexual drive, the opposite was almost certainly true. In 1932 Bern committed suicide in mysterious circumstances, and it was stated at the inquest that he was sexually underendowed. Shortly after M-G-M was established, he had an intense affair with Joan Crawford, a young newcomer who attached herself to him eagerly as a man of influence. He did much to advance her early career, rounding off the sharp edges of her tough, streetwise personality. Bern was responsible for the imitation Bernhardt shots of Crawford in black tights and doublet as Hamlet. In turn, she made his life miserable by demanding of him sexually more than he was able to give and then—to his great distress—finding consolation with other men. An M-G-M writer once saw them embracing in a corner of the studio. Bern was weeping on Joan Crawford's shoulder.

Thus Thalberg surrounded himself with men who were totally unlike the more carnal Hollywood executives who chased starlets around their offices. Thalberg's circle included Hunt Stromberg, an energetic, all-purpose producer and former journalist who alone did not fit the physical pattern because he was tall. Also on staff was Harry Rapf, a former vaudevillian nicknamed the Anteater because of his large nose. Rapf was solid, hardworking, and anything but an intellectual and was usually placed in charge of routine projects.

It was a strong team, but one that catered to Thalberg's intellectual aspirations rather than complementing them. The limitations of Thalberg's group become more evident when one looks at the kinds of pictures he did not make. There was, for instance, no one to lead him beyond the lure of his childhood reading and his growing fascination with Broadway—no one encouraging him to consider other possibilities, in particular the film genre that would come to represent Hollywood's most important contribution to American culture: the western.

5

IRVING'S WOMEN

But for his illness, Irving Thalberg would have been Hollywood's most eligible bachelor. His condition was common knowledge in the movie community, and Mayer was not the only father who did not want a young widowed daughter on his hands. So Thalberg was feted but kept away from marriageable daughters. Now approaching thirty, he continued to live with his parents in his rented home in Hollywood. For the most part his social engagements tended to be work-oriented. He had also formed an unlikely association with a group of bachelor carousers, hard workers and hard drinkers given to macho exploits both sexual and otherwise. Included in the group were the directors Howard Hawks, Victor Fleming, and Jack Conway and the romantic star John (Jack) Gilbert.

Through his circle of friends Thalberg came to know his way around the Hollywood night scene. When it came to sexual activity, however, he was a fringe member, physically too frail and temperamentally too cautious to be a full participant. He got a vicarious charge from the sex talk of his companions and occasionally from watching, say, Jack Gilbert building up to a seduction. Not that he was impotent; but the lack of development of the lower half of his body extended to his sexual organs, and this may have accounted for his limited sexual drive. He was likely to be seen at the establishment of Lee Francis, the Beverly Hills madam, reading the early morning *Los Angeles Examiner* while waiting for his more sexually active companions to rejoin him.

The beautiful women he squired had two things in common. All had been around and all qualified for Henrietta Thalberg's deep disapproval. Bessie Love, who was to star in more than one Thalberg picture, including his first talking movie, was at least five years older. Peggy Hopkins Joyce, a leggy Ziegfeld showgirl who towered above him, made a career of marrying and divorcing wealthy businessmen. Marie Prevost, the talented comedienne whom Thalberg had brought over to Mayer's company from Universal, was briefly his regular companion. Later she failed to make the transition from silent movies to talking pictures and drifted into alcoholism. A few days after the first anniversary of Thalberg's death, she would be found dead in her Hollywood apartment, aged thirty-nine. Trapped and famished, her dachshund had taken a few bites out of its owner's flesh.

Henrietta would complain to friends, such as the Mayers, about Irving's "bad ways," his late nights with the boys, and his even later nights with—in her eyes—thoroughly unsuitable women. But none of Thalberg's relationships was serious until one Sunday he was invited on the yacht of Joseph Schenck, Nick's brother and the head of First National Pictures, and his wife, Norma Talmadge. Also on the yacht was Norma's sister, actress Constance Talmadge, and Thalberg fell in love for the first time in his life.

Constance Talmadge, who was known to her friends as Dutch, was a playgirl, negligent of her own career, and a cocaine user. At the time that she was being pursued by Thalberg, one of her favorite diversions was to trawl the gay spots with the gay actor William Haines and help him pick up sailors. Haines had been a Metro actor before he was fired by L. B. Mayer after being arrested for homosexual offenses.

On the face of it, no one could have been less suitable than Talmadge for Irving Thalberg, with his straitlaced mother and his equally straitlaced double-breasted suits, with padded shoulders to add to his build, and his grave precocity. But she tickled the nerve ends of whatever it was in him that wanted to break out of the constraints imposed by his own ambition, his self-discipline, his background, and his illness. And perhaps, ultimately, his fascination with Constance Talmadge, Peggy Hopkins Joyce, and all the others was an attempt to free himself from his own programmed, complex personality.

Had she returned his interest, it's arguable that he would have devoted less of his energies to moviemaking and died earlier, probably with a satisfied smile on his face. But Dutch was not impressed by a boyish suitor who took work seriously. Thalberg's main competitor was Allaster Mac-Intosh, a member of the British aristocracy and playboy companion of the Prince of Wales. When Talmadge married her aristocrat, Thalberg's affair with Rosabelle suddenly intensified—until a quarrel ended it once and for all.

It happened when Thalberg was visiting New York for meetings at Loew's Inc. Running late for a theater opening to which he was to escort Rosabelle, Thalberg telephoned to say that he would send his limousine to pick her up so that he would have time to change at his hotel. He proposed to join her at the theater. Rosabelle's reply was that she did not arrive at functions unaccompanied, and that she went either with him or not at all. Quietly furious, Thalberg raced home to dress and then to the Laemmle house to pick up Rosabelle. Shortly after that, he and Rosabelle parted company. Taken by itself, the incident was a poor excuse for breaking up a romance; but Thalberg's infatuation with Rosabelle belonged to a past dimly remembered, and besides, she had committed the unpardonable sin of coming between him and his work.

By 1925 he had added another occasional date to his list, a young Canadian actress under contract to his studio named Norma Shearer. She came to Hollywood in the spring of 1923 from New York, where she progressed from photographic modeling to regular work in small-time East Coast pictures. Thalberg had screened some of the pictures in which she had appeared and her name had gone into his notebook as an actress who showed promise despite the generally low quality of the productions. He had sent her a six-month contract at $150 a week, plus railroad fares for herself and her mother, Edith.

Her arrival at the Mayer company's Mission Road studios was the occasion of another of those stories of mistaken identity that festoon the early Thalberg chronicles. In this version, Norma is met by a young secretary or office boy in a dark suit, very polite and deferential, who leads her down a long corridor to a small, modest office. Then he shuts the door, sits behind the desk, puts his feet up, and calmly, critically, looks Norma up and down. Disconcerted, Norma changes her mind about the young man whom she now regards as insolent. Then he introduces himself as Irving Thalberg, vice president of the company.

Thalberg derived a quiet enjoyment from such moments, so like scenes from one of his own movies. The joke had its uses, too, since the moment of revelation immediately placed his interlocutor at a disadvantage. But because he was already a legend, the youngest and most creative executive in the business, it was becoming harder to surprise anyone—at any rate, anyone in Hollywood.

Attempting to regain ground, Norma told him grandly that she had received other offers from Hollywood over the last year, including one from Universal at $200 a week that she had turned down because of other commitments in New York. Thalberg smiled and said he was responsible for the offers: in 1921 he had run a couple of Norma's recent pictures and proposed a Universal contract—and they both knew without his having to say so that the Universal offer had been for less than $200—and, more recently, about to leave Universal and go to work for Hal Roach, he had suggested Norma to Roach, who needed a new face for a comedy serial. It was when he'd learned that the deal with Roach had fallen through that he'd sent a Louis B. Mayer Productions company contract.

Her first screen test was a disaster, but a kindly cameraman who had seen her distress at the result ran the test that same day, decided that she had been poorly handled, and obtained the studio's permission to make a second one. Both Thalberg and Mayer were impressed with the new test, and Norma was given the female lead in *The Wanters*. Thalberg then cast her as a flapper in *Pleasure Mad,* but after a few days' shooting the director complained to Mayer that the new girl was not satisfactory. When Mayer summoned Norma, she was certain the end had come for her. She began telling Mayer that the director bullied her and made her nervous, but Mayer staged an alarming outburst, calling her a fool and a coward and accusing her of throwing away her career.

Unaware that she was the target of one of Mayer's staged, blustering pep talks, Norma responded with tearful defiance. She was no coward: she would show him what she was capable of. No director was going to intimidate her! At Mayer's suggestion she also saw Thalberg, who, involved at the time with Constance Talmadge and Rosabelle Laemmle, was distant and businesslike and told her he understood the problem and would speak to the director in question. Back on the set, she launched into her next scene—as she later put it—"lock, stock, and barrel, fur, fin, and feathers."

Norma would shrug off their occasional dates with the explanation that she was "Irving's spare tire." She would say, "When Rosabelle or Constance are away, or someone stands him up, I'm always available." Norma Shearer was not in the same league as Constance Talmadge. Norma was a young M-G-M contract player, attractive, vivacious, but not outgoing by nature. Constance Talmadge was a glamorous star, sparkling, beautiful, and well connected socially. But Constance was a wonderful optical illusion, a trick of the light, whereas Norma was always there, real, ready, and willing to oblige her boss.

The reference to a spare tire was apt because as a photographic model in New York, Norma had been Miss Lotta Miles of the Springfield Tire and Rubber Company. On a large billboard in Columbus Circle, floodlit at night, her smiling face and swimsuited figure were caught in the act of surfacing through the middle of a tire. For this daughter of a Montreal lumber merchant, pushing tires had been a first step on the road to stardom.

Like Thalberg, Norma was strongly influenced—in some respects dominated—by her mother. Like Henrietta, Edith Shearer supplied the drive, but the urge to become somebody and the strength of will to succeed despite handicaps were Norma's. Unlike Thalberg, however, Norma made no sudden leap to the top of the ladder. When her father's business failed, her mother took her and her elder sister, Athole, to New York to try to get them into the movies. Athole was quickly discouraged, but not Norma. The modeling was interspersed with work as a five-dollar-a-day movie extra and from 1921 in small speaking roles starting with *The Stealers,* in which Norma played the dowdy daughter of a minister.

Seven pictures and almost three years later, Thalberg brought her to Hollywood. But after her shaky start, the Mayer company had quietly spread the word that she was available to be loaned out to other studios. Loan-outs were useful because they built up "credit" with other studios for when the Mayer company might want to borrow a star for one of its own pictures. They also gave young contract players the opportunity to gain experience—in another studio's pictures.

In this way Norma raced through six pictures in eighteen months, none of them for her own studio. Thalberg showed very little interest in her professionally and none personally. Sooner or later, according to Norma's biographers, he learned that she was having an affair with Victor Fleming, the director of *Empty Hands,* one of her loan-out movies. It was Norma's first love and correspondingly deep, but for Fleming it was another adventure, even if an especially torrid one.

Whatever Thalberg thought of Norma's adventure with one of his macho friends, he was sufficiently impressed with her performance in Fleming's picture to cast her at last in an M-G-M movie—the merger having taken place in the meantime. In *He Who Gets Slapped,* the movie version of Russian playwright Leonid Andreyev's circus melodrama, Norma played a bareback rider who is loved by a sad clown but is herself in love with the circus lion tamer. The picture was Thalberg's first attempt at an all-star production: Jack Gilbert played the lion tamer and Lon Chaney, whom Thalberg had lured from Universal, the clown.

In one way it was not an ideal role for Norma: she wore a tutu throughout the movie, and by her own admission, her legs were not one of her best features. Another problem was a slight cast in her right eye. In later years, when she ruled the roost at M-G-M, she was able to dress to disguise the first and learned to control the second. Yet Thalberg was sufficiently impressed with the chemistry between her and Gilbert in *He Who Gets Slapped* to team them again right away in *The Snob.*

If Thalberg had little interest in Norma, he exercised great care with Gilbert, who was not only the studio's number one leading man, but also his protégé in the sense that without Thalberg's restraining hand, Mayer would long since have fired him. Morals tightened up in Hollywood in the early 1920s following a series of highly publicized scandals, notably the death in mysterious circumstances of a young woman following a wild party at the home of comedian Fatty Arbuckle. The incident ended Arbuckle's screen career, and Hollywood drew heavy fire from churches and concerned groups throughout the country for its lack of morals. The movie industry managed to forestall the introduction of government-sponsored film censorship by launching its own system. In 1927 Will Hays, former postmaster general in the Harding administration, was appointed the first head of the Motion Picture Code, which originally had a list of eleven don'ts and twenty-seven be carefuls.

In reality, the Hays Code, as it was called, created a double standard. On the screen, as long as six reels of fornication ended in contrition and a change of heart, and criminals got what their exciting lives deserved, the public could still dream of "sin" before it woke up to the need for respectability. Off screen, stars were expected to lead worthy private lives, and a "morals clause" was written into their contracts. In practice this meant being discreet about their love affairs.

It angered Mayer that Gilbert had not changed his reckless, party-loving, slightly mad, silent screen star personality to conform to the new mood of respectability and self-restraint. It got worse when Gilbert, on two separate occasions, spoke disparagingly of his mother in Mayer's presence—a grave sin in Mayer's eyes—and both times Thalberg had to intervene to save him.

In the second and most explosive episode, Gilbert came to Mayer's office to discuss a story idea. Impossible, said Mayer after Gilbert had outlined the story, the woman in the picture was a mother and also a whore, an inconceivable combination. Not at all, Gilbert replied, his mother had been a whore. Mayer demanded that he retract the remark and when Gilbert refused chased him with a knife, threatening to perform surgery on his private parts. As Gilbert raced for the door, he said, "Go ahead. I'll still be more of a man than you!"

Once again Thalberg dissuaded Mayer from firing Jack Gilbert. The star could be difficult, he agreed, but he was earning a lot of money for the studio. Besides, he said, it was unrealistic for Mayer to expect to like and be liked by everyone who worked for him. Mayer found this hard to accept. To him, the studio was a family—with him as its undisputed head.

It was initially Gilbert who alerted Thalberg to Norma Shearer's interest in him. Though Norma had gone from Victor Fleming to an affair with Monta Bell, her director in *The Snob*, Gilbert still sensed from his conversations with her that it was Thalberg who exercised the greater fascination. But Thalberg was too much under Constance Talmadge's spell to take much notice. In addition, his only personal contact with Norma at the time was when she complained that the studio cast her in too many routine pictures.

She had a point. Her last dozen films had all made money and earned her good reviews. She had built up a popular following. Yet the best roles were going to others, the ones with connections—Marion Davies, for example. Most of Marion Davies's pictures lost money, but she still had first call on many of the film parts because she was the principal star of her lover William Randolph Hearst's film company, Cosmopolitan Pictures Corporation, and Cosmopolitan had a production agreement with M-G-M. Another reason why Mayer considered it important to remain on good terms with Hearst was that Hearst owned the country's largest chain of newspapers. Eleanor Boardman was another example. She was a fine actress, but less popular than Norma; still, she was living with and would soon marry King Vidor, and in the meantime she was his favored leading lady. Thanks to her protector, Paul Bern, newcomer Joan Crawford had landed the starring role in *Our Dancing Daughters,* a major M-G-M production. Greta Garbo had moved into John Gilbert's Tower Road home in Beverly Hills, and in addition, Thalberg was taking an interest in her development. Only Norma, with no patron, seemed at the mercy of an indifferent system.

Her pleas to Thalberg for better material produced no results. Occasionally she dissolved into tears, but, she recalled, "it made no more impression than rain on a raincoat." He listened sympathetically, told her that Mayer valued her highly and that he did, too, but reminded her that it was the studio's prerogative to choose her pictures.

Thalberg always professed respect for actors, but he believed they were not the best judges of which roles were best for them. "In my many years of experience with artists of importance," he once wrote to the British actor Brian Aherne, "they have had a great deal more success in the roles that they objected to than in the roles that they desired. This may be a coincidence, but . . . close scrutiny would reveal that it isn't." Since it was Thalberg who chose the roles the actors did not want to play, the clear inference was that he was the better judge. He said as much to Norma, pointing out that the films she complained about had made her popular, so he must be doing something right. He did, however, arrange for her contract to be revised upward from $1,000 to $5,000, with the increase spread over five years. A decade later he was to use the same argument with Joan Crawford, right down to the pay increase, when she complained that Norma was getting all the best parts.

Yet as Norma continued to argue about her assignments, she captured Thalberg's attention. There was no improvement in the films she starred in, but a personal rapport of sorts was established. It was a one-theme relationship, but she had connected. Two days after Thalberg's first heart attack, Monta Bell proposed to Norma in Tijuana, across the Prohibition border, where Hollywood spent its weekends drinking and gambling. Norma's mind was on the man fighting for his life in Los Angeles, the man with whom she felt, increasingly, she had unfinished business. And when Thalberg returned to work, they picked up where they'd left off.

Then, one evening in July 1925, she received a telephone call in her dressing room. It was Thalberg's secretary asking if she would like to accompany Mr. Thalberg to the premier of *The Gold Rush*. Later, Norma was to say that she was sure Irving was listening on the extension for her answer. After the movie Thalberg took her to the Coconut Grove, where she was to discover that he was a good dancer. The evening was spent in small talk, and when Thalberg drove her to the home she shared with her mother and sister Athole, there was no mention of another date. After that evening, however, Norma knew she was going to marry Irving Thalberg.

This would have been news to Thalberg had he known it. In 1927 Constance Talmadge returned to Hollywood to make a film after a short-lived marriage and came back into his life. This time around, the interest seemed less one-sided than before. In the early days of his infatuation he used to park his car near her house at night to see who brought her home, relieved when it was Haines or another of her gay friends, insulted in a way that she found them more entertaining than him, but often driving away "close to despair" (according to Anita Loos).

Now, the woman F. Scott Fitzgerald once described as "the deft princess of lingerie and love . . . the flapper de luxe" agreed to be escorted on dinner dates and other social occasions; and she and Thalberg were a magical pair who seemed to take an immense delight in each other. He behaved with her as he did with no other woman, and it was clearly with immense self-satisfaction that he observed himself being smitten. She brought out all his charm and intelligence, and a humor few people suspected he possessed. They glowed like a couple in one of his movies, and seeing him like this, observers found it possible to forget the shadow over him. Ironically, the fact that Constance had told him she was fond of him but not drawn to him romantically made things easier: it meant he did not face the pressure of having to prove himself sexually, and she was saved the eventual disappointment.

Henrietta was alarmed. There were too many parties and too much dancing. She began to praise Rosabelle Laemmle, something she had never done before: what a good wife Rosabelle would make for Irving, how life-threatening Constance was: "She's frivolous, she's not concerned with his health, with his future. Rosabelle would understand." Then, on one of Constance's periodic trips, Thalberg began seeing Rosabelle again, and Henrietta began to complain how spoiled and overbearing Rosabelle was. The Mayer sisters, who followed the progress of Thalberg's amorous adventures closely, always knew which of the two women he was seeing, because Henrietta would praise the other.

In the fall of 1926 Monta Bell again asked Norma to marry him. She turned him down, telling him, "I'm going to marry Irving Thalberg." As far as the cheerful, rangy director knew, Thalberg was still madly in love with Constance Talmadge, so he surmised that Norma was inventing an excuse to end their relationship. But it was not an excuse. Dutch had once again faded out of Thalberg's life. A year after *The Gold Rush* evening, Thalberg had asked Norma to the premiere of King Vidor's film *Bardelys the Magnificent.* This time Norma and Thalberg were joined by two other couples, Vidor and Eleanor Boardman, Garbo and Jack Gilbert, the star of the film.

For Norma this was heady company. Walking into the Coconut Grove on Thalberg's arm after the movie, wearing a shimmering gown cajoled out of the studio wardrobe department, she had risen to another level of existence. If there was another man out there somewhere destined to sweep her off her feet, he had yet to appear, and Norma was twenty-four. Meanwhile the evening helped deepen her resolve to marry Irving Thalberg.

There was no immediate follow-up invitation, no signal that Thalberg considered her in any way special. When Norma began filming *The Student Prince* in the spring of 1927, she complained to Thalberg that director Ernst Lubitsch worked too fast. Lubitsch liked to keep the pace brisk, filming scenes with very little rehearsal to retain the actors' freshness and spontaneity. Norma relied on meticulous advance preparation and requested several takes of each scene until she was satisfied that she'd got it just right. Following Norma's complaint, Thalberg came to the set, listened to both her and Lubitsch, and then told her quietly, "Everyone has a lot to learn from Mr. Lubitsch." So Norma quietly adapted to Lubitsch's style.

Meanwhile she waited patiently for Thalberg to make his next move. When he next asked her out, she was ready, as she was the time after that—until their dates, though still infrequent, were at least regular.

Norma's interest in Irving was soon common knowledge in Hollywood; the cliffhanger was what Irving was going to do about it. Admire her he certainly did, especially as a gifted professional who had grown steadily in stature as an M-G-M star, often giving an outstanding performance in pictures he knew she had not wanted to make in the first place. He liked her occasional flashes of individualism, as when she appeared at a Mayfair Club ball, organized by Hollywood's crème de la crème at the Biltmore Hotel, in a shocking scarlet dress even though the women had been asked to wear white.

There was a noticeable absence of passion in the relationship, yet several people, among them Louis Mayer, thought Norma and Thalberg perfectly suited to one another. Not that either was devoid of passion, but Thalberg's was still directed elsewhere, and Norma seemed cool, even distant, when in reality there was a fierce inner tension that she had learned to keep under control.

Thalberg's appreciation of her increased as he dealt with more difficult stars. For example, the studio had signed

Lillian Gish to a million-dollar contract and found her brilliant but dated and unbending, as well as inclined to be difficult. In *La Bohème,* her first M-G-M picture, she decided that the eroticism of the plot would be heightened if Mimi and Rudolph, played by John Gilbert, never embraced. At Thalberg's insistence that Gilbert's fans expected at least one kiss, she agreed to a chaste peck. In *The Scarlet Letter* Gish gave one of the finest performances of the silent screen, but the picture flopped. When her next film, *The Wind,* did the same thing, Thalberg told her her image was old-fashioned for the jazz age and suggested that the studio "arrange" some sort of "scandal" that would "knock her off her pedestal." Shocked, she rejected the idea. After his experience with Gish, Thalberg preferred to develop the studio's own stars, and in this respect Norma was a role model.

Professional admiration may not seem a strong reason for marriage. In this case, however, it was a shared interest with a man who had no other. Norma and Thalberg had one more thing in common: their love of the theater—Irving from his teens, Norma from her days in New York. Whatever acting training Norma had was from sitting in the gallery watching the leading Broadway stars of her day. In addition, Thalberg faced a stark reality: he was twenty-eight and had been told he would not live long after thirty, and he wanted a taste of married life. More important, he wanted children. He wanted to found a dynasty. Sometime early in 1927, Thalberg decided that marriage to Norma would answer very well to his specific situation.

One essential preliminary was to win Henrietta's acceptance. To his mother any woman Thalberg dated on more than one occasion signaled danger. But Norma never missed an opportunity to ingratiate herself with Thalberg's mother. She was friendly to Sylvia, Thalberg's unmarried sister, but to Henrietta she was deferential. Whenever Thalberg escorted both Norma and Henrietta to a party or premiere, Norma insisted on being brought home first, and they said their good-nights while Henrietta waited in the car. She showed concern for Thalberg's health, making a point of not keeping him out on late dates: Norma wanted him alive as much as Henrietta did. In the summer of 1927 Thalberg rented a house on the beach in Santa Monica. By now Irving's relationship with Norma was sufficiently advanced for Henrietta to agree that she should spend the summer as their house guest to spare Thalberg the exertion of taking her home.

It was during this summer that Norma discovered the limitations of Thalberg's sexual drive, including his tendency toward premature ejaculation. Norma held back her considerable ardor and prepared herself for a married life of sexual self-restraint.

6

MRS. IRVING THALBERG

Thalberg pondered every aspect of the Norma Shearer situation with his customary thoroughness, but meanwhile life went on in its usual steady flow of problems and decisions claiming his attention. One of the problems he faced at the time was Greta Garbo or, more precisely, her mentor, Mauritz Stiller.

Thalberg had not at first been impressed with Garbo. She was overweight, her hair was worn in a style that made her look matronly, and her teeth needed fixing. Her first test had not been encouraging, and he wondered aloud to his associates what had possessed Mayer to give her a contract. As with Norma, a second test saved Garbo from oblivion. Stiller had persuaded Thalberg to try again, and this time Thalberg was more favorably impressed. He sent her to the studio dentist and the studio hairdresser, and he recommended a strict diet.

After waiting ten weeks, Garbo was one day summoned to Thalberg's office. He handed her a large brown envelope. "Here is the script for *The Torrent*," he told her. "Go to your hotel and study the role of Leonora." Garbo meekly took the envelope from his hands and without a word turned around and went to her hotel. It was her one display of total obedience in a Hollywood career spanning fifteen legendary years and twenty-four films.

To her great distress and Stiller's disappointment, the director was Monta Bell. Both had assumed that Stiller would be asked to direct his protégée in her first Hollywood picture. But *The Torrent* was a vehicle for Ricardo Cortez, M-G-M's Valentino look-alike. The film was based on a novel by the Spanish writer Vicente Blasco Ibáñez, better known as the author of *The Four Horsemen of the Apocalypse,* and Thalberg was probably hoping that it would do for Cortez's career what *The Four Horsemen* had done for Rudolph Valentino's. But he knew that if Stiller directed the picture, he would favor Garbo and ignore Cortez.

Bell directed Garbo on the set, but Stiller coached her in the part every night at home and was responsible in large measure for her performance. When Thalberg watched her in front of the camera, she didn't seem to be doing much of anything, and he began to feel uneasy about having cast her in the picture. On the screen, however, she created an immediate, unique impact. Here was an actress who could convey the intensity of her feelings with remarkable economy of expression. The arching of her eyebrow or the shrug of her shoulder was more eloquent than a dozen speeches.

The Torrent was a mediocre film except for its foretaste of Garbo's particular magic. *Variety* pronounced her "the find of the year," which was, of course, an understatement. The cinematographer assigned to the production, William Daniels, who was to film all but five of her American pictures, said her face "had no bad sides and needed no special lighting."

Thalberg instructed Lewin to find another suitable property quickly. What Thalberg had seen on the screen, as he wrote to Bern and Lewin, were the makings of "a captivating femme fatale, dangerous but also vulnerable. She never walks away unharmed herself. Nobody we have [in the studio] is so naturally suited to romantic tragedy."

The best Lewin could do at such short notice was another Blasco Ibáñez novel, *The Temptress*, which was already being developed for someone else. This time Garbo played a highborn siren luring men to their destruction. Garbo didn't like the script any more than she had the first one. But this time Thalberg asked Stiller to direct the picture.

The Swedish director had a "free form" way of working. He had no shooting schedule: he filmed scenes as the mood took him, out of sequence and following no particular order. He would plan to shoot a scene requiring a crowd of extras, then leave them standing idle because he had decided to switch to another scene. Having shot the picture, he would spend weeks shaping it in the cutting room.

Thalberg was astonished by this display of lush disorder. "Is the man mad?" he asked Lars Hanson, who had a role in the picture. The Swedish actor had been in the cast of *The Atonement of Gösta Berling* and Mayer had given him a contract as well. "Has he never been behind a camera before?" When Thalberg tried to explain that directors at M-G-M were expected to work within the system, Stiller—whose English was poor and who communicated with Mayer and Thalberg in Yiddish—was insulted and accused Thalberg of trying to teach him how to direct.

Stiller had been working on *The Temptress* for ten days when he was called to Thalberg's office. The meeting was late at night. Thalberg's suite was on the second floor of the M-G-M administration building. It had large windows that overlooked an alley from which, when it was dark, anyone passing by could observe what was going on inside the lighted room. One passerby that night was Albert Lewin.

"I looked up into Irving's office," Lewin remembered. "He and Stiller were talking. Irving was walking back and forth—he always walked around when he talked. . . . It was plain that a very lively discussion was in progress."

Then Lewin saw Garbo pacing up and down in the dark alley. She would look up at Thalberg and Stiller, watch them talking for a moment, and then walk away. Lewin watched her for quite a while, but he had not met her then and did not speak to her. "She was very agitated," Lewin said. "She knew that a great decision was being made that night, and she was waiting for the word."

Stiller came out of Thalberg's office with the news that he had been fired from *The Temptress*. In March 1927 the picture was turned over to Fred Niblo. Garbo was never personally informed of the switch: Niblo simply appeared on the set the following morning and took over the filming. Desolate and resentful at the loss of her mentor, but too new and intimidated to protest, she continued to report for work every morning—this time without the benefit of after-hours' help from Stiller, for the director was too preoccupied about his own plight to pay much attention to her. Thalberg had succeeded in driving a wedge between Garbo and the director. Stiller's costly working style was reason enough, in his eyes, to remove the Swede from the picture, but his real aim may well have been to detach his new, rising star from Stiller's influence. Thalberg disapproved of stars having mentors: they interfered with the studio's control.

Shortly afterward Stiller left M-G-M and moved to Paramount, where he directed two pictures with only moderate success. The gap between him and Garbo widened when Thalberg, upgrading her material, cast her opposite Jack Gilbert in her third picture, *Flesh and the Devil*, and they started an affair. Gilbert called her Swede; she called him Jacky, which she pronounced "Yacky." On the set,

Garbo and her lover made no secret of their affair, and M-G-M threw caution to the winds and publicized their affair to the limit. Their on-screen love scenes are still electric in a film that in other aspects seems dated.

Yet when Jacky asked her to marry him at the end of the filming, she refused. Gilbert, who wasn't accustomed to being rebuffed, continued to propose at regular intervals throughout their stormy relationship, and he continued to receive the same answer. Their affair fascinated Thalberg, as did all unconventional sexual relationships among his friends. Gilbert had confided that Garbo was terrific in bed. "Why don't you marry Jack?" Thalberg once asked her. "Don't you see him as a husband?"

Garbo replied, "No, and I don't see myself as a wife, either."

By her third film Garbo was already established as a star for whom critics delved deep into their reserves of superlatives. "Never before has a woman so alluring, with a seductive grace that is far more potent than mere beauty, appeared on the screen," said the *New York Herald-Tribune* in its review of *Flesh and the Devil*.

Taking his cue from references to her seductiveness, Thalberg tried to rush her into *Women Love Diamonds*. She was to have played a New York socialite who discovers on the eve of her wedding that she is really in love with her chauffeur. But Garbo's timid phase was over. She said, "No more bad women." When Thalberg promptly suspended her for breach of contract, Garbo went home to Sweden for six months.

It is reasonable to ask why Mayer had bothered to bring Stiller to Hollywood if he was expected to conform to an unfamiliar production system. It was established custom for Hollywood executives to bring home stars and/or directors from their European trips, like trophies from an African safari. The foreign names—the more unpronounceable the better—were thought to add prestige to the studio. In addition, a sufficient number of these transplants were successful (for example, Lubitsch) to keep the practice alive. On a more practical level, M-G-M was expanding so rapidly that it needed all the experienced directors it could engage, and the addition of a few European filmmakers made the mix more interesting. Under the heading "Top Box Office Attractions for the Next Twelve Months," the studio listed sixty productions, or four times the number scheduled in its first year, and it had twenty directors under contract to make them.

Stiller had committed the unpardonable sin of slowing down the flow of "product." By the late 1920s Loew's Inc. had a theater chain totaling a quarter of a million seats. It was an insatiable beast that had to be fed constantly. By 1926 the Metro-Goldwyn-Mayer lot was the centerpiece of Culver City, named after a developer named Harry H. Culver. Movies had started there in 1916 with Thomas Ince, who sold out to Triangle, and the latter subsequently leased the place to Sam Goldwyn. By the time M-G-M sprang into being the lot was forty-three acres.

In all, six stages were presided over by the most famous sign in Hollywood movies: a roaring lion encircled by the words *Metro-Goldwyn-Mayer Studios* and the smaller but not to be forgotten "Controlled by Loew's Inc." Over a thousand people were employed at the studio, which boasted the best of everything required for top-class motion picture production—the best stars, directors, writers, camera crews, stages, back lot, wardrobe, properties, makeup, and publicity, even the best studio commissary, the best dentist, and the best children's school, to say nothing of the best security force.

As production increased, Thalberg and his small team of producers each carried responsibility for more pictures. There was no reason for them to be less than creative, but they were expected to be brilliant, decisive managers and Thalberg the most decisive of all, since all major problems and unresolved questions were funneled to him for a final decision.

Early in 1927 Marcus Loew, who had been in poor

health, died, and Nick Schenck became president of Loew's. It was to Schenck, or the General, as he liked to be called, that Mayer reported Irving Thalberg's demand for another raise in salary. Thalberg was beginning to live at least that part of the legend that said he deserved more money than he was getting. His income also had to be factored into his thinking about marriage: he was earning $100,000 a year, but Norma Shearer, at twenty-four, was earning almost $260,000.

Schenck was hardly in a position to refuse. The motion picture industry was going through one of its periodic economic crises, owing in part to the phenomenal growth of radio. In an effort to lure audiences into their resplendent movie houses, producers danced around their own censorship rules. Censorship boards cropped up everywhere, and the local press rang with calls for vigilance against screen immorality. Talk of organized labor kicked up in Los Angeles, and union leaders targeted the high-profile movie industry as the obvious shop to close. Yet M-G-M was about to announce a net profit of $6,388,000, putting it ahead of every other Hollywood studio.

Mayer went to New York on his own to negotiate for both of them, and following a period of statutory haggling, Mayer and Thalberg each had their respective salaries raised to $2,500 a week. This was still half what Norma made per week, but Mayer also secured an increase in their percentage guarantees. Thalberg was to get $125,000, although later he learned that Mayer was to receive $500,000, a discrepancy that fed the growing rift between them. Still, he celebrated his raise by buying a new black Cadillac and inviting Norma to dinner, at which they discussed the eternal subject between them, her film roles.

At the time, Norma was shooting retakes for *The Student Prince*. As she left the set one evening, she was called to Thalberg's office. She found him sitting behind his desk, gazing at a tray of diamond engagement rings. He looked up with a faint smile and asked her to choose the ring she liked best. Rosabelle Laemmle was out of his life. He had come to terms with the fact that Constance Talmadge was a lost cause. So after testing endlessly for the part of Mrs. Irving Thalberg, Norma Shearer finally got it. One of her biographers states that Norma decided tears were not appropriate for the occasion, so she "caught her breath, smiled, and chose a ring."

That night Louis Mayer went home breathless with excitement and announced: "Irving's decided to marry her! There's no risk—everything will go on as it was, Henrietta's accepted the situation." After the ring had come the small print, for Norma had to pay a price for Henrietta's acceptance. Norma would move in with the family: any radical change in Thalberg's domestic arrangements had to be avoided. Henrietta needed to be on hand to teach Norma how to look after her husband. And Thalberg's future wife had agreed to the arrangement without complaint. She did not think a confrontation at this stage would work to her advantage.

What Thalberg told Norma about his condition is not known, but it would have been out of character for him not to have been totally frank. But Norma had prenuptial revelations of her own for Thalberg. Her sister, Athole, had become a depressive, and a live-in nurse had been engaged to take care of her. For the Shearers, as for most people at the time, any kind of mental illness was a deep and almost unmentionable shame. Thalberg had to be told, of course, and he almost certainly agreed that Athole's condition had to be kept secret. So it was with this additional anxiety looming over her that Norma prepared for their marriage, which was announced by M-G-M on August 17.

Norma wanted a small wedding, at least by Hollywood standards, and Irving was only too happy to oblige. The ceremony took place at four-thirty in the afternoon on September 29, in the garden of 9401 Sunset Boulevard, the home Thalberg was now renting from silent screen star Pauline Frederick. In the garden Cedric Gibbons had designed a flower-covered trellis as a backdrop. Norma wore a gown of soft ivory velvet studded with pearls, with a yoke of handmade rose lace. The diamond pin glittering in her bodice was a gift from Thalberg. The five bridesmaids wearing organdy dresses and matching organdy hats were Marion Davies, Bessie Love, Sylvia Thalberg, and Mayer's two daughters, Irene and Edie, with Athole—sufficiently recovered for the occasion—as maid of honor. Bessie Love was included at Thalberg's suggestion. She had been first a romantic attachment and then a shoulder to cry on when Constance Talmadge proved unresponsive. Thalberg remained friendly with her and gave her the second female lead in M-G-M's first talking picture, *Broadway Melody*. The bride's and groom's respective mothers wore black.

Mayer was best man, and most of the guests were Thalberg's studio colleagues—senior executives, members of the Thalberg team, directors Howard Hawks, Fred Niblo, and Robert Z. Leonard. Also invited was William Randolph Hearst. William Thalberg, good-natured but ineffectual, watched from the sidelines. Norma's father, Andrew Shearer, still living in Montreal, was absent. Norma had not seen him for nearly a decade. Besides Athole and mother Edith, however, Norma's family at the wedding included her brother, Douglas, who had recently come to Hollywood and was employed in the M-G-M special effects department.

Even while dressing for the ceremony, Thalberg conducted a story conference on a new Ramon Novarro picture with screenwriter Laurence Stallings. The bride had spent the morning nervously practicing her Hebrew responses for the Jewish ceremony with Rabbi Edgar Magnin. Like Thalberg, she had no strong religious beliefs, but at Henrietta's request she studied Judaism with Rabbi Magnin of the Wilshire Boulevard Temple in Los Angeles, who was known as the rabbi to the stars because of his close contacts with the movie industry. When the time came she muffed her lines and insisted on repeating them, with some whispered help from the rabbi. It was the only hitch in the production. A photo session followed the wedding ceremony, and then came a supper with bootleg champagne. In the late afternoon the newlyweds left by train for the Del Monte Lodge, a resort hotel three hundred miles up the coast on the Monterey Peninsula, for a short honeymoon that would bring no surprises.

Inevitably, the marriage of Hollywood's number one bachelor was the subject of a great deal of Hollywood gossip. The cynics said Thalberg had married Norma to show that he was different from his more conventional Jewish colleagues. Writer Edmund Wilson, visiting Los Angeles, noted in his diary a Jewish woman friend's theory that "Jewish men thought themselves ugly, so had to keep proving to themselves what they could do in the way of getting Gentile girls . . . any dumbbell from Indiana . . . Thalberg and Norma Shearer had nothing for each other . . . Thalberg just wanted to show what he could do." Rabbi Magnin suggested that Hollywood executives had affairs with Gentile girls because it made them feel less Jewish. "Sleeping with a pretty Gentile girl," the rabbi said, "made them feel, if only for a few minutes, 'I'm half Gentile.' No wonder they made idols out of shiksa goddesses. They worshiped the blue-eyed blondes they were forbidden to have."

Thalberg had taken things one step farther by marrying a Gentile, but the socioreligious implications were not likely to have worried him unduly. He may even have argued that mixed marriages were a good way for bright Hollywood executives to assimilate.

Thalberg was not the first Jewish movie mogul to marry a Gentile. Two years earlier Sam Goldwyn had caused a stir in top movie circles by marrying the beautiful Frances Howard as his second wife. Unlike Norma, Goldwyn's wife did not become Jewish; she even insisted upon her engagement that any children be brought up as Catholics. Interestingly, Sam Goldwyn admired Thalberg more than anyone else in the movies and often sought the younger man's advice on production problems. Thalberg respected the veteran producer's individualism. The fact that both married Gentiles had set them somewhat apart from their community and could have contributed to the bond between them.

But what about Norma? She was an easy target for accusations that she had married Thalberg for her career. "She doesn't love him, you know," Joan Crawford told writer Adela Rogers St. John. "She's made a sacrifice for what she can get out of him, knowing he's going to die on her." Anita Loos, who knew them both, observed: "Norma was bent on marrying her boss, and Irving, preoccupied with his work, was relieved to let her make up his mind. . . . Their relationship had put Irving safely in a groove of his own choice."

The dividends for Norma were both immediate and enormous. When director Bayard Veiller was casting M-G-M's second talking picture based on his own play, *The Trial of Mary Dugan,* several stars vied for the title role, including Joan Crawford and Ann Harding. Then Thalberg told Veiller, "Norma wants to play it. If you want her to play it, you can have her," and that ended Veiller's search.

A word from Thalberg that "Norma wants to play it" worked wonders in concentrating the mind of a Metro producer or director, and the competition was immediately annihilated. Joan Crawford's plaintive lament, "What chance do I have now? Norma sleeps with the boss," reflected the sentiments of every woman under contract at M-G-M—with the exception of Garbo, who was in a class all her own. The situation was particularly galling for Joan Crawford—first because she herself had never aroused much interest in Thalberg, and second because she felt Norma had patronized her even before marrying Thalberg and now patronized her even more.

Years later Norma was to admit to a member of her family that Thalberg had never in so many words told her he loved her, but he had shown it in the way he had always

treated her. The same could be said of Norma's own feelings about Thalberg. From the first day of their marriage
she had made it plain in public and private that her husband had priority over everything else. So if there was no
grand passion in the marriage, there was a partnership
based on mutual respect, advantage, and friendship—all
within a time frame that neither mentioned but that over-
shadowed and conditioned their life together.

If Norma was a bigger star at the studio, she was a
diminished one at home. In reality she was not "at home"
at home. Number 9401 Sunset remained Henrietta's house;
she sat at the head of the table. At the other end sat
William. When Irving and Norma entertained, Henrietta
invited the guests, planned the menu, and acted as hostess.
According to Eddie Lawrence, Strickling's deputy at M-G-M
and Norma's publicity handler, Norma once planned a Saturday dinner party at the house and invited several guests,
including Monta Bell. On Friday she learned from one of
them that they had all been disinvited by Henrietta, who
said Thalberg had had a very tiring week and needed to
rest. Since Henrietta had made Thalberg's health the point
at issue, and Thalberg's health was sacrosanct to both
women, Norma could hardly force a showdown. On another
occasion when the Thalbergs were planning a dinner,
Norma had decorated the dining room with a profusion of
yellow roses. When she returned from a day at the studio,
the roses had all gone and Henrietta's flowers were arranged in the dining room.

Norma and Thalberg slept in separate bedrooms at
opposite ends of the house, rooms assigned to them by
Henrietta, and at night she continued her routine of giving
her son his various medicines and literally tucking him into
bed, just as she had done before his marriage. Yet somehow,
observed Irene Selznick, "Norma and Henrietta managed,
but there could never have been real peace between the two
women."

There was the consolation that aside from enhancing her

status at M-G-M, marriage had also pitchforked her into the top echelons of Hollywood society. Inner-circle names she had previously known only from the society columns of the newspapers now invited her to their homes. She found herself a frequent visitor to Pickfair, home of Mary Pickford and Douglas Fairbanks, Sr., and to San Simeon, Hearst's imposing castle 250 miles north of Los Angeles, and to Ocean House, the 118-room beach house Hearst had built for Marion Davies in Santa Monica.

At Pickfair Norma impressed Fairbanks and astonished other guests with her athletic party tricks. She would do cartwheels or stand on her head. Another of Norma's performances was to kneel with a glass of water balanced on her forehead and then rise gracefully to her feet without spilling a drop. For Thalberg this was a new side to Norma, and he looked quizzically tolerant, as he always did when confronted with eccentricity.

At San Simeon the protocol was stricter and the castle itself a formidable retreat: 150 rooms boasted a wealth of European antiques, from Gobelin tapestries to Renaissance Madonnas; it offered a mosaic-tile indoor pool, medieval towers with thirteen bells that carilloned the hours, and a magnificent view of the 350,000-acre estate that included a zoo and a mausoleum for Hearst's favorite dachshund. Because of the distance from Los Angeles, San Simeon parties were weekend affairs, and guests arrived and departed in a special train. At the castle they assembled for a single glass of sherry before moving to the refectory for a four-course dinner without wine. They were then seated in the Gothic library for the inevitable movie screening.

Besides the socializing at home, there was the high-style travel. Five months after their marriage—on February 15, 1928—Thalberg and Norma set off on their first trip to Europe. For Norma it was the first of many royal departures. Mayer, Eddie Mannix, Will Hays, Joe Schenck, Jack Gilbert, the Thalberg team, and others saw the departing couple off at Los Angeles Central Station as they boarded the train for New York. Six days later the Loew's Inc. brass, led by Nick Schenck himself, escorted them to the Port of New York, where the SS *Mauritania* would spirit them to Cherbourg.

Mayer, showing off his Washington connections, had sent a telegram to Secretary of Commerce Herbert Hoover asking him to arrange for "my young associate Irving G. Thalberg" to receive "letters and credentials similar to those you secured for me from the State Department, which were very helpful and a great source of comfort when I made my trip to Europe three years ago." The State Department obliged with letters to American embassies in Europe requesting them to give the Thalbergs any assistance they might require; Hoover added personal introductions, and the young couple traveled to Britain, Italy, Germany, Switzerland, and France as VIPs. On March 1 they crossed by train into Germany. Hearst had recommended a heart specialist at Bad Nauheim, a spa near Frankfurt. Dr. Frenz Groedel examined Thalberg, pronounced his condition generally good but added the usual refrain about the dangerous consequences of taxing his heart through overwork and the importance of avoiding chills.

In the museums of Europe Thalberg discovered a visual feast. His eyes devoured paintings, statues, frescoes, and buildings. For nearly three months Norma trailed dutifully behind her husband, watching him gobble up culture and file away images. She listened to him vow that soon they would be sufficiently well off to spend part of the year in Europe, and that dream was to become a fixed point in his thinking and somehow to be connected with postponing the end.

For Norma, the trip provided an opportunity to perfect the role of the top Hollywood executive's wife, which she was to play flawlessly from then on. At each stop, M-G-M's overseas staff lavished attention on the couple, organizing receptions and press conferences and seeing that they met the right people. Norma looked and behaved perfectly, rarely saying much and gazing intently at Thalberg while he held forth with his charismatic self-assurance.

On May 28 the Thalbergs returned to the United States with their memories and their trophies. The latter included French director Jacques Feyder, whom Thalberg had signed after seeing his film *Thérèse Raquin* in Paris, and a sixteen-year-old Viennese dancer named Eva von Plentzner. The combination of Greta Garbo's spectacular success and the Thalberg-Mayer rivalry made it inevitable that Thalberg would attempt to outdo Mayer by bringing back another Garbo. Mayer characteristically took the credit for recognizing the potential of the young Swedish woman he had so grudgingly hired. If anyone, besides Garbo herself, was responsible for her instant impact, it was the man who had chosen her pictures and steered her early career, Irving Thalberg. But at M-G-M Garbo was now touted as Mayer's greatest find.

When Thalberg's discovery landed in New York, the staff of M-G-M were not impressed. She was a beautiful brunette, but too heavy and awkward. Still, the New York staff remembered the newly arrived Garbo and gave Eva von Plentzner the benefit of the doubt. Her name was changed to Eva von Berne, after Paul Bern; she was given a role in *The Masks of the Devil*, an important M-G-M production starring John Gilbert and Alma Rubens. When Thalberg watched the first rushes of the picture, he realized that his discovery was no actress. She could not take direction, she moved clumsily, and she was incapable of conveying any emotion. So, after only a few days on the set, Thalberg ordered her taken off the picture. The studio's beauty specialists were immediately instructed to transform Eva von Berne as Garbo had been transformed, and then Thalberg put her back into the movie and gave her another chance.

She finished the film, but the result was no better. On the screen she was slimmer, her looks were striking. But if anything, correcting the physical flaws brought into sharper focus the real problem. She was without talent. Thalberg's Garbo was not assigned another picture, and when her initial six-month contract expired, the studio dropped her and bought her a passage home. Thalberg was not at the station to see her off; nor had he made himself available to say good-bye when she left Culver City for the East Coast and home.

The New York office had been given strict instructions to arrange her departure without fanfare. She had been booked on a ship that was leaving the same night that her train arrived because the studio wanted to avoid spending money on her hotels and meals. Distressed and bewildered, she sailed to Europe on a little German ship, a far cry from the luxury liner in which she had arrived.

7

QUALITY
TALKING PICTURES

Irving Thalberg's life strad-
dles one of those seismic
cracks in the surface of
history, with the silent movie era on one side and the
introduction of sound on the other. The arrival of the
"talkies" ushered in a new age in motion pictures—the most
important technological development in mass communications after radio. Yet it was some time before Thalberg
accepted its long-term significance. On December 28, 1927,
he and Norma had accompanied the Goldwyns to the Los
Angeles premiere of *The Jazz Singer*. All of Hollywood
turned out that Wednesday evening, and at the end of its
eighty-nine minutes the audience sat for a long time in
stunned silence. Then they gave the film a standing ovation.
But Frances Goldwyn remembered seeing "terror in all their
faces"—the fear that "the game they had been playing for
years was finally over," and in the car going home Goldwyn
and Thalberg both brooded in silence.

With hindsight, the addition of music and dialogue to motion pictures seems a natural progression, but at the time Thalberg, perhaps because M-G-M's silent films had been so successful, either failed to grasp or blocked out the enormous potential of this development. Experiments in sound technology had been going on in Hollywood since the mid-1920s, but not at M-G-M. In 1926 Warner Brothers launched the Vitaphone sound-on-disc system and that year released *Don Juan,* which had sound effects and music but no dialogue. Departing for Europe, Thalberg had told his associates, *"The Jazz Singer* was a good gimmick, but that's all it was. We shall continue to rely on quality pictures to enhance our prestige and bring in the profit."

In New York he had discussed the matter with Nicholas Schenck and found him skeptical and unwilling to undertake the huge expense involved in equipping Loew's theater chain for sound films. Thalberg did not try to persuade him. He did not seem to recognize either the magnitude of the technological leap or the potential of films with a full-length sound track. In Thalberg's absence Warner had gone farther than the experimental few words in *The Jazz Singer* and produced the all-talking *Lights of New York,* and Paramount released its first sound film, *Interference.* Both were box office successes, and their popularity with movie audiences was certainly not attributable to the quality of the pictures. So Schenck switched signals and instructed M-G-M to tool up for sound movies.

Slowly, skeptically, Thalberg began the process of converting M-G-M to the new sound technology. His lack of conviction is reflected in the decision to ask his brother-in-law, Douglas Shearer, to form a sound department. Shearer was an engineer with a keen interest in electronics, but he had no knowledge of sound techniques. A Thalberg who was focusing on the problem would have scoured the country for the leading expert and, in the best M-G-M tradition, hired him regardless of cost. Fortunately for M-G-M, Douglas Shearer was both thorough and resourceful. "[Mayer and

Thalberg] ordered me to do the job," Shearer recalled. "They didn't just give it to me." Shearer went to Bell Laboratories in New Jersey, where the latest equipment was being developed, "to see what I could learn." Then he put together a crew—"which I stole from every which where. I had a guy from Bell, another from somewhere else, a few from the colleges."

By the summer of 1928 other studios were releasing more full-length sound pictures, and in the teeth of increasing panic calls from Loew's Inc. exhibitors clamoring for "talkies" from Metro, Thalberg's approach remained unrelentingly cautious. He started experimenting with sound effects and musical tracks. In August 1928 audiences heard Leo, the studio's trademark lion, roar for the first time from the screen in *White Shadows in the South Seas*. Then he added dialogue to another already completed silent film, *Alias Jimmy Valentine*, a mystery thriller starring William Haines, Lionel Barrymore, and Leila Hyams. The scenes with sound were shot at Paramount because M-G-M's sound stages were still under construction at the time.

Next Thalberg turned his attention to the studio's contract players. The introduction of sound had cut like a scythe through the ranks of Hollywood's silent stars, who suddenly had to produce voices as attractive as their faces. Stutters, heavy foreign accents, and voices that recorded higher-than-normal pitch were suddenly exposed on the screen. Business was booming for elocution and speech teachers. Vilma Banky, whose English was heavily larded with her native Hungarian, struggled with elocution lessons for a while and then left to work in Europe. Nazimova, realizing that she was out of her depth, retired from the screen. Constance Talmadge, who had a thin, light voice, also quit the movies, remarking, "Leave them while you're still looking good and thank God for the trust funds Mama set up." She supplemented the trust funds by marrying Chicago millionaire Townsend Netcher.

Thalberg's main concern was how audiences would react

to hearing the stars speak for the first time. "Audiences have formed their own idea how each star sounds," he said. "They've heard the voices in their head in picture after picture, and what they hear coming from the screen may be disappointing. It's very risky." To reduce the risk he brought in speech coaches to work with the contract players—behind closed doors, to reduce the risk of leaks and malicious rumors. Then some of the leading stars made recordings at the University of Southern California's cinema department, where their voices were analyzed to determine whether they were "dyaphonic," or suitable for talkies.

Norma Shearer had to face the anxiety of speaking with a Canadian accent, which was not quite American but not foreign, either. However, when she took the test her voice was pronounced excellent, medium pitch, and fluent. Joan Crawford's low, husky voice suited her screen persona, and Marion Davies's stammer disappeared. Mae Murray's voice was squeaky and her star quickly faded, as did Ramon Novarro's for the same reason.

Thalberg himself also tested and was told his voice was too "white," or high-pitched, which hardly mattered in his case, but did in the case of Jack Gilbert, whose voice on the screen turned out to be what was kindly described as a "light tenor." The great screen lover's first talking performance brought giggles from the audience. Metro's sound engineers corrected the problem, and in subsequent films Gilbert's voice registered at respectable levels. His failure to make the transition after that was more a matter of style and—ultimately—alcoholism. In *His Glorious Night* (a silent movie title if ever there was one) and subsequent films until his death in 1936, Jack Gilbert remained the silent star in manner and gesture and both on the screen and in life looked sadly anachronistic.

Besides the challenge of radical changes in technology, the introduction of sound confronted the studios with one crucial question: Where was the story material to come from? From the start the answer was obvious: from an even heavier reliance on stories with a proven track record. In fact, the introduction of sound brought less original material to the screen than before. Although this may have been good marketing strategy, reducing the odds of box office failure, it amounted to a lost opportunity.

Thalberg seemed to see talking pictures as an extension of the theater rather than as a medium in its own right—a way of bringing the theater to a wider audience through filmed plays. He may have seen this fusion as a means of legitimating the movies. "The making of pictures is a career just as honorable, just as exciting, and a good deal more profitable than the stage," he wrote to Brian Aherne, and one gets the impression that this was a line he had used before to entice leading stage stars to M-G-M. Thalberg was also influenced by Paul Bern, whom he had sent to New York to sign up actors and buy as many plays as possible.

Playwrights, too, figured prominently in the equation, because the advent of sound had almost overnight radically altered the techniques of writing for the screen. ("A silent film was like writing a novel, and a script for a talking picture was like writing a play," said Lenore Coffee, one of Thalberg's early writers for talking pictures.) Sound movies started a drift of established writers to work in the movies and altered Hollywood's intellectual landscape. Humorists such as Donald Ogden Stewart, George S. Kaufman, and S. J. Perelman, leading novelists including William Faulkner and F. Scott Fitzgerald, all spent time in the studios, attracted by the money and the weather.

By now M-G-M's first two sound stages were completed, cavernous, bunkerlike buildings with eight-inch-thick concrete walls to keep out the noise and soundproof camera booths synchronized with recording equipment in an adjoining building. Thalberg inaugurated them with *Broadway Melody,* which started off as another part-sound movie but blossomed into the studio's first full-length talking picture as shooting progressed and pressure built to complete the transition to sound.

Thalberg's original intention had been to include very little dialogue. *Broadway Melody* was the backstage story of a sister act (Bessie Love, Anita Page) broken up by a song writer (Charles King) who is loved by one sister and in love with the other one. To write the songs, Thalberg chose a relatively unknown composer-and-lyricist team, Arthur Freed and Nacio Herb Brown, and their score produced three hits—the title song, "You Were Meant for Me," and "The Wedding of the Painted Doll." About a third of the way through the filming, Thalberg felt he could surrender to pleas from Loew's Inc. to deliver an all-sound film, and a Broadway playwright, James Gleason, was brought in to add contemporary backstage slang.

When the shooting was finished, Thalberg decided that "The Wedding of the Painted Doll" song-and-dance sequence was too static and ordered it redone with added zest. To reduce the cost of the already overbudget production, Douglas Shearer suggested that the cast could mime for the cameras to the already recorded music played back to them over loudspeakers.

"Can that be done?" Thalberg asked.

"Well, it should work," Shearer replied, unsure of a procedure that was to become standard in Hollywood.

Broadway Melody was hailed by both critics and audiences. Costing $280,000, it was to gross $4 million. It was also the first M-G-M production to win Best Picture Award from the Academy of Motion Picture Arts and Sciences, founded two years earlier.

The film caused a row between Norma and Thalberg, a row that was both trivial and, as far as is known, unique. Trivial because it was apparently caused by Norma's discovery that Thalberg had sent Bessie Love flowers on her first day on the *Broadway Melody* set—something he had never done for Norma; and unique in the sense that it was the only known open conflict between them. But living at 9401

Sunset had not become any easier for Norma. She moved in with her sister, Athole, by then married to director Howard Hawks.

The separation lasted three or four days. Then Thalberg sent his chauffeur to pick up his wife and return her to the house.

He never referred to the incident, and neither did Henrietta, but behind the facade of politeness, the estrangement between wife and mother-in-law deepened into an underground hostility, and Norma was more determined than ever to persuade Thalberg to move out.

However, it was shortly after Norma's return that Thalberg let her have the title role in M-G-M's first planned all-dialogue movie, *The Trial of Mary Dugan*, an adaptation of Bayard Veiller's Broadway hit. Originally he had thought of giving the role to the stage actress Ruth Chatterton.

The Trial of Mary Dugan was in the literal sense a filmed play. The entire action took place in a courtroom, where a showgirl is on trial for the murder of her wealthy boyfriend, and since all the early sound equipment was cumbersome, the single set was a point in its favor. Coached by former stage actress and Belasco star Mrs. Leslie Carter, now sixty-seven and playing character parts in Hollywood, Norma gave her emotional all in a performance that, like the movie itself, now plods and creaks slightly. But at the time the picture was well received and established her as a leading lady of talking pictures. While most of M-G-M's major players were eased into sound production in *The Hollywood Revue of 1929*, a pastiche of star turns, Norma had taken the plunge in a full-length role and given a virtuoso performance.

"M-G-M is still behind the other studios in sound production," Mayer admitted in a memo to Thalberg, written in October 1929, "but quantity is not important . . . what matters is that M-G-M becomes identified with the quality talking picture!"

Quantity, however, was what the front office in New

York was demanding as the public clamor for sound movies increased. "When sound came in, everything was new all over again," David O. Selznick once said. "It was the first western with sound, the first war picture with sound, the first swashbuckler with sound." Filming on the new stages went on day and night. Work was slowed down, however, by a widespread lack of experience and the vagaries of the new sound system. Voice levels varied wildly in the same scene from a whisper to an ear-splitting shout, and take after take was ruined by microphones picking up unwanted noise. Basil Rathbone, the British actor who was one of the recent Broadway imports, recalled a typical noise problem of this kind on the first day of filming on Norma's next sound picture, *The Last of Mrs. Cheyney.* "Norma's dress was very beautiful, but as she walked around in it ... the materials used gave the impression of a heavy storm at sea," Rathbone wrote. "From 9 A.M. to 5 P.M. attempts were made to silence Norma's gown, and we never shot a foot of film! The next day Norma wore a new dress and all was well."

The advent of sound set off a flurry of expansion, especially of the most successful studios. Stock certificates flew like bullets in a western. Warner Brothers merged with First National and then moved to a new studio First National had built for itself in Burbank. Joseph Kennedy muscled into the Pathé organization, which he merged with the Keith-Albee-Orpheum theater chain and David Sarnoff's Radio Corporation of America into the Radio-Keith-Orpheum corporation. Meanwhile, William Fox had built his Fox Movietone studios in an area between Beverly Hills and Culver City and was quietly buying up Loew's stock with the aim of taking over the country's largest movie theater chain.

The operation, of course, would have put Fox in control of Metro-Goldwyn-Mayer Studios, yet Fox had Nick Schenck's secret support because Schenck stood to make over $8 million from the sale of the stock. But they had reckoned without Louis B. Mayer, who was not about to see his livelihood disappear without a fight. His political hero Herbert Hoover was now in the White House, and Mayer urgently appealed for help to powerful friends in Washington. In March 1929 the Justice Department filed an antitrust suit against Fox.

But Fox pressed on with his takeover bid. He had borrowed more than $50 million from the Chase Manhattan Bank and other financial institutions with which to buy Loew's stock on the open market. On March 4, 1929, the *New York Times* reported that he had purchased 400,000 shares of Loew's Inc. from Loew's widow. The acquisition of the family shares gave him virtual control of the company and for a while Mayer and Thalberg faced an uncertain future.

When their fate seemed sealed, events took a sudden turn in their favor. On the morning of July 17, Fox was badly injured in an automobile accident on his way to play golf (ironically with Nick Schenck). While in the hospital his friends advised him to sell his Loew's stock, for the market had risen to unprecedented heights, and he could turn a profit on them. But Fox refused, still determined to gain dominance of M-G-M. In October a crash of another kind finished off his designs on M-G-M. The 660,900 shares of Loew's stock, for which he had paid over $73 million, lost 50 percent of their value overnight. With his finances severely damaged, he was forced to sell a sizable portion of his Loew's stock to service his bank loans and to meet other obligations and was slowly eased out of his controlling interest in Loew's.

Fox's raid had one lasting effect: Nick Schenck found himself on Mayer's permanent shit list, and he was usually "Nick Skunk" whenever Mayer referred to him after that. Thalberg would in due course use the deep antagonism between Schenck and Mayer to his advantage. Mayer's hostility toward Thalberg deepened when he learned that his partner's silence on Fox's takeover bid had been bought by

Schenck and Fox for $250,000. But Thalberg was aware that Mayer had later made his own deal with Fox and was to receive over $1 million and a new contract once the merger was completed. But aside from the implications of Fox's raid, Thalberg was facing a double crisis of his own.

In the summer of 1929, Thalberg found himself in hot water with the Internal Revenue Service. His tax returns had been audited, and he was accused of fraud. The IRS challenged the deduction he claimed for employing his father as his manager and the gift of stocks he had made to Henrietta. An inspector had visited 9401 Sunset, where William had cheerfully denied that he was his son's manager. Thalberg had also engaged his sister, Sylvia, as a script writer at M-G-M but was paying her salary out of his own pocket and claiming it as a deductible expense. The IRS took a dim view of that, too.

His plea that the deductions had been made at the recommmendation of his tax adviser, Margery Berger, and her bookkeeper, Mae Muller, was rejected. He was informed that were fraud to be proved, he would have to pay a stiff penalty or even serve time in jail. The matter hung like a cloud over him, making him unusually tense and testy. He offered to pay the shortfall in an emotional letter to the IRS on July 5, in which he attempted to correct the impression that he had earned a great deal of money. "The first years of my connection with the motion picture industry brought hard work and small pay," he wrote.

Success came gradually, he went on, and because of the demands on him he'd decided that members of his family could be of assistance to him. He'd consulted his father on business matters and employed his sister. He defended the gift of stock to his mother as a well-established principle of law. He added: "I have attempted to show that this transaction was made for the purpose of providing [Henrietta] funds which would protect her from the hazards of speculation and accumulate for her future security. This purpose was uppermost in my mind and not the question of how it should be done for income tax purposes." Thalberg never had much regard for his father's business ability, and the claim that he had sought William's advice is a highly improbable one. Sylvia Thalberg's name was listed in the credits of eight movies, all of them undistinguished, and there is no doubt that she owed her career to her brother.

When the IRS remained unsympathetic, Thalberg reluctantly turned to Mayer for help. Through his Washington connections Mayer managed to arrange for the IRS to drop the charges, but only on condition that Thalberg pay a hefty reassessment, with interest.

To placate the IRS, Thalberg had to borrow heavily, because on top of his tax troubles he had taken a beating in the stock market crash. Mayer had invested in real estate and was not hit hard, but Thalberg was virtually wiped out. He had invested heavily in stocks and bonds, and his losses amounted to upward of $250,000. Ironically he got a welcome windfall of around $150,000 when Rubin and Mayer forced Schenck to pay an indemnity of $750,000 to the partners for supporting William Fox's raid, but that was not enough to bring about his financial recovery, and he was once again forced to press Mayer for more money.

Thalberg was now earning almost $4,000 a week at a time when banks were closing and Loew's stock had lost 35 percent of its market value in two weeks and was still falling. Mayer judged it a bad moment to be asking Schenck for a raise, but Thalberg insisted. So Mayer asked for a redistribution of the percentage deal with Loew's—at his own expense. His share in the studio's profits was reduced by 10 percent, which was added to Thalberg's share, increasing it to 30 percent and cutting Mayer's down to 43. Rubin's share remained unchanged at 27 percent. Mayer regarded this as a personal sacrifice, Thalberg as a more accurate reflection of his worth to the studio.

In 1928 he had supervised the production of fifty-one movies, masterminded M-G-M's successful transition to sound, and guided its stars into the new medium with a minimum of casualties. So his claim of being essential to the studio's success was hardly an exaggeration.

Thus, as he approached thirty Thalberg suddenly found himself with what he at any rate considered relatively little to show for ten successful years in movie production. In 1929 M-G-M posted a record profit of $10.5 million, of which his share under the new arrangement was over $3 million, most of which went to repay the loan he had been forced to take out to cover his tax shortfall. Norma was also nearing the peak of her earning power, but the Thalbergs kept their money separate (to the point of retaining different financial consultants), and Thalberg always regarded it as his sole responsibility to provide for the family. Starting again financially was a limited option, because if his doctors were right, he was now living on an overdraft and could die at any moment. So making money, which had always been high on Thalberg's list of priorities, was now placed even higher.

Those who worked with him felt he was now increasingly driven by some inner compulsion to leave as large a legacy as possible. Others worried about the pace he set himself, but he seemed oblivious of the impact his condition sometimes had on those around him. For example, during one of the numerous script conferences on *Grand Hotel,* he was discussing with Paul Bern and the writers of the picture how to film the death of Kringelein, the Lionel Barrymore character, from a heart attack. "What I would like," Thalberg said, "is one more line. Kringelein says: 'It doesn't matter that life be long, but that one feel it entirely—drain it to the last,' then collapse." Then he recalled that when he had seen the play, "it came as a terrific shock to the audience—when he says 'drain it'—and then he collapses. . . . That scene can make a picture." While Thalberg went on with his explanation, totally unconscious of the irony, those present looked at one another meaningfully.

Perhaps partly because he was in a hurry to get things

done, his philosophy of leadership was autocratic and he knew it. But he saw himself as a benevolent despot, acting in the best interests of his "subjects."

"Scottie," Scott Fitzgerald says Thalberg told him over lunch one day, "supposing there's got to be a road through a mountain, a railroad, and two or three engineers and people come to you, and you believe some of them, and some of them you don't believe, but all in all there seems to be half a dozen possible roads through these mountains. Now suppose you happen to be the top man. There's a point where you don't exercise the faculty of judgment in the ordinary way, but simply the faculty of arbitrary decision. You say, 'Well, I think we will put the road there,' and you know in your heart, and no one else knows, that you have no reason for putting the road there rather than in several other different places. . . . But when you're planning an exercise on a grand scale, the people under you mustn't know or guess that you're in doubt because they've got to have something to look up to." All of which is as clear a rejection of collective leadership as one can possibly get. No wonder Thalberg found it impossible to sympathize with the revolutionaries when he was producing *Marie Antoinette.*

Though not vindictive by nature, he was as decisive and unsentimental about firing an actor or writer whom he thought served him no useful purpose as he was in cutting from a script a scene that didn't work. In the late 1920s David O. Selznick was employed at M-G-M as an assistant production supervisor. The son of Lewis Selznick, who had been a New York–based film pioneer, young Selznick was just starting in the movie business but already showed the energy and pugnacious manner that were to become marked features in the man who produced *Gone With the Wind.*

One day he got into an argument with Hunt Stromberg over which director should be assigned to the movie *White Shadows in the South Seas.* When that was settled, they had a further dispute over the storyline in the picture. For a junior story editor to question the decision of a senior production supervisor even once was foolhardy; to repeat the transgression was seen as insubordination. Selznick then compounded his error by trying to go over Stromberg's head to Thalberg—and doing so in public. Selznick marched up to Thalberg in the commissary and complained in what he later described as "the rather strong language of youth," and the confrontation decided his fate. Thalberg backed Stromberg, and Selznick shouted that neither Stromberg nor Thalberg knew what they were talking about.

Thalberg told him, "If you don't apologize to [Stromberg], you're going to have to leave. We must have authority here."

"I've already cleared my desk," Selznick replied, and stormed out.

Thalberg turned his attention to other matters, and Selznick was gone from his mind. Neither man could know that six years later, Selznick would return to M-G-M as Thalberg's equal—more than an equal since he was then married to Irene Mayer.

Thalberg could be tough with stars, too. When Garbo refused to appear in *Anna Christie,* which Thalberg had chosen as her first talking picture, he told her business manager, "I understand Miss Garbo's bank has gone under and she's lost most of her savings. I try not to take people off salary, but if she turns down this role, I will stop her paycheck." Garbo dutifully appeared when called.

He encouraged his staff to give him an argument, but this did not mean that decisions were reached by consensus. His word was final, even when it came to writing scripts.

"Let's play the scene," he said to director Edmund Goulding during a script conference on *Mata Hari.* What he meant was "let me play the scene."

This was a sequence toward the end of the picture when Garbo's young lover arrives unexpectedly at the house of her spy boss Shubins, whom she has just killed. She has stolen secret plans from her lover and passed them to the enemy. Now, as the net draws in around her, she is trying to avoid implicating the young airman in her crime. Thalberg says: "To me it's clear. Garbo comes out of a door and says, 'What are you doing here?' He says, 'I came to find you.' She says, 'I didn't want you to find me.' He says, 'I can't get you out of my life.' She says, 'What do you want of me—I'm a bad woman; I'm no good—what do you want of me? Keep out of my life.' He says, 'I can't.' She says, 'What—knowing all these things about me?' He says, 'Of course.' She says, 'But I can't—I've tried—I admit I've loved you, but now I realize that I do want to forget about it—forget about you.' He says, 'That's how much it means to you. . . . Come.' He takes her out of the place."

Goulding accepts this monologue without the slightest hint of a question. "You have the scene right there," he says.

Thalberg replies, "Yes. But, of course, it has to be properly written. . . . She's trying to send him out of her life. She doesn't say why she sends him away: 'For God's sake, go—leave me alone—forget about me.' Finally she breaks down and goes into his arms. . . . Do you want a crack at it? But don't drop the mood."

On the screen, little is changed in the scene from the way Thalberg spelled it out. As he spoke he was pacing about his office as he always did when he talked, tossing a coin up in the air and catching it. In the early days of his career the coin was a silver dollar. By the time the decade ended it was a twenty-five-dollar gold piece.

The endless story conferences were an integral part of how Thalberg made pictures. "Let's try it this way," he would say to a roomful of writers, and the sequences would come flowing out of him. Not that his ideas were always the best to emerge from these sessions: but not everyone had the nerve to contradict him, and many of his ideas found their way onto the screen. Then he would realize they were not good and would order the scene to be rewritten and reshot. Going back into production for retakes on a wholesale scale was possible only in a studio where stars and technical resources were readily available. Even in those advantageous circumstances it was a costly business, but it was another integral part of the Thalberg approach. In reality, though, Thalberg's major overhauls were usually reserved for pictures that did badly before a preview audience.

Hollywood tested new movies the way detergent companies test new products, and the practice was to run completed pictures before at least one preview audience in advance of its release. The difference between M-G-M and other studios in this respect was that while most studios were willing to reedit a picture on the basis of the audience's response, Thalberg was prepared to remake it and to keep on remaking it until he got the desired effect.

On preview evenings a Pacific Electric railway car would arrive outside M-G-M studios on a spur extending from the main line to the studio. The car was stocked with soft drinks, cards, and picnic food supplied by the studio commissary. At six P.M. Thalberg and his team boarded the train, followed by Mayer and his guests for the evening. Their destination: a major movie house in the Los Angeles suburbs. Also on the train would be several cans of film, and occasionally an editor would still be splicing the footage together. Margaret Booth recalled one occasion when she was editing titles to a silent movie while the train swayed precariously from side to side.

En route the passengers had supper and played pinochle or bridge for high stakes. Sometimes Mayer sat in for a hand or two: he was not much of a gambler, and whenever he joined, the stakes were tacitly adjusted downward to penny ante. After arriving at the designated theater, the new film would be substituted for the one that was scheduled, and the executives would sit in the audience to gauge public reaction.

Thalberg usually sat at the back of the theater, dictating in an undertone to a secretary. Behind him sat Dean Dorn, a jovial Metro publicity man assigned to keep him supplied with mints and glucose tablets whenever he silently stuck out his hand during the performance. Before his promotion to Thalberg's candy supplier, Dorn was assigned to the

Barkies, a team of trained dogs that appeared in M-G-M short subjects. In those days his pockets would be full of dog biscuits with which to feed the dogs during filming.

On the return ride, Thalberg huddled with his staff reading the cards filled in by members of the audience and dissecting the reaction to the movie like tribal witch doctors examining the entrails of a sacrificial chicken. They contemplated the significance of every comment, collective gasp, groan, or giggle, timed periods of fidgeting and restlessness, and estimated the number of people who had left their seats to go to the toilets, classifying them by age and gender.

After a really bad preview Thalberg would sit alone staring out of the window into the darkness of the southern California landscape flashing past while, in a scene like one of those paintings of Napoleon in exile, his lieutenants stood grouped some distance away, eyeing their leader and talking together in hushed tones. On such occasions they knew that the following morning the movie would begin undergoing major surgery.

There were times when Thalberg would zero in on a detail that he felt was pivotal and that, if corrected, would make the difference between success and failure, and he was often right. He did not himself like gangster films, but in 1930 he decided to make *The Big House,* partly to show that Warner Brothers did not have a monopoly on stories about the seamy side of society. He personally supervised the production, allotted it a big budget, and cast Robert Montgomery, Chester Morris, and Leila Hyams in the leading roles.

The film was previewed twice, both times unsuccessfully, largely because Thalberg had to have a love interest—not a prerequisite in a gangster movie, but then this was an M-G-M gangster movie. Finally Thalberg decided it was the wrong kind of love interest. "I think I know what's wrong," he said after the second disastrous preview. "When Chester [Morris] gets out of prison he goes to see Bob Montgomery's wife and gets into a romance with her. Women don't like that."

After $25,000 worth of retakes, Leila Hyams became Montgomery's sister instead, and a potential box office flop gained broader acceptance and made a profit of $460,000.

One of his best rescue operations saved *The Sin of Madelon Claudet* from disaster. He had chosen the 1924 tear-jerker by David Belasco about a young girl who becomes a prostitute to support her illegitimate child as the screen debut of Broadway star Helen Hayes. It was when Thalberg opted for such sentimental drivel that his choice of material became indefensible. Hayes's husband, writer Charles MacArthur, protested strongly that modern audiences would find the melodrama out of date and that his wife deserved something better for her first picture. But with his eye on the theater, as usual, Thalberg argued that the play had been a hit both when it was first produced and in a subsequent revival. Moreover, he felt the drama would appeal to women, which was always his target audience. He believed that women took their menfolk to the movies, not the other way around.

The picture previewed so badly that Mayer advised him to shelve it and cut his losses, advice a young studio executive had once given him in different circumstances. He also told Thalberg to cancel Helen Hayes's contract. But Mayer's advice only hardened Thalberg's resolve to distribute the film and make a success of it. His assessment was that it was two-thirds viable, and he asked MacArthur to rewrite the last third to make the character less pathetically sentimental and then—to Mayer's intense irritation—put the picture back into production.

Mayer had meanwhile loaned Helen Hayes to Sam Goldwyn for *Arrowsmith* and was worried that he might be forced to cancel the loan-out if the actress had to work on her Metro picture. Thalberg managed to persuade her to appear in both movies simultaneously—that is, report to Goldwyn's studio on weekdays and secretly finish *Madelon Claudet* in Culver City on Sundays and occasionally at night. Inevitably Goldwyn found out she was moonlighting, protested to Metro, and forced Mayer to refund him part of the loan-out fee he had paid for exclusive use of Helen Hayes during the filming, thus increasing Mayer's anger.

Goldwyn also received an unexpected dividend and Mayer an equally unexpected rebuff. When *The Sin of Madelon Claudet* was released, Thalberg used the M-G-M block vote in the Academy Awards to ensure that Helen Hayes won the Oscar for Best Actress. By the time *Arrowsmith* reached the screen, she had become a bona fide star.

Whereas Thalberg's conferences and retakes made the pictures, Cedric Gibbons and Adrian gave them their distinctive, glossy M-G-M look. Thalberg said in an interview that Gibbons and Adrian—whose first name, Gilbert, was hardly ever used—and his own wife had been the most vital influences on his taste. The last may have been a formal compliment to his wife, but his acknowledgment to the other two was real enough, and it was consistent that his taste would come from the movies. Both Gibbons and Adrian had the kind of visual sophistication that he admired, coupled with a knack for theatrical statement.

Gibbons's sets combined Art Deco with a stylized version of reality that he called "architectural engineering." Thalberg would occasionally ask him to reduce the grand scale of his sets to more modest proportions. The Gibbons style found expression in the bedroom—a big bed, usually on a platform, large mirrors, thick pile carpets . . . this was the fantasy of women everywhere. But Gibbons's finest hour was yet to come—namely, his own version of the royal palace at Versailles for the 1937 production of *Marie Antoinette*. M-G-M's royal palace was larger and grander than the original. Thalberg was dead before filming began, and the handsome Gibbons's Versailles was to be his tribute to the man who had charmed, cajoled, and bullied him into stretching the limits of his considerable talents.

Adrian developed a similar aesthetic. Movie costumes had to do more than look good on the screen and were effective only if—as he said—"they helped an actress to realize her role." Most of all, Adrian was an expert at hiding a star's faults and highlighting her good points: for Norma, raised waistlines to make her legs seem longer and an extended shoulder to make her hips seem narrower; for Joan Crawford, exaggerated shoulders to detract from her short-waisted figure, frills everywhere to minimize her aggressive stride, extralarge brimmed hats to complement her wide mouth. The sensuous figure-line gowns he designed for Shearer and Harlow in the 1930s gave satin a bad name. Emotional and gnome-like, Adrian kept armies of seamstresses busy round the clock creating the extravagant clothes that became trademarks of M-G-M's grand style.

8

INTO THE
THIRTIES

It was not the best of times for the Hollywood studios. The switch to sound technology had required a heavy investment, and the economic uncertainty and shifts in the national mood kept the industry off balance, unsure what would work with the public and what wouldn't. The Depression was turning traditional values upside down: at Warner Brothers front-page stories were grist to the production mill. Warner's ground national headlines about gangsters, unemployment, civic corruption, and juvenile delinquency into hard-hitting naturalistic dramas. Mervyn LeRoy directed such gangster epics as *Little Caesar,* and *I Am a Fugitive from a Chain Gang,* making stars out of Edward G. Robinson and Paul Muni. In 1931 James Cagney squashed a grapefruit in Mae Clark's face and became the screen's public enemy number one.

Metro-Goldwyn-Mayer confronted the Depression by steadfastly ignoring it. Whatever the differences between Thalberg and Mayer, there was always consensus about M-G-M making "beautiful pictures for beautiful people," and "beautiful" was an adjective Thalberg used constantly when talking about movies. The company stock fell from sixty-four cents to fifty in the first weeks of the crash, but Garbo, Joan Crawford, and Norma Shearer helped the studio live up to its motto.

By 1931, despite the troubled national economy Metro-Goldwyn-Mayer had embarked on its best years of quality and profitability. In terms of the latter, it would be eight years before the studio would equal its amazing 1929 profit level, but M-G-M would be more successful than most of its Hollywood counterparts in staying afloat in the financial storms of the early 1930s. Most of its films were the product of Thalberg's vision from conception to final execution. A pattern was irrevocably established of steering clear of original source material, and the product was packaged as in a laboratory.

The established stars built up their stock of successes, and new stars were developed. Thalberg had a favorite pronouncement about that: "One picture in which a player makes a success is only one step in the career of a real star. It must be followed by more pictures of an equally important nature, or the success won by the first effort is soon forgotten." This systematic buildup is nowhere more evident than in the case of his wife, Norma. Building a star, Thalberg once told Brian Aherne, "cannot be left to chance, but to a definite plan of campaign," and it was becoming clear that Thalberg's plan of campaign for his wife was to propel her to the position of M-G-M's top star. He had discussed strategy with her before their marriage and now set about putting it into operation, with more than a little help from Norma herself.

In 1930, at Paul Bern's suggestion, Thalberg bought the movie rights of *Ex-Wife,* the best-seller by Ursula Parrott, a novelist whose beautiful, sophisticated heroines reflected the fantasies of women who were living conventional married lives but would rather be somewhere else. The film, renamed *The Divorcee,* was meant to be a Joan Crawford vehicle, but Norma wanted the role: "Very strong, almost ruthless," was how she described it to Ramon Novarro. "Perfect for me, but Irving won't give me the part, because he doesn't think I'm glamorous enough."

Glamour had nothing to do with it. To Thalberg his wife was simply not believable as a hard-edged, sensual, provocative woman. But Norma had a plan that would correct that perception. She had herself photographed in a silver lamé wrap by portrait photographer George Hurrell and sent the pictures to her husband. They showed a woman half reclining on an arm chair, hair tumbling over one eye, her wrap left open to suggest nakedness underneath, and the body language charged with sexual promise. Thalberg was first astonished and then excited. It was a Norma he had never seen before. Thanks to Hurrell's pictures, Norma landed the part in *The Divorcee.* And by the end of the filming she was also pregnant.

Privately Norma did not welcome motherhood, but she knew Thalberg wanted children, and she therefore considered it her part of their marriage bargain. The situation also had its up side. It offered her a means of escape at last from 9401 Sunset. In a rare moment of candor she said as much to Mayer's daughters. "It was the only way I could get out of there," she told Irene and Edith shortly after medical tests confirmed what she already knew about her condition.

Thalberg agreed that it was time to move into a home of their own, but he couldn't bring himself to break the news to his mother. Norma, on the other hand, could and did. "Alas, we will be too many," she said sweetly. "I just can't live here anymore. Isn't that a pity."

The birth of the Thalbergs' son on August 24, 1930, at the Good Samaritan Hospital was a quasi-royal event in Hollywood. It was reported in the press and noted by all the leading columnists. At Norma's insistence, the baby was named Irving Grant, Jr. To Norma's immense satisfaction mother and child returned from the hospital not to Henrietta's home, but to a house in Beverly Hills that Thalberg had rented from Gloria Swanson while their new residence on the beachfront in Santa Monica was under construction.

Free from Henrietta, and the focus of public congratulation, Norma felt for the first time that she was Mrs. Irving Thalberg, mistress of her own house, mother of Irving's child. But Norma Shearer film star was impatient to return to the limelight, and in less than three months she was back at work. The film was *Strangers May Kiss,* based on another sexual adventure by Ursula Parrott, and Norma followed that up with yet another role balanced precariously on the edge of the movie morality code in *A Free Soul.*

In *A Free Soul* she played Jan Ashe, the spoiled debutante daughter of a famous criminal lawyer who finds sexual excitement down market in the arms of a handsome young mobster. Lying on the couch in his apartment, avidly eyeing her new conquest, she breathes, "A new kind of man, a new kind of world." From the start she makes it clear that her interest is exclusively sexual. When he starts to talk about himself, she cuts him off and demands, "Come on, put 'em around me." When she decides to leave him, the gangster shoves Norma violently back on the couch and orders her to "take it and like it." Norma being manhandled sent audiences into frissons of excitement, and though Lionel Barrymore as the famous lawyer chewed up the scenery in the courtroom for the last couple of reels, earning himself an Academy Award, audiences remembered Shearer's rich bitch and her rough-diamond boyfriend.

The latter was a young actor destined to become one of M-G-M's all-time greats. Lionel Barrymore had brought him to Thalberg's attention, and Thalberg had signed him to a contract, protruding ears, bad teeth, and all—not out of personal conviction, but because Eddie Mannix and other M-G-M executives saw his potential. *A Free Soul* was Clark Gable's first role as a contract player, and he created something of a sensation with audiences. True to his strategy,

Thalberg gave him the full star-making treatment: publicity and a number of movie roles in quick succession playing opposite already established stars in order to ensure maximum exposure.

M-G-M had never until that time had a male star with an action-man image, and the studio was breaking new ground in projecting Gable as a rugged outdoorsman equally comfortable with a hunting gun or a gold-tipped cane. In just over one year he appeared in seven pictures, including one each opposite Garbo (*Susan Lenox: Her Fall and Rise*), Crawford (*Possessed*), Marion Davies (*Polly of the Circus*), and Shearer (*Strange Interlude*). By the fall of 1931, when Thalberg, convinced of Gable's potential, gave him top billing in his own picture, *Red Dust*, Gable was immovably fixed in his star persona as Metro's leading man. Playing opposite him in *Red Dust* was the most recent newcomer earmarked for star treatment, Jean Harlow, and the process had thus come full circle.

If *A Free Soul* launched Gable's career, it also ended a phase of Norma's as the screen's most sophisticated "other" woman. In a decade in pictures she had played a remarkably wide range of roles, including a cigarette girl, a dowdy secretary who turns out to be not so dowdy with her hair down and without her glasses, an international jewel thief, an actress, and a double role as a taxi dancer and a judge's respectable daughter. To Thalberg this added up to a remarkably versatile talent, and he decided that Norma had what it took to become the screen's equivalent of a first lady of the theater. The concept combined Thalberg's interest in—almost fixation for—the theater and his dedication to his wife's career. Norma would bring to the screen the major successes of Broadway's famous actresses—Katharine Cornell, Lynn Fontanne, and Gertrude Lawrence.

Of Norma's eleven film roles over five years after 1931, all but one had recently been performed by a leading stage actress. Only two of the films made serious money at the box office, and several never broke even. But one of

Thalberg's strengths was his skill at damage control, and the mixed success of Norma's later films coincided with the emergence of his truly inspired concept of the "prestige" picture.

A successful studio, he began to say in 1933, was justified in making a few high-quality pictures every year that would enhance its prestige without necessarily making a profit. The innovation was carefully contained within the star system: there was no question, for instance, about making a picture with total unknowns or about giving a director creative freedom; but within its limitations the concept, inimical to the basis of the studio system from Biograph on, was brilliant. It meant that if any other producer failed to make money on an expensive production, the picture was regarded as a flop. If one of Thalberg's high-budget pictures bombed at the box office, it could always be classed as a prestige production.

Thalberg's "prestige" movie thesis had several ramifications, one being that M-G-M was, or appeared to be, prepared every so often to make a picture that was likely to have limited public appeal but would enhance the studio's image. Another was that the studio looked at its output as a whole, not as a series of individual motion picture releases, and was ready to invest the returns of a box office success in another picture that was not expected to show a profit.

Thalberg's prestige picture policy began to wobble when it turned out that his prestige pictures were for the most part movies starring his wife on which he had lavished money, talent, and attention (*Private Lives, Romeo and Juliet, The Barretts of Wimpole Street*) with little to show for it at the bottom line beyond a few favorable reviews. A case in point was *Private Lives,* the first of Norma's succession of stage roles. The film version of Noel Coward's mannered comedy was a critical success for Thalberg's wife but showed no profit for Thalberg's studio. Yet M-G-M held on to the idea of prestige pictures even after Thalberg's death, enabling Mervyn LeRoy to produce one of Hollywood's most famous movies, *The Wizard of Oz,* in spite of its prohibitive cost and what were seen as its dubious chances of being a box office success.

Norma, who had no stage experience whatsoever, was at first doubtful about following in the footsteps of the grande dames of the Broadway theater. Partly to help his wife, and also to give himself a basis for writing the screenplay, Thalberg introduced a practice that became standard procedure for every current Broadway play that he acquired. A performance of the stage play was filmed with the original cast—Noel Coward, Gertrude Lawrence, Laurence Olivier, and Jill Esmond—to serve as a guideline for production, pacing, the timing of the individual lines for laughter, and individual performances. Thanks to the filmed play Norma had the opportunity to study Gertrude Lawrence's interpretation as often as she wanted. And to further bolster his wife's confidence, Thalberg assigned her favorite director, Sidney Franklin, to direct the picture.

Thalberg talked a lot about the importance of writing in the movies ("If it isn't for the writing, we have nothing"), but he said little about the directing. Working with Erich von Stroheim and a few other independent directors had shaped his preference for cooperative, dependable craftsmen who functioned under his close supervision. Often a director was not assigned to a picture until the script was virtually completed. In many instances the director, even when he had been selected, did not attend script conferences. Moreover, only some of them had a say in editing their own pictures.

Among Thalberg's regular standbys, W. S. ("Woody") Van Dyke, Clarence Brown, and Victor Fleming coped imaginatively with dramatic action; Edmund Goulding and Sidney Franklin were at home with plushy interiors; and Monta Bell handled light comedy. Only King Vidor was occasionally given a chance to make a picture of his choice, such as *The Crowd* or *Billy the Kid.* There was also Tod Browning, who had followed Thalberg from Universal. His eerie melodramas with Lon Chaney were original creations that had a large following. After Chaney died in 1930, Thalberg allowed Browning to make *Freaks*.

But directors were also constrained by the shooting script, which at the time had become the central need of studio filmmaking. Not only did the script "break down" the story and systematize the continuity; it also dictated what was to be shot and how. All scheduling and budgeting came down to the shooting script; that was where the money men got their hands on the elements of the story, and that was where the writers, typically, were left behind. Directors were left even farther behind. Thalberg's script instructions were so detailed that there was rarely much room for a filmmaker to maneuver, and his "regulars" provided him with plenty of footage from which to edit the picture.

Thalberg labored over the script with the writers for months, sometimes years. Story and script conferences for *Grand Hotel* stretched intermittently over more than a year, but later *Marie Antoinette* was to take the prize for longevity. The script was in preparation for five years. Transcripts of story conferences that show clearly Thalberg's grasp of detail, his feel for pacing, and his dominance of the proceedings were then distributed to everyone concerned with the production and became the hallowed word—until Thalberg changed everything at the next conference.

Thalberg's writers have always characterized their working relationship with him as a lively, intellectual debate, full of argument and spirited give and take. After his death most writers romanticized him because, in contrast with other studio bosses, he listened to their arguments. "We battled it out," said playwright Donald Ogden Stewart, one of Thalberg's favorite collaborators.

But did they? Half a dozen transcripts, chosen at random, contain several skirmishes but no victories for the writers. When all was said, Thalberg prevailed. He was not sparing in his criticism, nor particularly respectful of the writers' material. "There isn't one thing that's said between pages thirty-six and forty-three that's funny or entertaining," he told Goulding in his opening salvo at one of the *Grand Hotel* conferences.

"You're pulling [*sic*] story," Goulding replied defensively.

"Yes, it's telling story, but you can tell story and at the same time have a humorous touch," Thalberg snapped back. "I think this is awfully dull stuff." And for the next fifteen minutes he reeled off one change after another for improving the pages.

There was no saying how long these solos would last once Thalberg got going. At times he progressed from one scene to another through half the picture. But always there was a sense of direction, with few deviations or asides. Discussing *Grand Hotel,* he bombarded Goulding with specific instructions: "Have Preysing [the tough, unsympathetic industrialist played by Wallace Beery] called 'Director General Preysing' someplace in the script: in Germany everyone is called by their title." Cut down on the length of Lionel Barrymore's speeches, Thalberg ordered: "He deliberates . . . and it will take six reels."

Thalberg had seen Vicki Baum's play *Menschen im Hotel* in Berlin and on his return to California had acquired the movie rights. Then, faithful to his policy of filming Broadway successes, M-G-M financed the New York production of *Grand Hotel* and waited for it to become a hit before starting the movie version. In the script conferences, the German text was often consulted and borrowed from. Thalberg was under no illusions that it was a great play, but he saw its potential as a movie. "To me this is a lousy play that only succeeded because it is lousy," he admitted to Paul Bern. "It's full of life—a painted carpet upon which the figures walk. Audiences love these damn things, if they are properly done."

In *Grand Hotel* Thalberg pioneered a formula that is now familiar (*Stagecoach, Airport, California Suite*) but was then innovative. The interaction of a number of characters hitherto unknown to each other, brought together in one setting, ran counter to the industry's conventional wisdom. If putting more than two stars in one picture was wasteful, using six stars was sheer folly, and Thalberg had a lot of explaining to do when he began to pile stars into his production.

Grand Hotel is a diagnosis, a dissection, and a requiem. The characters are all failures in one way or another, and in the bustling old central European hotel each confronts a personal crisis, which in the case of two results in death. Garbo was the obvious choice for Grusinskaya, the prima ballerina who is past her prime; and Joan Crawford was immediately announced in the role of Flaemmchen, the stenographer who uses sex to get ahead. Then the wife of Douglas Fairbanks, Jr., she had cornered Thalberg at a party with one of her periodic laments that she was not getting any good roles, and he had promptly given her the *Grand Hotel* part, which had been his original intention.

For the Baron von Geigern, the hotel thief with whom Garbo falls in love and who is killed in the picture, Thalberg had initially wanted Clark Gable. John Barrymore got the part when Thalberg decided to cast both brothers in the picture: Lionel played Kringelein, the terminally ill clerk who checks into the *Grand Hotel* for one brief fling at the good life before dying. For a while plans went forward to pair Gable with Crawford. He was to play Preysing, the self-made industrialist and in his way also a failure, with whom Crawford has an affair; but in the end Thalberg opted to cast the rough-hewn Wallace Beery.

Thalberg had script meetings with his writers and director between mid-winter 1930 and early 1932. In their first meeting he outlined his view of the film in his own rambling style. The speech was an attempt to convey a total concept of the picture, and it is interesting to note that throughout subsequent meetings he always brought his writers back to that original perception: "In the play there was this mood," he said. "A group of men and women with terrific problems. . . . But then we come down to a music-filled room in which the characters of our story are, and they all make light of it. Kringelein, Flaemmchen, and the Baron, they're all enjoying life. Kringelein tells the doctor how wonderful, how marvelous, living in the hotel is, how excited he is about it—but, of course, he's dying. Flaemmchen laughs at Preysing, but Preysing gets her in the end. In the last analysis Flaemmchen must have clothes, she must live, she has to accede to Preysing. You get profound philosophy from the lower classes, but no matter how much they fight against the certainties of life, in the end they have to succumb to it, and they do.

"The Baron's love is wonderful assurance to Grusinskaya. His constant buoyancy gives her confidence. She goes out to the theater, buoyant that she will be a success, confident that he will get the money and he'll be on the train with her, but the fact is that he's lying dead and we know it. . . . You get suspense against hope. . . . It was so beautiful in the play. Not a woman in her prime, a disillusioned woman who had faith again. I can see Gable play the Baron."

The atmosphere on the set was edgy when both screen divas were working. Garbo followed her usual routine of arriving on the set on time, sunbathing alone in a screened-off area near her dressing room between takes, and leaving promptly at six P.M. on the dot. Convinced that she was being snubbed by Garbo, Crawford, according to an M-G-M insider, "would arrive late on the set each day, rolling up in her mobile dressing room, to the tune of 'I Surrender, Dear' played as loudly as her gramophone could play it." Crawford's behavior reflected her insecurity at being thrown into such distinguished company. Determined not to be left behind, she hired an acting coach and put every ounce of effort and experience into her performance.

Goulding shot 270,000 feet of film on the Berlin hotel set, which was not a replica of an existing establishment, but Cedric Gibbons's wonderful composite of features from various hotels in Mittel Europe to create a mood-filled setting. Then Thalberg began the lengthy process of producing a 10,000-foot final cut. Several scenes were reshot as Thalberg fussed obsessively over detail. In one editing conference, Thalberg, among other things:

Wrote his own version of the first love scene between Garbo and John Barrymore while Edmund Goulding wrote another version—and then approved Goulding's to be filmed in the retake!

Decided that the sequence in which Garbo, unaware that the Baron has been killed by Wallace Beery, telephones the Baron's room had to be recut to include shots of the Baron's dog in the empty room with the telephone ringing.

In the scene in which Preysing propositions Flaemmchen, he called for a concluding sequence "that will tell you that Flaemmchen has agreed to Preysing getting a room for her that night in the hotel."

Ruled out adding background music to the gambling scene.

On March 17, 1932, Thalberg, Bern, and Goulding carried six reels of film in three suitcases onto a plane bound for Monterey, in northern California, where that evening *Grand Hotel* was sneak-previewed before a regular paying audience. The general reaction was overwhelmingly positive, but some commented that Garbo was too somber, and Thalberg "ordered that Garbo be recalled for [still more] retakes," according to *Variety*.

The work was quickly finished, and on a warm, foggy evening in late April "huge searchlights scraped the low-hung heavens, and pots of incense perfumed the air" outside Grauman's Chinese Theatre in Hollywood for the gala opening of *Grand Hotel*. The premiere was typical of the send-off major studios gave their important productions—black-tie dinner parties beforehand, with guests transported by special limousines to the five-dollar-top-ticket event, twenty thousand fans lining the streets and sidewalks of Hollywood Boulevard, five thousand of Los Angeles' finest to keep them at bay, and the studio's top echelon of stars and executives in attendance.

The first to arrive were the M-G-M top brass—Mayer, Nick Schenck (on hand from New York for the occasion), Mannix, Rapf, and their wives and the top executives from rival studio Warner Bros., including Hal Wallis, Jack Warner, and Darryl Zanuck, also with their wives. "Seldom have I seen so many men and women with their spouses," commented Louella Parsons. Then the stars appeared— Norma, with Thalberg, the latter wrapped carefully in a topcoat and wearing a white silk scarf, Clark Gable, Marlene Dietrich and her husband, Rudolf Sieber, and Jean Harlow with Paul Bern.

Every premiere had a gimmick, and in this case the gimmick was that the arriving guests were escorted by bellhops to a hotel desk in the theater lobby to sign the *Grand Hotel* register. "Do we need luggage?" inquired Harlow. Joan Crawford arrived with Douglas Fairbanks, Jr. She was "suntanned as a berry, dressed in an electric blue dress, with her hair in the new 'bangs style.' Her eyes sparkled, and her voice choked with emotion when anyone spoke to her."

The film had cost $700,000 and returned a clear profit of $950,000. It also went down well critically, winning Best Picture Award for 1931–1932. Though Garbo's role was smallish, she dominates the picture. If Crawford provides the film's drama, Garbo endows it with its magic. Somewhat implausible as a prima ballerina, she is what she plays—a star.

Emboldened by her success in *Grand Hotel,* Joan Crawford asked for the role of Nina Leeds in Eugene O'Neill's *Strange Interlude.* But Thalberg told her there was only one M-G-M star with the right temperament to play Nina Leeds. "Don't tell me," Crawford said. "Let me guess: Marie Dressler," and walked out of his office.

Strange Interlude was Thalberg's next theatrical project for Norma. The actress's role in this commercially risky production called for her to age from eighteen to her sixties in a complex characterization that she didn't quite pull off. To Joan Crawford's not very secret delight, the movie was one of Thalberg's failures. It lost money and with its lukewarm critical reception couldn't even be called a prestige success.

It brought complaints from Mayer and Schenck that Thalberg resentfully considered unjustified. Mayer argued that Thalberg had not only squandered the studio's money, he had also risked the career of a top M-G-M star. By now the Mayer-Thalberg rivalry for control was a fact of life at Metro. Thalberg steered clear of open comment, except to his immediate circle. Mayer complained to all and sundry. Alexander Korda, the British producer, lived briefly in Hollywood at the time. When he decided to return to London he said the greatest relief was not to have to listen anymore to L. B. Mayer complain about Irving Thalberg.

So their relationship continued to veer a dotty course between guerrilla tactics, open warfare, and occasional demonstrations of Mayer's affection. Sometimes it was hard to tell Mayer's immediate intentions, perhaps because Mayer wasn't sure himself. In 1931 Thalberg was trying to secure the services of Edmund Goulding for a series of picture assignments. Mayer questioned the wisdom of this choice, but when he voiced his doubts in a telegram to Thalberg in New York, it was hard to tell whether the tone was friendly or ironic: SCHULBERG [B. P. Schulberg, then production chief at Paramount] THRU WITH GOULDING. ADVISED PICTURE HE MADE NIGHT ANGEL COST $600,000. HIS DIRECTION SO IMPOSSIBLE, UNBELIEVABLE DONE BY A SOBER MAN. HOWEVER, YOU KNOW HIM. HIS SALARY WITH THEM $50,000 A PICTURE. HE OWES THEM EIGHT WEEKS WITHOUT PAY IF THEY KEEP HIM. THEY ARE WAIVING THAT TO GET RID OF HIM. NOT SAYING YOU SHOULDN'T TAKE HIM, BUT THIS INFO FOR YOUR GUIDANCE. URGE YOU TO ACT IN ALL MATTERS AS IF YOU OWNED THE COMPANY 100 PER CENT. DON'T AGREE YOU SHOULD HOLD BACK. CLOSE DEALS WHENEVER YOU FEEL IT IS GOOD FOR US. YOU WILL MAKE MIS-

TAKES, SO WILL I. WE WORRY TOGETHER ON OUR MISTAKES AND GLORY TOGETHER ON OUR WONDERFUL ACCOMPLISH-MENTS. Thalberg hired Goulding anyway.

Mayer and Thalberg began to disagree more frequently over the choice of films, and a case in point was *Red-Headed Woman*. Mayer opposed the un-Metro-like story about a small-town girl who sleeps her way to the top with breezy promiscuity, but Thalberg was intrigued by the personality and thought the audience would be as well, even though he knew the film would be a borderline case with the censor. Possibly it was his way of demonstrating that he was capable of handling bawdy material.

Red-Headed Woman was Jean Harlow's first movie for M-G-M. She had made her mark in *Hell's Angels* when under contract to Howard Hughes, uttering the memorable line, "Wait until I slip into something more comfortable." As she was wearing very little at the time, audiences gasped either in anticipation or disapproval. From then on there was never very much between Harlow and her leading man except some flimsy creation that defined her curvy figure and outlined her nipples, which seemed to be on permanent sexual red alert. By the time M-G-M bought her contract from Hughes, she was no longer a novelty and had been relegated to low-budget productions. Things changed for her when Paul Bern fell for her blatant charms and made it his mission to save her from impending obscurity. Bern had been insistent that M-G-M sign her, and somehow Mayer had agreed.

She was an odd bird among Metro's refined women stars, and for a while Thalberg was unsure how to handle her. He already found Joan Crawford's sexuality too obvious, and Harlow's was even more overstated. Tight censor-ship added to his doubts about finding suitable material for her. In *She Done Him Wrong*, released in 1932, Mae West was able to get away with saying to Charles Osgood, "Is that a gun in your pocket, or are you glad to see me?" But as the Hays Code tightened up, couples had to be shown in twin beds, and in bedroom scenes involving two people of different sexes one of the pair had to have a foot on the floor. As Thalberg saw it, almost any picture focusing on Harlow's sexuality was bound to run into trouble.

Because Bern was his friend, and he was still uncertain who would play the role, Thalberg let him test Harlow for the redheaded Lil Andrews in *Red-Headed Woman*. He felt Harlow tested well, but he wanted an established star to play the role. The top contender by common consent was Joan Crawford, but Thalberg resisted such obvious casting and tested a number of other actresses, including Colleen Moore. Then Bern virtually forced him to run the Harlow test again and cajoled him into taking a chance on her.

On the day she met Thalberg so that he could make an appraisal of her, Harlow had been ordered to the makeup department to be fitted with a red wig. Anita Loos, who was present, recalled that Harlow didn't seem at all nervous in the presence of the man who could skyrocket her into fame.

"How did you make out with Howard Hughes?" Thalberg asked her.

Harlow replied: "One day when he was eating a cookie he offered me a bite." As Thalberg smiled, she went on, "Don't underestimate that. The poor guy's so frightened of germs, it could darn near have been a proposal."

Then Thalberg asked her the question that was uppermost in his mind: "Do you think you can make an audience laugh?"

Harlow replied: "With me, or at me?"

"*At* you," said Thalberg.

"Why not? People have been laughing at me all my life."

As she breezed out of the office, Thalberg commented, "I don't think we need worry about Miss Harlow's sense of humor."

But audiences didn't find her funny—not at first, at any rate. The picture previewed badly, and that night the train ride back to Culver City was a grim one. At the following morning's postmortem, Thalberg diagnosed the problem as the audience's failure to recognize *Red-Headed Woman* as a comedy. "People don't know whether they're supposed to laugh or not," he told Anita Loos, who had written the final version of the script. "We need an opening scene that will set the mood."

Loos wrote a sassy prologue in which Harlow, at the beauty parlor, admires herself in the mirror, then turns to the camera, winks, and says, "Gentlemen prefer blondes? Sez who?" (This was also an inside joke, of course, because Anita Loos was the author of *Gentlemen Prefer Blondes*.)

Then there's a quick wipe to a shot of Harlow in a department store, trying on a dress. "Is this dress too tight?" she asks the salesgirl.

"It certainly is," the salesgirl replies with obvious disapproval.

"Good!" says Harlow, and sashays happily toward the exit.

This time the audience got the point: they were supposed to laugh at this gold-digger—and they did. One reviewer called the picture red hot, which it was in more ways than one. *Red-Headed Woman* drew fire from groups all over the country. Loew's theaters were picketed, and the film was denounced from Catholic pulpits. In Britain, the film was rejected by the censor and never released. The central objection was the absence of retribution. Not only had Lil slept her way to the top, but she got away with it. After attempting to kill her husband and then throwing him over for an aging millionaire, she leaves a racetrack in Paris in the closing shot with an even older millionaire—but the same chauffeur (Charles Boyer), who is also her lover.

Faced with widespread protest, M-G-M eventually withdrew the picture from distribution. By then Harlow was repeating her role as a lady of easy virtue in *Red Dust*, the picture in which Thalberg paired her with Clark Gable. It was obvious from the early footage that they were a perfect match—she was no lady: he was no gentleman. When he saw the sequence in which Gable leers at Harlow taking a bath in a rain barrel, a worried L. B. Mayer, who had hated

Red-Headed Woman, warned Thalberg to make sure *Red Dust* did not land the studio in more hot water with Hays's censorship rules.

Thalberg assured Mayer in an interoffice memo that for the benefit of the censor, Ventine loses out in the final reel to a classy dame (Mary Astor) who did not bathe in rain barrels. Then he added that in Gable and Harlow, "we are bringing to the screen two people who are modern and attractive, and reflect contemporary ideas, feelings, and values."

None of this reassured Mayer, whose values and feelings were traditional and old-fashioned. He blamed Thalberg for the debacle of *Red-Headed Woman.* He had suggested that the film be reissued with a "moral" ending, and Thalberg had flatly refused.

9

707 OCEAN FRONT

The Thalbergs' ten-room Santa Monica beachfront mansion was an M-G-M production. It was built in the French provincial style, chosen by Irving and Norma from a number of designs prepared by Cedric Gibbons. Thalberg had bought the land, and like the Mayer family's Spanish-style home up the road, the house at 707 Ocean Front (later Pacific Coast Highway) was built by studio craftsmen and studio labor. Thalberg had wanted more rooms, but Norma—doubtless fearing an invasion by Henrietta—persuaded him to settle for what by Hollywood mogul standards was a modest-size home. Next door was the Pickford-Fairbanks beach cottage, and from his garden Irving Thalberg Jr. would watch wide-eyed as Douglas Fairbanks, Sr., "used to jump out of the window on the second floor of his house, bounce off the first-floor awning, do a flip, and then go into the pool."

Despite its French shell, the decor of 707 Ocean Front was "contemporary neutral." It was comfortable and uncluttered, the walls were surprisingly bare, and the thirties furniture could have come from a set by Cedric Gibbons. Upstairs was the nursery, two guest suites, and Norma's and Thalberg's bedroom suites in opposite wings. Henrietta's influence was hard to shake.

The Thalbergs' home was the first beach house in Santa Monica to have air-conditioning. Irving's doctors had advised him that the damp salt air would be bad for his lungs. The house also had sealed windows to shut out the roar of the ocean, which kept Thalberg awake at night. Thick wall-to-wall carpeting deadened footfalls. From the highway, nothing was visible. A high wall screened the house from view. Day and night this set was closed, except when the Thalbergs entertained.

The atmosphere was affluent, antiseptic, and a little impersonal, as though it really were a movie set, or as though its occupants were transient tenants reluctant to put down roots. Only Thalberg's library escaped this feeling. There were framed photographs everywhere, and the walls were lined with books recalling Thalberg's boyhood reading, Dickens, Alexandre Dumas, Prosper Mérimée, and a variorum edition of Shakespeare's plays. A movie screen rose automatically from the floor. It was perhaps a consequence of Thalberg's condition that he had never been an accumulator of possessions; and until she was past twenty Norma didn't possess much that was worth preserving. Besides, neither spent much time at 707 Ocean Front, and what was most important to both of them was its suitability as a domestic setting for their public lives.

An invitation to 707 Ocean Front amounted to a royal command. Norma quickly slipped into the real-life role of one of Hollywood's leading hostesses. She liked to entertain on a grand scale, even if she sometimes got carried away. For one party in honor of Helen Hayes she collected an impressive array of Hollywood personalities—the Goldwyns, the Selznicks, Fredric March, his wife, Florence Eldridge, Ernst Lubitsch. When the guests were seated in the dining room, a forty-piece orchestra took up positions in the adjoining sitting room, and at the end of the dinner the guests had to wait for the orchestra to dismantle their paraphernalia and disperse before they could get out. Thalberg gave his wife the same impassive stare reserved for her party pieces, the handstands and glass-balancing acts. She had done it again.

For the most part, the Thalbergs entertained—and were entertained by—the same inner circle of friends. Others were added occasionally, particularly visitors from the East or from abroad, but the hard-core group included Paul Bern and (after her marriage to Bern) Jean Harlow; King Vidor and Eleanor Boardman; producer Arthur Hornblow and Juliet Crosby; David Selznick and his wife, Irene Mayer; the writer Herman Mankiewicz; the Barney Glazers; Edmund Lowe and Lilyan Tashman; director Carey Wilson and his wife, Carmelita; Jack Gilbert and (while they were together) Greta Garbo; the actress Colleen Moore; Basil Rathbone and his wife, Ouida; Sam and Frances Goldwyn; and Cedric Gibbons and his wife, Dolores del Rio. All were movie people, and most had an M-G-M connection. Components of the group met at least once a week at Sunday brunches, a movable feast that convened at the house of one of the group, most frequently Jack Gilbert's. The movie community always started work early in the morning, and the Sunday brunch gave everyone an opportunity to retire early.

The Sunday brunch was immortalized by F. Scott Fitzgerald in his short story "Crazy Sundays," his fictionalized portrait of the Thalberg-Shearer relationship, which together with the unfinished *The Last Tycoon* formed the writer's twin hagiographic works about Irving Thalberg.

Fitzgerald was powerfully, hypnotically fascinated by Thalberg. Here was a man who was everything the writer wanted to be: young, attractive, glamorous, commercially successful without loss of artistry—and at the same time tragic. Fitzgerald was then close to being a burnt-out case, his early success having vanished in a haze of alcohol. He had pinned his hopes on Hollywood to give his career a new lease on life, but not all successful writers made the transition to screenwriting, and Fitzgerald was one of the failures. Thalberg had hired him on the basis of his literary reputation and assigned him to write the script of *Red-Headed Woman*, but he had not liked the result. "Scott tried to turn the silly book into a tone poem," he complained to Anita Loos when he put her to work on a new version. "I'd like you to go ahead and make fun of its sex element."

Dropped from *Red-Headed Woman*, Fitzgerald then proceeded to shoot himself in both feet by behaving badly at a Thalberg Sunday brunch. As with all the Thalbergs' productions, food, service, and cast were perfect. Besides the usual group, the guests included Robert Montgomery, Ramon Novarro, Scott Fitzgerald, and Dwight Taylor, the son of Laurette Taylor. The two writers had agreed in advance that Taylor would make sure Fitzgerald did not drink at the brunch. After briefly resisting temptation, Fitzgerald began sneaking cocktails hidden behind large houseplants and furniture. It was when Fitzgerald decided to become the life and soul of the party that Taylor realized he had failed.

Robert Montgomery entered in riding clothes and was not amused when Fitzgerald asked him why he hadn't brought his horse. Then the writer announced that he was going to sing a song. Ever the impeccable hostess, Norma Shearer inquired courteously if he had a particular song in mind. Why, yes, Fitzgerald said, he had composed a ditty about a dog. Smiling, Norma sent the maid to fetch her poodle. Cradling the dog in his arms, Fitzgerald launched into an embarrassingly sophomoric song about the dog being man's best friend, accompanied by Ramon Novarro at the piano. Norma listened with rapt attention, but after a couple of almost incomprehensible refrains, the other guests became restive and lost interest.

Taylor watched Thalberg, a little figure "standing in the

As others saw him: Man-about-town IRVING THALBERG with hat, CANE, AND GLOVES, IN A MAGAZINE CARICATURE PUBLISHED IN HIS BACHELOR DAYS IN THE MID-1920S. *ACADEMY OF MOTION PICTURE ARTS AND SCIENCES*

THALBERG, NICK SCHENCK, AND MAYER GREET LILLIAN GISH AT LOS ANGELES CENTRAL STATION, 1925. ALSO PRESENT IS HARRY RAPF.
UPI/BETTMANN

THE YOUNG PRODUCER WATCHES LILLIAN GISH ON THE SET OF *LA BOHEME*, 1925. GISH WAS ONE OF THE ESTABLISHED STARS THALBERG SIGNED TO BRING PRESTIGE TO METRO-GOLDWYN-MAYER.
BETTMANN ARCHIVE

AN EARLY PUBLICITY SHOT
OF THALBERG WELCOMING
NEWCOMER NORMA
SHEARER TO THE STUDIO.
*ACADEMY OF MOTION PICTURE
ARTS AND SCIENCES*

THE HOLLYWOOD BRASS TURNS OUT TO WELCOME NICHOLAS SCHENCK,
PRESIDENT OF METRO-GOLDWYN-MAYER, INC., ON A VISIT TO THE COAST.
LEFT TO RIGHT: DEADPAN COMIC BUSTER KEATON, HARRY RAPF, THALBERG,
SCHENCK, MRS. SCHENCK, LOUIS B. MAYER, EDDIE MANNIX, AND
HUNT STROMBERG. *USC CINEMA-TELEVISION LIBRARY AND ARCHIVES OF PERFORMING ARTS*

THE PUBLIC FACE OF THE
MAYER-THALBERG PARTNERSHIP.
EVEN WHEN THE WARM
RELATIONSHIP OF THE EARLY
YEARS EVENTUALLY GAVE WAY TO
JEALOUS RIVALRY AND SQUABBLES
OVER MONEY, THALBERG AND
MAYER COULD STILL MUSTER
A CORDIAL HANDSHAKE FOR
THE CAMERAS. *ACADEMY OF MOTION
PICTURE ARTS AND SCIENCES*

AT THE THALBERG WEDDING.
NEWLYWEDS IRVING AND
NORMA EXCHANGE SMILES
ACROSS HENRIETTA. WILLIAM
THALBERG (LEFT) BEAMS,
BUT HENRIETTA— WEARING
BLACK— STARES GRAVELY AT
THE CAMERA. EDITH SHEARER
(RIGHT), ALSO IN BLACK,
LOOKS ALMOST SAD. *ACADEMY OF
MOTION PICTURE ARTS AND SCIENCES*

THE WEDDING GROUP LINES UP IN FRONT OF CEDRIC GIBBONS'S FLOWER-COVERED TRELLIS AFTER THE MARRIAGE CEREMONY.
LEFT TO RIGHT: CEDRIC GIBBONS, BRIDESMAID BESSIE LOVE, DOUGLAS SHEARER, MARION DAVIES, THE NEWLYWEDS, SYLVIA THALBERG,
WHO WAS MAID-OF-HONOR, L. B. MAYER, IRENE AND EDITH MAYER, EDDIE MANNIX. *ACADEMY OF MOTION PICTURE ARTS AND SCIENCES*

PROUD PARENTS IRVING
AND NORMA POSE
WITH IRVING JR., AGED
ONE. WHILE IRVING
GAZES HAPPILY AT HIS
SON, NORMA POSES
FOR THE CAMERA.
UPI/BETTMANN

NORMA AND IRVING
WITH SIDNEY GRAUMAN
AT THE OPENING OF A
NEW FILM AT GRAUMAN'S
CHINESE THEATER IN
HOLLYWOOD, 1932.
UPI/BETTMANN

"IT ISN'T UP TO ME TO SAY,"
SHRUGGED THALBERG AS
CORONER FRANK NANCE
PRESSED HIM FOR SOME
REASON WHY HIS FORMER
ASSOCIATE, PAUL BERN,
SHOULD HAVE ENDED A
BRILLIANT CAREER. A
VERDICT OF SUICIDE —
REASON UNKNOWN — WAS
RETURNED BY THE JURY.
HERE, THALBERG IS ON THE
WITNESS STAND DURING
THE BERN INQUEST.
UPI/BETTMANN

THALBERG AND MAYER
RIDING IN LOS ANGELES,
1932. *UPI/BETTMANN*

GRETA GARBO AND JOHN
BARRYMORE IN A ROMANTIC
SCENE FROM THALBERG'S
ALL-STAR PRODUCTION OF
GRAND HOTEL, 1932, ONE
OF HIS MOST SUCCESSFUL
PICTURES AS AN INDEPEN-
DENT M-G-M PRODUCER.
THALBERG ORIGINALLY
CONSIDERED CLARK GABLE
FOR BARRYMORE'S ROLE AS
THE HOTEL THIEF. *SPRINGER/
BETTMANN FILM ARCHIVE*

ANOTHER SCENE FROM
GRAND HOTEL, WHICH SET
A VOGUE FOR ALL-STAR
PRODUCTIONS. *SPRINGER/
BETTMANN FILM ARCHIVE*

A TIRED AND GRIM-FACED IRVING THALBERG SHOWN AT HIS DESK
SHORTLY AFTER HIS OUSTER AS METRO-GOLDWYN-MAYER STUDIOS' HEAD
OF PRODUCTION. *BETTMANN ARCHIVE*

IRVING AND NORMA IN GERMAN OPERETTA COSTUMES AT A BON VOYAGE PARTY
GIVEN FOR THEM BY M-G-M STAR MARION DAVIES (LEFT) PRIOR TO THEIR
DEPARTURE FOR EUROPE. COSTUME PARTIES WERE MARION'S FAVORITE FORM OF
ENTERTAINING. THE THEME OF THIS PARTY WAS "A NIGHT IN HEIDELBERG,"
POSSIBLY BECAUSE THE THALBERGS WERE GOING TO GERMANY.

ACADEMY OF MOTION PICTURE ARTS AND SCIENCES

NORMA AS ELIZABETH
BARRETT IN TWO SCENES
FROM THALBERG'S PRODUC-
TION OF *THE BARRETTS OF
WIMPOLE STREET*, 1934. IT
WAS THALBERG'S FIRST
"PRESTIGE" FILM FOR HIS
WIFE. HE WAS DETERMINED
TO ESTABLISH HER AS THE
FIRST LADY OF THE SCREEN.

LEFT: SHE WATCHES
SYMPATHETICALLY AS THE
AUSTERE MR. BARRETT
(CHARLES LAUGHTON) GIVES
HIS YOUNGER DAUGHTER
(MAUREEN O'SULLIVAN) A
HARD TIME. *SPRINGER/BETTMANN
FILM ARCHIVE*

ABOVE: NORMA
WITH FREDRIC MARCH
AS THE POET ROBERT
BROWNING WITH WHOM
ELIZABETH BARRETT ELOPES.
BETTMANN ARCHIVE

TWO SCENES FROM *MUTINY ON THE BOUNTY*, 1935, ANOTHER OF THALBERG'S SUCCESSES, STARRING CHARLES LAUGHTON AS THE CRUEL CAPTAIN BLIGH AND CLARK GABLE AS FLETCHER CHRISTIAN, UNWILLING MUTINEER ON BLIGH'S SHIP, *H.M.S. BOUNTY*. *SPRINGER/BETTMANN FILM ARCHIVE*

THE THALBERGS RELAX ON BOARD BARON LONG'S YACHT, THE *NORAB*,
ANCHORED OFF SANTA CATALINA ISLAND. *UPI/Bettmann*

THE SOCIAL THALBERGS: NORMA AND IRVING, THE LATTER WELL PROTECTED AGAINST THE NIGHT AIR, ARRIVING AT THE PREMIERE OF *THE GREAT ZIEGFELD*, 1936, AT THE CATHAY CIRCLE THEATER. WITH THEM ARE MAYER, LESLIE HOWARD, AND MRS. LESLIE HOWARD. *UPI/BETTMANN*

"I HAD FIVE VERSIONS OF IT,"
M-G-M FILM EDITOR
MARGARET BOOTH SAID OF
THE BALCONY SCENE FROM
ROMEO AND JULIET, 1936.
"ONE WITH TEARS, ONE
WITHOUT TEARS, ONE PLAYED
WITH CLOSE-UPS ONLY,
ANOTHER PLAYED WITH
LONG SHOTS ONLY, AND
THEN ONE WITH LONG-
SHOTS AND CLOSE-UPS CUT
IN." LESLIE HOWARD WAS A
RELUCTANT ROMEO; HE
THOUGHT HE WAS TOO OLD
FOR YOUTHFUL ROMANCE.
SPRINGER/BETTMANN FILM ARCHIVE

THALBERG'S FLOWER-COVERED COFFIN IS CARRIED OUT OF A WILSHIRE BOULEVARD TEMPLE AFTER THE FUNERAL SERVICE, SEPTEMBER 1936. AFTER HIS BURIAL AT FOREST LAWN MEMORIAL PARK, L. B. MAYER WAS REPORTED TO HAVE SAID, "AIN'T GOD GOOD TO ME?" *UPI/BETTMANN*

doorway at the far end of the room, with his hands plunged deep in his pockets, his shoulders hunched slightly in that characteristic posture of his which seemed to be both a withdrawal and a rejection at the same time. There was a slight, not unkind smile on his lips as he looked toward the group at the piano."

The next day, depressed and angry with himself, Fitzgerald sat alone, looking green, in the M-G-M commissary. A group of midgets, pinheads, and Siamese twins from the cast of Todd Browning's *Freaks* bustled in en masse and occupied the next table, causing him to turn even greener. The day improved somewhat when he received a telegram from Norma—I THOUGHT YOU WERE THE MOST AGREEABLE PERSON AT OUR TEA—but Fitzgerald was still scared of Thalberg's reaction. And he was right to be fearful: a week later he was fired.

Fitzgerald was convinced that his dismissal was a result of the incident at 707 Ocean Front. But Thalberg had a high tolerance for eccentric behavior and more likely had simply come to the conclusion that Fitzgerald's particular talents were not suited for screenwriting. In short, Fitzgerald was no longer useful to him.

Although the writer left Hollywood vowing never to return, he was hired again by Metro in 1937. By then Thalberg was dead, but Fitzgerald was no more successful than he had been the first time. After working on a few pictures but receiving screen credit for only one, he was loaned briefly to Selznick International and served time on the *Gone With the Wind* writers' chain gang. Then M-G-M notified him that his contract, which had expired, would not be renewed, and he quit Hollywood, this time for good.

In between Hollywood stints, Fitzgerald had written "Crazy Sunday," a magazine short story churning with conflicting passions of hero worship and revenge for his subject, Miles Calman, who is not hard to recognize as Irving Thalberg. In the story, the writer/narrator starts making love to Calman's movie-star wife, Stella Walker, equally identifiable as Norma Shearer. The wife responds, but they are interrupted by a telephone call. Calman has been killed in a plane crash.

Fitzgerald's love-hate for Thalberg found fullest expression in *The Last Tycoon*, which fueled the Thalberg myth. The bane of Thalberg biographers, Fitzgerald's novel is a classic case of a victim's identification with his tormentor, a portrait of Thalberg on the surface but ultimately Fitzgerald's fantasy of himself as Thalberg. Long after the death of both men, Norma Shearer would be involved in an attempt to film *The Last Tycoon*, which she eventually abandoned. Irving could have told her that any story in which the central character is really two people is well-nigh impossible to film.

One thing Fitzgerald did capture was the glossiness of the Thalbergs' marriage. *Vanity Fair* had previously published Edward Steichen's portrait of the Thalbergs, proclaiming them Hollywood's leading couple: Norma in a blouse with a polka-dotted scarf, Irving for once out of his business suit in a trendy V-neck sweater but still wearing a tie—all in all, a picture of self-assurance and casual elegance. She held his hand; he leaned toward his wife, smiling with evident satisfaction.

Outwardly they were an ideal couple, successful, influential, at the very center of the motion picture community. In a stratified society they were at the top of the social "A" list, and their presence at a function amounted to royal patronage. They had few really close friends because neither Norma nor Irving was comfortable with chumminess or personal intimacy. Norma had a way of sounding as if she were taking people into her confidence, but it was part of her act. Thalberg rarely dropped his guard. He would gaze at people with the clinical look of a scientist scrutinizing a laboratory specimen.

From all accounts their domestic relationship had the intimacy of friendship rather than sexuality. Professionally Thalberg admired his wife and was prepared to give her preferential treatment to advance her career. But the favoritism stopped short of indulging any star behavior. During the filming of *A Free Soul,* Norma began to arrive late on the set, full of apologies but with no explanation. Fearful that the production might fall behind schedule, production manager J. J. Cohn mentioned Norma's tardiness to Thalberg. "Irving never took any nonsense from anyone, Norma included," Cohn said. "He promised to take care of it." Norma's late arrivals stopped.

The sex in their marriage, which got off to a poor start under Henrietta's surveillance, remained low key. Thalberg's sexual drive was hardly supercharged, and he was conscious of being anything but well endowed. He once told Anita Loos that he saw sex as comic rather than dramatic material and personally was more interested in "the deep emotional rapport that can be attained outside the bed." But Anita Loos also recalled that "Irving could spot sublimated sex in every human relationship." One day she told him, "If you ever make a movie on *Frankenstein,* you'll try to prove he had a mad crush on the monster he created!" To which Thalberg replied, "Why not? That old yarn is about due for a new twist."

Sexual proclivities seemed to fascinate him. On one occasion Ernst Lubitsch complained to him that he was being blackmailed. A woman with whom he had had a brief affair on a trip home to Berlin, he said, was threatening to publish his love letters unless he paid her fifty thousand hard-earned dollars. Thalberg was immediately interested. "And what's in the letters?" he asked. Lubitsch produced copies sent to him by the woman and reluctantly handed them over. Thalberg scanned a few pages and told Lubitsch, "Look, my friend, if you can keep *these* out of print for fifty thousand dollars, you've got a bargain. Grab it!"

On another occasion, Anita Loos had a discussion with him about *Mädchen in Uniform* (*Girls in Uniform*), the German semipropaganda film about young women in the Hitler Youth Movement (Thalberg liked to watch German films). He had pointed out the lesbian overtones in the picture and said he wished he could get away with the same scenes in a Hollywood picture.

Norma needed more than deep emotional rapport, but she held her sexual drive in check throughout his life. The variety and number of her affairs immediately after Thalberg's death suggested a woman anxious to make up for lost time. But in his lifetime, her one means of escape was the sexual fantasy of the screen. It was as if her screen character in *A Free Soul* and other such films made up for the sexual shortcomings in her life. Marriage to Thalberg brought satisfaction in almost every respect but left a hollow core of disappointment where the sex should have been.

She readily indulged Thalberg's only sexual oddity, and that—according to two Hollywood figures who knew them well—was his occasional cross-dressing. Because he carefully watched what he ate, Thalberg's thin frame never varied, and Norma's dress size fitted him well, as did her shoes. One of their private jokes was to dine together by candlelight wearing each other's clothes, Thalberg in an Adrian creation complete with makeup, Norma wearing one of his suits.

Fancy dress parties were all the rage at the time, and on such occasions cross-dressing was not uncommon. But though Thalberg went to one Hearst party as a little boy in a sailor suit, there is no indication that he ever appeared in drag in public.

Whatever her unfulfilled sexual desires, Norma did an effective job of juggling the manifold responsibilities of wife, star, mother, and nurse. And daughter-in-law, since Henrietta made surprise raids on 707 Ocean Front to check on her son's condition. Thalberg maintained a clinical attitude toward his illness, carefully noting shifts, changes, and new details in the way he felt and comparing his notes with a pathologist friend, a specialist in degenerative diseases, with whom he shared a vital interest. Dr. David Perla's heart had also been weakened by rheumatic fever, and like Thalberg himself, he faced an uncertain future.

Thalberg and Perla had been friends since their teens in Brooklyn. Perla had married Jessie Marmorston, a heart specialist at Montefiore Hospital in New York. Thalberg had become one of her patients and at her suggestion had begun reading Freud, which had in turn kindled an interest in the growing field of psychoanalysis. He would discuss his illness in letters to Jessie Marmorston or David Perla, but it was never mentioned to others, not even to Norma.

Thanking the Perlas for their gift of a first edition of Freud's collected works on his thirty-second birthday, Thalberg wrote that Freud had joined Epictetus, Kant, and Bacon as his favorite writers. "They stimulate me," he wrote. "The philosophers are brain sharpeners, and Freud has helped me to understand myself and given me courage to confront my particular future, which in the past I had tried to block out."

But Thalberg's birthday party was cheerful enough, with a specially made and very appropriate silent movie, filmed without his knowledge, in which some clever cutting shows him slowly disappearing behind a growing mountain of film in his editing room. These short films on 35 millimeter were a standard feature of Hollywood parties. "Usually very dirty," according to Maurice Rapf, they poked good-natured fun. For Rapf's eleventh birthday Metro made a futuristic picture in which he is running the studio and Thalberg and Harry Rapf, the boy's father, are sitting in Thalberg's waiting room to see him. "Then I'm riding in Thalberg's car with his chauffeur, now a very old man, all whited up," Rapf recalled. Thalberg was always willing to take part in such jokes.

10

THE HEART
OF THE MATTER

Irving Thalberg is what Hollywood means by M-G-M," said *Fortune* magazine in its December 1932 cover story on the studio.

The accolade was amply justified. It had been a vintage Thalberg year. He had supervised the making of thirty-one Metro productions. *Grand Hotel* had paid good dividends, winning the Best Picture Oscar for 1931–1932 amid a shower of generous reviews and netting $950,000 profit. The success of Norma's latest picture, *Smilin' Through,* was another high note. Released in December, it was an instant box office hit—"a showman's dream come true," in the words of the *Motion Picture Herald.*

For all that, Thalberg was despondent and irritable, surprising his staff and friends with uncharacteristic angry outbursts. When he threw his twenty-dollar gold piece up in the air, he would fail to catch it, always with him a sign of extreme exhaustion. But the problem went deeper than that.

The year 1932 had been one of the worst of the Depression. Audience figures were slipping, and some studios were hard hit. Metro's annual profit dropped to $5.3 million, reminding Thalberg and the studio leadership that the studio was not immune from the country's rampant economic malaise.

A new sobriety had settled on the movie community. The frenzy of the jazz age was gone forever, and more sedate rhythms were in vogue. The Thalbergs' dinners and receptions reflected Hollywood's new attempts at restraint and responsibility: on such occasions Norma would often have a harpist strumming quietly in the corner of the living room. But as Thalberg drove to Culver City in his black Cadillac, signs of human misery and deprivation flashed past his window—long lines for food, groups of aimless, wandering souls in the streets.

Invariably a large crowd was stationed at the main gate of Metro-Goldwyn-Mayer Studios. Inside was a world of glamour and fantasy; outside was harsh reality. As Thalberg approached each morning, eager faces pressed against the windows, hoping for a glimpse of a star. But when they saw no star occupying the backseat, the faces withdrew, disappointed. Thalberg stared ahead impassively or read his papers. But he once observed to Lawrence Weingarten that the day there were no crowds peering into his car window, he would start to wonder what he was doing wrong. He never forgot the importance of the moviegoing public. Attending the Hollywood premiere of *Smilin' Through*, he stood calmly beside Norma as she was mobbed by fans, signed autographs, and did a sidewalk radio interview. Watching him, L. B. Mayer muttered to Eddie Mannix, "How does Irving stand it?" In reality, Thalberg's mental scanner was estimating the size of the crowd and making comparisons with other recent premieres. Had the concept existed then, Thalberg would doubtless have been described as a "computer brain."

He was now earning about $500,000 a year, yet he still

grumbled about money—the high cost of medical insurance, his payments of back taxes to the Internal Revenue Service, the expense of bringing up a son. He claimed that he still had not recovered from his disastrous losses in the stock market crash. More than ever he felt unappreciated by Mayer and Schenck—and above all underpaid. His constant complaint was: "I work my butt off so Mayer and Schenck can get rich and sassy." His associates would find him doing calculations on the backs of envelopes and scraps of paper to work out how much Mayer made or Schenck, and the answer always left him gloomy.

For a man facing a virtually certain early death, leaving the family—which he counted as wife, son, parents, and sister—adequately provided for was understandably a pressing concern. Thalberg was thirty-three. On the basis of the doctors' predictions that he would not survive past thirty, he was now living on an overdraft. His state of mind was not improved by the situation of his friends David Perla and Paul Bern. Perla's heart condition was worsening, and Jessie Marmorston had told the Thalbergs that Perla might not have more than another year to live. Even more traumatic was Bern's suicide three months after marrying Jean Harlow.

Norma and Irving had been witnesses at their wedding on the evening of July 2, 1932. Jack Gilbert was best man, and all three attended the wedding reception the following morning in the garden of Bern's hillside house in Beverly Hills. To Thalberg and many others of his circle, it had seemed an odd match—"probably the single most beloved person in Hollywood," as Irene Selznick had described Bern, and Harlow, Metro's reluctant sex symbol. It was inevitable that eventually one of Bern's series of frustrating relationships with drug-addicted or promiscuous actresses would end in marriage. But although her past fitted the pattern, Harlow at least seemed to see marriage as a way out of that past. She had confided to Irene Selznick that her greatest desire was to have a child.

Thalberg liked Harlow and was glad that Bern had found an actress who was not exploiting him. Seeing them together stirred his fantasies, but privately he doubted that the marriage would last. Harlow was then twenty-one, Bern twenty-one years older. He was an intellectual, while she had dropped out of high school, and the Pygmalion overtones added to the unreality of the situation. Still, Thalberg had never expected it to end so quickly, and in such a melodramatic fashion.

On September 5, Norma and Irving were entertaining Sam and Frances Goldwyn at a Labor Day luncheon on the porch of 707 Ocean Front. The butler called Thalberg to the phone, and Mayer told him that Bern was dead. Thalberg immediately telephoned David Selznick, also a friend of Bern's, and then the Thalbergs drove to Bern's house with Selznick following close behind.

They found Mayer already there with the faithful Howard Strickling. It was a measure of M-G-M's pervasive power that Bern's household had alerted the studio before notifying the police, and Mayer was first on the scene. He quickly recounted what he knew to Thalberg. Earlier that morning, Bern's butler had entered the bedroom to ask about breakfast and had discovered his employer lying naked on the bathroom floor, shot in the head. Beside him was a small automatic pistol. Of Harlow there was no sign; the butler believed she had spent the night at the home of her mother and stepfather.

Mayer had found a mysterious suicide note. Scribbled in a green morocco-bound notebook in what appeared to be Bern's handwriting, it read: "Dearest Dear: Unfortunately this is the only way to make good the frightful wrong I have done you and to wipe out my abject humility. I love you." As if that weren't puzzling enough, there was an equally cryptic postscript: "You understand that last night was only a comedy."

Mayer sniffed scandal and quietly slipped the note into his pocket. Later, when they were alone, he showed it to

Strickling. Afraid of the consequences of suppressing evidence, the publicity man persuaded Mayer to hand it to the police. Thalberg arrived in time to see Bern's body being removed from the house. He sat in stunned silence, but somebody had to find Jean. So Thalberg and Norma drove to the home of the star's mother and stepfather, Marino Bello.

Norma, waiting in the car, had a low-angle view of an upper-floor bedroom through a long glass window opening onto a balcony. She could see a pair of trouser legs she recognized as Thalberg's and then the skirt of a pale negligee and slippers. At one point the figure in the negligee almost collapsed and had to be helped onto a bed by Thalberg. This had been Harlow's reaction to Thalberg's news. He told her the contents of Bern's letter, but she seemed not to understand it either. She told Thalberg that Bern had quarreled with her the previous night, and the quarrel was the reason why she had left the house and gone to her mother.

The shock of his friend's violent death left Thalberg incapable of decisive action, but the situation brought out Mayer's gift for effective damage control. Through his city connections, he was able to keep the press and even the police away from the grieving star while the studio concocted a story to protect her from a major scandal. But what story?

Considering her screen persona—to say nothing of her reputation—it was going to be hard for the public to see Harlow as the innocent young widow. The memory of *Red-Headed Woman* was still too fresh, and lurid speculation immediately began to circulate about her role in Bern's death. Despite the evidence of suicide, the Los Angeles district attorney at one point even considered indicting her for murder. Bern's household staff had heard the sound of raised voices around the pool, and shortly afterward neighbors had heard a car drive away from the house at speed. Things looked grim for Harlow.

Mayer consulted his doctor, E. B. Jones, whom he

knew had for a time also had Bern as a patient, and Dr. Jones mentioned that Bern had an unusually small penis. Mayer knew a lucky break when he saw one. The studio's publicity department immediately went to work leaking the story that Bern was impotent and Harlow the innocent victim of a cruel deception. Shortly afterward, the autopsy report confirmed that Bern had an "under-sized penis" but went on to say that it had not been possible to determine whether or not he had been impotent.

The press—primed by M-G-M—was not nearly so reti-cent. When Harlow's engagement was announced, wrote columnist and author Adela Rogers St. John, "I learned that Paul hadn't told her about himself. So I told her." But Harlow loved Bern, the writer went on, and "entered into a marriage that would be in name only."

Along with the leaked stories about Paul Bern's sup-posed impotence came a flow of revelations from "friends and associates" about his suicidal tendencies. David Selz-nick: Bern had told him "a man should be ready to die by his own hand when he had outlived his usefulness." Jack Gilbert: "Paul once told me that should the time come, 'I will not hesitate to snuff out the candle.'" Louis B. Mayer: Bern had long been preoccupied with suicide. Dr. Jones, who was on vacation in Honolulu, wrote to the coroner that Bern suffered from "acute melancholia," the result of "trivial things becoming exaggerated in his mind," and that his suicide was "a personal act." In short, Bern's wife was not involved.

Approached by Mayer, Harlow refused outright to cooperate in spreading the studio's story, but she readily agreed to let Metro's lawyers arrange for her to be excused from the coroner's inquest. Thalberg was appalled by Mayer's strategy. He knew of Bern's physical deficiency, but he also knew Bern wasn't impotent. His friend's problem had been mental rather than physiological. Thal-berg was particularly repelled by the rumor that "the frightful wrong" referred to in the letter had included penetration by a dildo and beating Harlow out of frustration. The fact that his own physical attributes were hardly more generous and his own sexual drive not much stronger than those of the man being vilified must have made the whole story doubly unpleasant. Yet he showed less resolution than Bern's young widow and appears to have made no move to dissociate himself publicly from the studio's insinuative portrayal of his friend and valued associate as a sexual incompetent possibly given to sadism.

At the inquest he listened to the testimony in silence. When it was his turn he was asked to comment on the suicide note, and he replied that he could offer no explanation. Bern was dead: life had to go on. And life to Thalberg meant movies. He understood the need to protect Harlow very well. *Red Dust* was soon to be released. Three more Jean Harlow films were in preparation, and Thalberg was already conferring with writers about a fourth, *The Girl from Missouri.*

So the wave of hostility toward Harlow was skillfully turned into sympathy at the expense of her dead husband's reputation. Irene Selznick, who had initially blamed Harlow for Bern's death and was not aware of M-G-M's campaign, now thought her "truly a heroine."

On the day of Bern's funeral service at Forest Lawn, a large crowd gathered outside the chapel. They saw Harlow arrive with her mother, and Mayer flanked by Eddie Mannix and Howard Strickling. Thalberg came without Norma and sat alone staring at the casket smothered in orchids from the studio. Many of the mourners seemed nervous, but this was usual: unscripted things tended to happen at Hollywood funerals. Sometimes, for example, the officiating minister or rabbi would seize the opportunity for a fervent denunciation of sin in the movie colony. But to everyone's relief, the service came to an end without any additional embellishments.

Or had it? Before anyone had time to leave, the

funeral director bounded to the front of the chapel, took his stance beside the casket, and with pride offered Bern's friends the opportunity of saying a last fond farewell. At that the casket mechanically moved into an upright position, the top of the lid gradually slid down, and there was Bern's face staring out at the congregation. The curtain fell slowly to the sound of Jack Gilbert throwing up. Thalberg broke into tears, perhaps more out of anger than grief, or from a sense of guilt at having done nothing to prevent the public slurring of a friend.

Bern's death shattered Thalberg. For several days he shut himself away in his home, refusing to go to the studio or to receive visitors at 707 Ocean Front. When he emerged he was unusually broody and short-tempered. He insisted that M-G-M hire private investigators to inquire into Bern's death. But the tragic story had not yet run its course. Two days after the funeral a former New York actress named Dorothy Millette took her own life by throwing herself in the Sacramento River in northern California. She apparently left no note, but when the Sacramento police searched her hotel room, the trail led straight to Paul Bern. They found a stack of letters from him, most typewritten on M-G-M notepaper, some referring to payments he had made to Millette.

It gradually emerged that Dorothy Millette was the ghost in Bern's past. They had met as drama students in New York in 1911 and had lived together for a number of years, first in an apartment in Jersey City and later in the Algonquin Hotel in Manhattan, as "Mr. and Mrs. Paul Bern." In time their marriage became a casualty of Bern's success as a producer. According to one report, when Bern left New York and Dorothy Millette for Hollywood, she had a nervous breakdown and entered a sanatorium. But in another published account of the relationship, Dorothy Millette continued to live in the Algonquin as Mrs. Paul Bern.

The two versions have one common factor: in both instances Bern paid the bills. The second account quotes Frank Case, the manager of the Algonquin, as saying that Bern would visit Dorothy Millette when he came to New York—usually about twice a year.

Both stories agree that about the time of Bern's marriage to Jean Harlow, Millette appeared in Los Angeles and insisted on seeing him. Bern appears to have made an appointment and then staged a quarrel with Harlow that was "only a comedy" to get her out of the house. Millette arrived late on September 4. Their argument was heard by the staff, and then came the sound of the departing car. After she left, Paul Bern shot himself, for whatever reason, and after the funeral Dorothy Millette drowned herself.

The story does not clear up the mystery of Bern's suicide, particularly since Jean Harlow had known of his past association with Millette; and given their close friendship, it was highly likely that Thalberg had known as well. But the public knew next to nothing about this story. With William Randolph Hearst's cooperation, Mayer succeeded in arranging a press blackout of the whole affair. Following the inquest, the story was buried, and the Metro version of events remained unchallenged until some two decades later, when fuller accounts of the tragedy began to appear in print.

Harlow paid the expenses of Millette's burial in San Francisco. Two days after Bern killed himself, the Plaza Hotel in San Francisco had received a check signed by him and made payable to "Miss D. Millette," who was a guest in the hotel. By then Dorothy Millette was also dead.

Two of Millette's sisters contested Bern's will, which left his estate of $48,000 to Jean Harlow, on the grounds that Bern and Dorothy Millette had established a common-law marriage. Thalberg saw to it that Harlow was represented in the case by a phalanx of M-G-M lawyers, but four years later—in April 1936—an out-of-court settlement was reached in which the sisters received $2,000 from the estate.

Bern's death deprived Thalberg of a valuable associate, burdening him with more work because, as Albert Lewin recalled, "Irving was the team captain and the team was small; only about half a dozen of us made the entire product." Moreover, Thalberg "was a perfectionist. . . . He would push and push to get every bit of excellence into a production." In an era when the producer dominated picture making, Thalberg was—to paraphrase *Fortune* magazine—what Hollywood meant by total control. It wasn't just the choice of material and the scripting, to which he paid meticulous attention, or the editing, for which he was justly famous. "Thalberg always wanted to know everything," remarked Douglas Shearer, "what was going on with sound, costumes, photography. . . ."

Conferences and meetings dominated his working style. Meetings were a way of life or, rather, a suspension of real life in favor of the shadow world. He held meetings through lunch, at the hospital during his illness, in men's rooms, at wedding receptions, and once even at a funeral. He had begun a conference on *Billy the Kid* with King Vidor and Laurence Stallings in his office, then received a call that his limousine was ready and asked them to ride with him. All the way, Thalberg never stopped "talking story," and there was no opportunity to ask him where they were going. The limousine finally stopped outside a chapel where a funeral had just started.

"Too many murders," Thalberg commented to Vidor quietly as they took their seats.

For an instant Vidor thought he was talking about the body in the chapel, but then he realized that Thalberg was still commenting on the script. Vidor recognized many movie people among the mourners and asked Eddie Mannix, who happened to be sitting next to him, whose funeral this was.

"Mabel Normand," Mannix replied.

As the service progressed, Thalberg leaned toward Stallings: "Why not kill him before he gets to the hotel?"

He spent half a day with director Leo McCarey and writer Zelda Sears, going over the script of *Prosperity* scene by scene. *Prosperity* was one of a series of relatively low-budget Marie Dressler–Polly Moran comedies (others were *Politics* and *Caught Short*). Thalberg's suggestions for one sequence went like this: "This next scene is of the two old women, and we cut outside and there's John. He comes in—his mother says he shouldn't see the bride. Then a romantic scene to make the audience feel that the two kids are in love with each other. Don't plant laughs . . . Marie [Dressler] can lean on a line and do it well. Marie can be trusted, but Polly [Moran] never—she breaks it. The minister comes in—it's a very funny idea, having two ministers come in, but there should be some definite understanding about how two ministers got there. . . ."

Margaret Booth, M-G-M's chief editor, remembers that during editing sessions, Thalberg "made his points by mumbling. He'd mumble all the way through: 'I don't like that bit,' 'I wish you'd done so-and-so,' 'See what you can do with that.' " Donald Ogden Stewart described working for him as exhilarating: "He would never praise you. You would take a scene in to him and he'd read it, and then the best he would ever say to you was, 'Hmmm . . . not bad.' "

But he had his critics among writers, too, people who resented his view of writing as a collective endeavor, his tendency to treat his word, once pronounced, as set in stone. James M. Cain, the novelist, remembered him as "the most unpleasant of guys. . . . I was ushered into the Presence. This pale guy sat there: whether he was listening or not was hard to say." Director Gregory La Cava referred to him as the Pagoda—"I've been summoned by the Pagoda," he would say. Hired by Thalberg to write the script of *Greenwich Village*, S. J. Perelman and his wife, Laura, spent four frustrating months in Hollywood because—according to Perelman—"we never got a clear reading from Mr. Thalberg whether he wanted *la vie Bohème* or another *Rip Tide: The Story of a Woman's Conflicting Emotions* or a singing disaster film like *San Francisco*." In the end, after numerous rejected versions of the script, Thalberg decided to cancel the production, and the Perelmans took the train back east.

Perelman got his revenge in a famous *New Yorker* piece, "And Did You Once See Irving Plain?" on the theme of waiting in Thalberg's outer office, an endurance test to which all M-G-M employees were regularly subjected. Perelman had such difficulty getting to see Thalberg that he "seriously began to question whether Thalberg existed, whether he might not be a solar myth or a deity concocted by the front office to garner prestige." When he was finally given an appointment, he found himself sharing the waiting room with "a dozen artisans of note: Sidney Howard and Robert Sherwood, George S. Kaufman, Marc Connelly, S. N. Behrman, and Donald Ogden Stewart. . . . I discovered that everybody there had been seeking Thalberg's ear without success and was seething." Anita Loos, who had also done time sitting on the same leather couch, used to pass the time knitting a scarf, an occupation she reserved exclusively for the long waits outside Thalberg's office. When it was finished it was twice the height of the diminutive writer, and she calculated that at her weekly salary of $2,500, it had cost M-G-M $20,000.

The unrelenting pressure, which would have taken its toll on a healthier man, regularly brought Thalberg to the brink of physical collapse. At meetings he would deliver a weary preamble about how he longed for a much needed break away from the studio, how he wanted to go to Europe. But then from somewhere deep inside his small frame he somehow unearthed fresh reserves of energy and concentration, and he would be as mentally alert and as decisive as ever.

As the end of 1932 came into sight, the first floor of M-G-M's administrative building was busier than ever. Writers and producers came—and waited. The weekly story meetings to discuss current and future productions, over which Thalberg presided, took longer and longer as the studio's output increased commensurately with the growing number of stars under contract. Thalberg's production schedule for early 1933 included *Mutiny on the Bounty, Dancing Lady, Night Flight,* and dozens of other pictures. He fully expected to persuade George Bernard Shaw to sell him the rights of *Saint Joan* for Garbo (Shaw eventually refused). Meanwhile, *Fortune* said, Thalberg "weighed 122 lbs. after a good night's sleep," but "in frantic moments he appears as a pale and flimsy bag of bones held together by concealed bits of string." There were nights when he left the studio so exhausted that his chauffeur had to help him to his car.

Shortly before Christmas the bag of bones told Mayer that he felt tired and sick and wanted to terminate his contract. Their correct but cool working relationship was about to erupt into a confrontation.

Thalberg had been brooding over the situation for weeks. He had come to regard Mayer as an absentee landlord. The legendary energy and drive that had gone into guiding M-G-M to preeminence among Hollywood motion picture studios was now channeled toward Republican Party politics (Mayer was chairman of the California Republicans), golf, ballroom dancing, and women. The press had reported that President Hoover had offered him the post of Ambassador to Turkey, and this was true, but Mayer had declined the post.

Mayer's wife, Margaret, the quiet little hausfrau who had always found the limelight an ordeal, was now a neurotic semi-invalid. She suffered from a hormone imbalance as a result of a hysterectomy, and she sank into such deep depressions that she began to spend most of each year in a Massachusetts sanatorium. Meanwhile Mayer found consolation with hopeful young starlets supplied by a cheerful bootlegger and demimonde figure named Frank Orsatti.

Thalberg observed Mayer's antics and felt he was being taken advantage of. But Mayer continued to have grievances of his own. He acknowledged Thalberg's value to Metro but was secretly jealous of it. He had not so secretly seethed about *Fortune*'s flattering description of Thalberg and the magazine's dismissal of Mayer himself as "essentially a businessman" and a "commercial diplomat." He quite rightly felt this view diminished his role in running a great empire. Furthermore their recent differences over money stuck in his memory as an attack on his self-perception as a generous, patriarchal boss.

Irving Thalberg and Louis Mayer had always been two divergent souls forced into compatibility by a common purpose, and the Paul Bern affair highlighted this contradiction. Thalberg could not have brought himself to go as far as Mayer had to protect their common interest. But he did not oppose Mayer, knowing that the studio head was being callous but pragmatic. Now Thalberg was saying he wanted out of the company where—according to a 1927 profile of him—"he knows how to make pictures better than any of the mob of directors, writers, artists, and businessmen."

Thalberg's request to terminate his contract spurred the patriarch to one of his operatic rages. Thalberg's contract had only a few months left to run, and Mayer suspected that Thalberg was softening the ground for renewal negotiations. But he also knew better than anybody that Thalberg's defection to a rival studio would be a blow to M-G-M's prestige, its organizational structure, and—at least in the short term—its ability to function. The studio had no plan that would permit operations to proceed smoothly without him.

Mayer called the General, and five days later the three met in Schenck's suite at the Beverly Hills Hotel. The conference was stormy: Schenck threatened Thalberg with a breach of contract suit, but Thalberg stood his ground. If Metro refused to release him, he would sit out the remaining time and then leave. Pressed by Schenck, M-G-M's physically fragile head of production coolly restated his complaint that Mayer fiddled while he, Thalberg, burned out. He was overworked and underpaid while the head of the studio did nothing and reaped the benefits.

White with rage, Mayer walked out of the meeting, and the General found his strategy in Thalberg's reference to money. A salary increase on any respectable scale was out of the question at that moment, he said, but would Thalberg consider a sizable stock deal—say, an option over a five-year period to purchase 100,000 shares of Loew's common stock at 20 percent of the market price?

Schenck's offer backed Thalberg into a corner. His decision to resign had not been a negotiating tactic. He was genuinely tired. He found coexistence with Mayer increasingly unpalatable. He was getting depressed with the lowering of standards at M-G-M and elsewhere in the face of the Depression. He despised the shoddy exploitation movies that even M-G-M was turning out in a desperate resort to triple bills of mediocre pictures designed to lure people back into the theaters.

Yet Schenck's proposal was tempting. Thalberg had no shortage of offers from other studios, from Joseph Kennedy at RKO to Sam Goldwyn, who more than once had urged him to become an independent producer, releasing his films through United Artists. But the new deal at M-G-M would increase his holdings in what was still the world's most profitable motion picture company and ensure the future for Norma and his son.

So he agreed to stay on, and there was a show of reconciliation with Mayer. But Mayer's feelings were even more bitter than before. And Schenck's strategy was to drive an even deeper wedge between the two. Thus he made the same offer of Loew's shares to Mayer, but for 80,000 shares only. Mayer, who was well aware of Loew's greater generosity toward Thalberg, at first refused and then agreed. For the first time his protégé had received better treatment from Loew's than he had. This was not something he would forget.

There was no indication to what extent Thalberg had discussed his intentions with his wife. Throughout the crisis Norma remained in the background, as discreet and in control of herself as ever. Yet the decision was as important to her as it was to Irving. If her husband left Metro, she would have to leave, too. The queen would be forced into exile at another studio at a time when M-G-M's protective mechanism was most useful to her.

She was thirty-one and the mother of a small child. Thirty-one was not in itself an advanced age; but her rival Joan Crawford was twenty-eight, Garbo was supposed to be twenty-seven (although in reality she was the same age as Norma), and the up-and-coming Myrna Loy a mere twenty-four. Sam Marx, however, believed that Thalberg had decided Norma would shortly retire—a decision announced unilaterally some three years later when he made known his plans to produce *Marie Antoinette*.

If Thalberg wanted to interrupt her career in order to give them more time together in his last years, Norma was not going to complain. No one ever questioned her deep concern for Thalberg's health and her willingness to do everything in her power to prolong his life for as long as possible. In any case, she had trained herself not to think about life after Irving. It was as if she somehow felt that by not thinking about it, she could somehow extend his life.

Meanwhile the tension in the topmost reaches of M-G-M's management made scarcely a dent in the flow of work at the studio. To some of his associates, Thalberg seemed more serious and pensive then usual, but his hand on the controls never faltered. There were now six associate producers under his direct supervision. They in turn were responsible for the work of eighteen directors and sixty-two writers. But the number of writers changed frequently as some left and new ones—those who had made their mark at other studios or in the literary world—were enticed to the studio.

Thalberg often hired leading writers for the prestige, and William Faulkner was a case in point. "We all knew Faulkner was a question mark when it came to screenwriting," Sam Marx recalled. But Faulkner was a respected and admired literary figure at the height of his reputation, and Thalberg couldn't resist the temptation of offering him a six-week contract at $500 a week, which—the author said—was like selling a short story every week for six weeks.

The studio's doubts were confirmed in Faulkner's first meeting with Marx following his arrival on May 7, 1932. Faulkner said, "How about my writing newsreels? Newsreels and Mickey Mouse, these are the only pictures I like." Marx told him he was assigned to Harry Rapf for a picture called *Flesh,* starting immediately. No Mickey Mouse, no newsreels.

Faulkner promptly disappeared and showed up again a week later at the studio with the laconic explanation that he had been "scared by the hullabaloo over my arrival." Lack of knowledge of the medium did not deter him from turning out one film treatment after another, but none made it into production. As the six weeks drew to a close, with little likelihood of a renewal, Howard Hawks asked him to write the script from his short story "Turn About."

When Hawks first approached Faulkner with the idea, the writer replied, "See you in five days."

"It shouldn't take you that long to think about it," Hawks answered shortly.

"I mean to write it," Faulkner said.

When Faulkner brought in his treatment five days later, Hawks took it to his wife's brother-in-law and waited as he read it. Finally Thalberg looked across his desk and said, "I feel as if I'd make tracks all over it if I touched it," he said. "Shoot it as it is."

But the decision had come too easily for it to be his final word, and Hawks probably knew it. As he brooded over it, he began to feel that the picture needed a woman. At the same time, Joan Crawford needed a picture. . . . Within a week Thalberg was doing what he had said he would not do. He was making tracks all over Faulkner's story.

When Howard Hawks informed Faulkner of Thalberg's decision, the writer remained silent for a moment. Then he said thoughtfully, "I don't remember a girl in the story."

Hawks replied, "That's the picture business, Bill. We get the biggest stars we can, and Joan's a nice girl, too."

Faulkner asked if he could write the script at home, and Hawks replied that he could, not realizing that Faulkner meant home in Oxford, Mississippi. M-G-M was not in favor of writers working at home even when they lived in Los Angeles, but Faulkner got away with it. Despite complaints from the studio manager, a onetime faro dealer named M. E. Greenwood who was responsible for keeping track of M-G-M's weekly operating expenses, Thalberg did not order Faulkner's recall.

"Several times I reminded Mr. Thalberg that Faulkner was away from the studio and yet had drawn his salary," Greenwood wrote to Marx. "A few days ago I again reminded him, and he said for you to advise me what the situation was."

Faulkner was left to complete his script in Oxford, possibly out of deference to his status or because he had quickly proved himself to be productive. But Thalberg was not inhibited from assigning two other writers to rework the famous author's version, even though Faulkner received sole credit for the film, which ended up with the title *Today We Live.*

A more weighty problem was finding a new movie role for Norma to follow *Smilin' Through.* The Thalbergs had attended the Los Angeles opening of the play *The Barretts of Wimpole Street,* which starred Katharine Cornell as Elizabeth Barrett, Basil Rathbone as her tyrannical father, and Brian Aherne as the poet Robert Browning, and Thalberg immediately saw it as a vehicle for his wife. Norma was not interested in playing a part that would seldom allow her to get up from a sofa, and she suggested he approach Katharine Cornell.

The actress told him she was committed to Joe Schenck. What's more, her contract gave her joint control of the play with its author, Rudolf Besier, and she had no intention of allowing it to be filmed in any other way. But this was a minor obstacle to Thalberg, who calmly maneuvered actress and playwright out of the picture by making Schenck an offer he couldn't refuse—double the $40,000 he had paid for the motion picture rights.

Having bought the play, he filmed a stage performance of it for future reference. Possibly, the play appealed to him on a more personal level. Finding the determination to overcome a serious illness was something he could relate to. Moreover, as an amateur Freudian he must have been fascinated with the incestuous overtones in the relationship between Elizabeth and her father. Still, he had to overcome Norma's lack of enthusiasm for playing the original couch potato.

Thalberg's condition and her sister Athole's illness brought the role of an invalid too close to home, and she found the idea of playing one extremely disturbing. The other reason, more private and at least partly subliminal, was that for Norma movies continued to be an antidote to the marginal role that sex played in her marriage. Too loyal and prudent to risk an affair in real life, she could at least escape into the illusion of sexual adventure in such films as *Strangers May Kiss* and *Lady of the Night,* encased in Adrian's clinging, revealing finery. Lying supine on a couch promised no such excitement.

Before the couple could resolve the debate over *The Barretts,* Thalberg suffered a serious reminder of his precarious health. On December 24 Metro shut down early for its annual Christmas party. Norma, making her first appearance at the studio since her husband's confrontation with Mayer and Schenck, smiled and was friendly but maintained her usual distance. Mayer appeared jovial, although his public display of affection for Thalberg must have galled him. Thalberg, who was the subject of much celebration for deciding not to quit, kissed more Metro female employees than usual for such an occasion, drank more than his customary quota of a single weak Scotch and soda. Unlike Norma, Irving stayed until about eleven o'clock, when he began to feel tired and was driven home. Then on Christmas morning he had his second heart attack.

For Norma, who had witnessed from close quarters the

tensions of the past few months, the crisis was not unexpected. She called Dr. Philip Newmark, Thalberg's doctor, who diagnosed "a mild coronary." He thought it unnecessary to move Thalberg to the hospital, prescribed complete rest, no visitors, and no phone calls. When Norma advised Metro, the studio's publicity department announced that Thalberg was confided to his bed with influenza. Within days, however, the real story had spread through the movie colony, and people began to ask how many such attacks Thalberg's condition could withstand. Henrietta rushed to see her son. But Norma, reinforced by Dr. Newmark's instructions, would not allow her in the bedroom. Mayer arrived a few days later and got no farther than the front door, as did Schenck. Sometime after New Year's, Thalberg began to recover, but he made no move to return to the studio.

One afternoon in late February, Louis Mayer appeared once again on the Thalbergs' doorstep, this time by prearrangement. As before, Norma Shearer met him at the door, but this time she took him to Irving, who was propped up in bed. Mayer was on a mission that he must have known was almost certain to widen the rift between them. He had come, he said, to tell Thalberg that he had hired David Selznick as a producer at M-G-M with his own independent unit. That meant Selznick would not be subject to Thalberg's supervision but would be answerable directly to the Metro front office—that is, to L. B. Mayer and to Nick Schenck.

Since his last employment with Metro, Selznick had married Irene Mayer. He had also fulfilled his early promise as a producer at RKO. He had vowed never to work for his father-in-law, but Mayer's offer had come at a moment when he was seeking more independence than RKO was prepared to give him.

Mayer told Thalberg an agreement with Selznick had already been worked out. In short, he was presenting Thalberg with a fait accompli. Then he produced a letter from the General that attempted to reassure Thalberg and sought retroactively to secure his very necessary consent. Thalberg was not only M-G-M's vice president in charge of production, he was also its second in command and entitled to approval of all major contracts. Moreover, word that Thalberg had accepted Selznick's appointment would help reduce the unrest the appointment was certain to create among Thalberg loyalists.

Schenck's letter pointed out that "by consenting to the execution of such a contract, you will not be deemed to have approved the terms of the same nor the special conditions therein set forth . . . and it is agreed that no concessions similar to that made to Mr. Selznick shall be made in connection with any other contract or employment without your express consent."

Mayer's news sent Thalberg into an icy rage. His quiet insinuations of betrayal rattled Mayer, whose angry protests echoed through the large, soundproof house. Thalberg had nothing against Selznick, whose work he admired. They were contemporaries and friends, brought closer by Paul Bern's death. A few months earlier Thalberg had shown Selznick's film *A Bill of Divorcement* on his living room screen with a newcomer named Katharine Hepburn playing the leading role, and he had been generous in his praise. Thalberg's anger was directed at Mayer, who had made the deal behind his back. He also suspected that Mayer intended to replace him with Selznick. When he accused Mayer of taking advantage of his illness to undermine his position in the studio, it was a cue to Mayer to make one of his outraged exits.

But Thalberg's anger did not deflect Mayer from his intention, and a few days later Loew's Inc. formally released the news that David O. Selznick had "signed a contract with Metro-Goldwyn-Mayer as an executive producer." If the official description of Selznick's situation sounded familiar, it was because it was similar to Thalberg's, and this inevitably raised the question of how the position of Metro's resident genius was affected by the appointment.

Rumors that Thalberg was out for good were denied by Schenck, but his prolonged absence was noted in the *New York Times*. Thalberg was still seriously ill, the paper reported, and "present plans were for him to go to Europe, probably to Bad Nauheim, for at least four months' rest as soon as he can travel." In fact, Thalberg had once again bounced back remarkably. He was still weak, but Dr. Newmark had been surprised by his patient's calm in the face of additional stress.

On March 23, 1933, a few days before Thalberg departed for Europe, Mayer—who hardly ever put anything in writing—sent him a long, conciliatory letter: "I regret very much that when I last went to see you to talk things over I did not find you in a receptive mood to treat me as your loyal partner and friend. I felt an air of suspicion on your part towards me, and want you to know, if I was correct in my interpretation of your feeling, that it was entirely undeserved. . . . Instead of appreciating the fact that I have cheerfully taken on your work, as well as my own, you chose to bitingly and sarcastically accuse me of many things, by innuendo, which I am supposed to have done to you and your friends. Being a man of temperament, I could not restrain myself any longer." He went on to say: "Regardless of how I felt, or what my nervous condition was, I am big enough to apologize to you, for you were ill and I should have controlled my feelings."

Selznick had been hired not to replace him, as Thalberg had surmised, but as his possible successor. Perhaps it had taken Thalberg's heart attack to focus Mayer's mind on the fact that his young production chief was more mortal than most, and Mayer's main intention had been to ensure continuity in the studio. He felt it would be necessary to replicate Thalberg, but in the more manageable person of his son-in-law.

Thalberg's reply to Mayer on March 25 rejected his olive branch. He too regretted "any words that I may have used that aroused bitterness." He had, however, "sustained a deep hurt." It was all very well for Mayer to talk about friendship, but there were "loyalties that are greater than the loyalties of friendship. There are loyalties to ideals, the loyalties to principles without which friendship loses character and real meaning."

Thalberg went on: "I realize with deep appreciation the effort you have been making for the company and in my behalf, and no one more than myself understands the strain to which you are subjected." Thalberg did, however, invite Mayer to visit prior to his and Norma's departure, "as nothing would make me happier than to feel we had parted at least good personal friends, if not better than before."

Two days later L. B. Mayer returned to 707 Ocean Front to say good-bye to the departing couple. Work was not mentioned, and there was much kissing, embracing, and back slapping. But both men knew that the cracks in the relationship were only being papered over.

A warmer leavetaking was organized by Marion Davies, who gave a bon voyage costume party for the Thalbergs at her rambling Santa Monica beach house. The theme of the evening, appropriately, was "A Night in Heidelberg." The men were dressed in Bavarian lederhosen or gold-braided jackets, and pillbox hats perched delicately on each head. The women's costumes ranged from beer garden waitress uniforms to heavily beaded gowns. Norma came as a waitress. Bavarian brass bands played in nearly every room, and beer was served in generous, decorated steins. After dinner things got lively, and conga lines of famous faces wandered down the beach, then snaked back in waves of frantic movement. The Thalbergs stayed exceptionally late and left only when Norma insisted that her husband needed to rest.

Thalberg was returning to Dr. Groedel in Bad Nauheim. Dr. Newmark had urged it, and Norma had insisted on it. Thalberg could have been treated in California, but Norma wanted to put as much distance as possible between him and the studio. There are indications that before Thalberg departed on March 28 he was considering leaving M-G-M on his return and forming his own company. A few days before sailing from San Pedro aboard the SS *California,* he sounded out Donald Ogden Stewart on joining forces with him in an independent production venture, and the writer had accepted. Thalberg's health was one good reason for not going back to the huge M-G-M workload. But his departure would also earn widespread sympathy for other reasons.

No one who knew Mayer doubted his determination to reduce Thalberg's power. No one who knew him could miss his need for control. Irving Thalberg had no hope of reforming L.B., but there was a Thalberg cult at the studio that would grow more potent in his absence. Irving treated his co-workers well enough for them to believe they might be his equals. Thalberg's collapse was seen as a symbol of the struggle for quality and integrity. What most did not know was the extent to which Thalberg's fights with Loew's had been, quite simply, for more money.

As usual, the Thalbergs traveled in style: the party consisted of Irving and Norma, plus Irving Jr., Norma's personal maid, and their friends Helen Hayes and Charles MacArthur, with their baby daughter Mary, her nurse, and a manservant. After passing through the Panama Canal, the *California* docked for a few days in Panama City. At their hotel the Thalbergs' party was told that in the red-light district the prostitutes used the names of their favorite stars, and the brothels displayed signs bearing these well-known names as a come-on. Charles MacArthur and Thalberg wanted to see this titillating sight, and the women went along. When the driver of their rented car learned that one of his passengers was Norma Shearer, he took them to a rundown house and there, on the front in bold letters, was Norma's name.

The others were amused, but not Thalberg, who found it deeply offensive. He wanted to confront the owner of the brothel and have the sign removed immediately. Usually quick to spot cinematic possibilities in real-life developments, he seemed not to be intrigued by this situation. He just became angrier as he realized that his traveling companions found it funny. But Helen Hayes noted that Norma, "who was so refined on screen and off, seemed pleased by this tribute to her name."

The Thalbergs were in New York when an earthquake hit Long Beach, California. The shocks were felt as far north as Los Angeles and Culver City, and Mayer rushed out of his office in alarm. The killer quake claimed over fifty victims and did more than $40 million worth of property damage, but as Thalberg was told when he telephoned the studio, its impact at M-G-M was minimal, merely a power failure and some overturned arc lamps. Relieved, the party boarded the SS *Conte di Savoia* and sailed for Genoa, where the Thalbergs took the train to Bad Nauheim and the MacArthurs went on to Paris.

Dr. Groedel told Thalberg that his tonsils were inflamed and there was risk that the inflammation could extend to his heart. He recommended a tonsillectomy.

In the spring of 1933 Hitler was chancellor of Germany, and his Nazi party was brutally consolidating its grip on the country. The Reichstag fire had started a witch-hunt for communists when in reality the incident had been engineered by Hitler to frame the Left. The monster of organized anti-Semitism was still not fully formed, but an anti-Semitic campaign was already doing deadly mischief. By day there were anti-Jewish demonstrations in the streets. The more sinister acts happened at night: the windows of Jewish-owned stores smashed, anti-Semitic graffiti daubed on the walls. Worse, individual Jews were beaten up by thugs who then melted into the darkness.

Years later Norma told Eddie Lawrence that the uneasy atmosphere had been evident from the moment they'd checked into the hotel. The following night they witnessed an attack on a couple from their window. As the couple were being beaten in the street below, Norma said, Thalberg alerted the hotel reception to call the police, but no police came. After that the Thalbergs saw at least one march of brown-shirted Nazi storm troopers, and Thalberg was able to translate the racist chants for Norma.

Dr. Groedel, himself Jewish, advised Thalberg to leave Germany and have the operation elsewhere. But Thalberg felt it was too risky to postpone the tonsillectomy and persuaded the doctor to perform it that same week at his clinic. As an American, Thalberg did not feel personally threatened. He also seemed to believe that international opinion, and especially Jewish international opinion, was making too much of anti-Semitism in Germany.

"A lot of Jews will lose their lives," he pronounced when he eventually returned to New York. But "Hitler and Hitlerism will pass; the Jews will still be there." When his astonished listeners questioned this judgment, he said world Jewry should not interfere. Hitler would "eventually disappear; the Jews will remain."

Thalberg's apparent insensitivity to the plight of German Jews shows him at his coldest and most detached, or perhaps his most pragmatic. Like many Americans at the time, he saw communism as the greater threat and felt that in the short term Hitler provided the best hope of an adequate defense against the menace of Soviet expansionism. He seemed to have bought the line fed to him by officials of the German film industry that Hitler's campaign against the Jews was a short-term political tactic to consolidate his position by playing on Germany's history of anti-Semitism.

An even less edifying reason for his refusal to publicly condemn the Nazis was the German film market. Foreign sales accounted for nearly half of M-G-M's revenue, and Germany was one of the studio's biggest single overseas customers ($4.5 million in sales in 1933). Tightening Nazi control to ensure conformity with Nazi values and moral standards and to limit "decadent" foreign influence was already reducing the importation of Hollywood films, but in 1933–1934 the market was still large enough to discourage the studios from giving offense to Hitler's regime. To Dr. Goebbels, the Third Reich's head of propaganda, most Hollywood movies were "degenerate." The number of imported Hollywood films was dropping every year—from eighty in 1932, to sixty-eight in 1933, to forty in 1934, and among the films rejected as unsuitable in 1934 were *The Thin Man, Flying Down to Rio,* and *The Devil Is a Woman.*

A purge of all Jews working in the German film industry was under way, with a disastrous effect on the national industry; Hollywood executives believed that Hollywood films were being increasingly shut out of German movie theaters at least partly because the Nazi regime perceived Hollywood studios to be run by Jews. The American Embassy in Berlin suspected the same thing.

"Censorship has become so severe," the embassy reported to Washington on June 26, 1934, "that the rejection of one film after another gives rise to the thought that some sinister purpose, probably the continuance of semitic antipathy, is the underlying reason."

11

MAYER'S PURGE

On the morning of June 13, 1933, Irving Thalberg was lying in bed in his suite in the Hotel Cap d'Antibes on the French Riviera. The Thalbergs had joined the MacArthurs there a few days earlier so that Thalberg could continue his recovery from his tonsillectomy. The surgery had gone off without a hitch, but Dr. Groedel had urged his patient not to hasten his convalescence.

A telegram from Los Angeles was delivered to Thalberg's bedroom, and Norma saw him read it, turn white, and slump back almost in a faint. Fearful that it might be another heart attack, she ran to the MacArthurs' suite for help. The three of them found Thalberg lying back in bed, breathing hard. "There was that delicate face, deathly white," Helen Hayes recalled later, "and all he said was, 'They knifed me, Charlie, they knifed me.'"

His hand shaking, he handed Norma the telegram.

It was an announcement from L. B. Mayer that he had

reorganized the studio and in the process had abolished the post of head of production. In short, Thalberg had been sacked. The gradual process of corrosion in the relationship between the two men had finally destroyed the partnership, and the formidable team that had built M-G-M was now history. Having thus torpedoed Thalberg's future, Mayer added a solicitous note: I AM DOING THIS FOR YOU.

Where the new setup left Thalberg was not clear from Mayer's telegram. Yet Thalberg made no attempt to contact the studio chief, nor did he send any reply to the telegram. Instead he remained firmly ensconced in Antibes like an exiled Balkan prince overthrown by a coup d'état in his country. For the second time in three months, Mayer had taken a major decision affecting Thalberg's position without prior consultation. Thalberg hunted down recent issues of *Variety* and from published reports pieced together the true extent of Mayer's betrayal.

Mayer, it turned out, had offered Thalberg's former associates—Al Lewin, Stromberg, Weingarten, and Hyman—contracts as independent producers with their own units. It was the same arrangement that David Selznick had enjoyed and that Mayer and Schenck had two months earlier promised Thalberg would not be repeated "without your express consent." Pressured by Mayer and uncertain about the actual state of Thalberg's health, all his associates with one exception had run for cover, accepting Mayer's offer. The holdout: Albert Lewin. Lewin asked for a leave of absence to think it over. *Variety* quoted Mayer as saying he hoped Thalberg would operate on the same basis. It was a classic way of cutting the master down to size: his group of subordinates would now be his equals.

Thalberg the pragmatist, the Jamesian, must surely have realized that whatever Mayer's personal motives, it could be argued that he had acted in the best interests of M-G-M. Mayer had done it with characteristic deviousness. Thalberg himself, in the same situation, would have opted for candor. But the end result was the same: reducing the dependence of a multimillion-dollar operation on the uncertain health of someone who, according to the doctors' predictions, should already be dead.

Thalberg had once commented wryly to Howard Dietz, M-G-M's director of publicity in New York, that he presumed he would work "until I drop." Had that happened while he was in charge of the studio's entire output, a large number of pictures in various stages of production would be thrown into disarray until a successor could be appointed. But in his bitterness over what he saw as Mayer's betrayal, Thalberg could only focus on one fact: Mayer was now in total control of movie production at Metro-Goldwyn-Mayer. He had abolished Thalberg's position altogether, which protected him from the emergence of another potential challenger to his authority. And the independent producers were under his overall authority.

Thalberg had to face the strong possibility that he was finished as a major producer. As he sat on his balcony in the French Riviera, he reviewed his options again and again: starting his own company, moving to another studio, or accepting a scaled-down position at the studio where until recently he had been kingpin. But what likelihood was there that the stars and writers he wanted would be willing to sign up with him following his widely publicized illness? And there was no immediate indication that Goldwyn and the others were rushing to renew the attractive offers they'd once made him. At least with the third option, staying on at Metro, there was the prospect of less work and the added advantage of leaving his family well provided for.

Meanwhile Thalberg was resting, putting on much needed weight, and getting stronger. In Antibes the Thalbergs were joined by Basil and Ouida Rathbone and the singing star Jeanette MacDonald and her husband. As Thalberg's health improved, the whole group went to the Monte Carlo casino to gamble. At the roulette table, Thalberg played twenty-five, the date of his heart attack, and won a thousand dollars.

Thalberg never smoked, and he drank in moderation, but gambling was the one passion he shared with other movie moguls. He taught Goulding how to set up the chemin de fer game in *Grand Hotel* ("Chemin de fer is not a game to play with friends," he observed to the director); and Thursday nights was a regular card night at 707 Ocean Front. Generally Norma greeted the players—Harry Rapf, Joe Schenck, Sam Marx, Sam Goldwyn, and Chico Marx—and then left them alone. She waited up until the game was over—usually about midnight—and Thalberg came upstairs to bed, but she never asked whether he had won or lost. With Thalberg it was usually the former. Sam Marx describes a typical game, not at Thalberg's home, where Thalberg stood up and said, "Fellows, I've got to go to work. This is as far as I go. Cash me in." He was $16,000 ahead.

Aside from gambling (occasionally) and pondering his future (continuously), in Antibes Thalberg also bought the film rights of a new biography by Stefan Zweig, *Marie Antoinette: Portrait of an Average Woman.* Norma read the book and had no difficulty seeing herself as the tragic French queen. So, on leaving Antibes, the Thalbergs visited Versailles, where Norma soaked up the atmosphere. From Paris they went to London, with a side trip to the Gleneagles so that Thalberg could play on the world-famous golf course. In London Thalberg dodged questions about his future plans. The truth was that he had not yet decided what his future should be. The one thing he was sure of was that he intended to star his wife in a succession of high-quality productions that he was determined would be his best work—and Norma's. It was the best way he knew of expressing his appreciation for the support she had given him, particularly during his recent crisis.

Arriving in New York in the second week of July on the SS *Majestic,* Thalberg looked older, heavier, but otherwise rested and remarkably fit. At a dockside press conference, Norma smiled silently beside him as he handled reporters' questions with his usual diplomacy. He was evasive about his future relationship with M-G-M but announced that his plans included producing the movie version of Zweig's biography, with Norma as *Marie Antoinette*. The Thalbergs then checked into the Waldorf-Astoria for an "indefinite stay," and the next day Nick Schenck invited them out to his Long Island estate for the weekend.

From Schenck, Thalberg learned more about the decision to oust him from Metro.

The scheme had been Mayer's, the General said, but he had endorsed it as an emergency measure because production commitments had to be met. He had not intended to remove Thalberg altogether. At the same time, the studio had to face up to the reality of Thalberg's illness and the very real possibility that he would not be physically capable of supervising every Metro movie in the future.

Whatever Thalberg's real intentions, he remained outwardly noncommittal. This was his kind of game, and he played it well. But Schenck continued to press him about returning to M-G-M. He would have his own independent production, make the movies he wanted to make, with Norma or with anyone he chose.

Thalberg pushed cautiously for an advantage. He was thinking of *Marie Antoinette* for Norma. He could make it at Metro, Schenck replied. Another idea was for Ernst Lubitsch to remake *The Merry Widow* as a musical. That too, Schenck said. Thalberg added that he would want people under personal contract. It could be discussed, Schenck said. So, after a five-month absence from Metro, Thalberg agreed to go back, and a deal was struck: Thalberg went to bed, and Schenck telephoned the decision to Mayer, who professed to be delighted.

It seems clear that one aspect of the deal made at Long Island was an agreement that Thalberg would not have to submit to Mayer's authority. Selznick and the other newly created independent producers were expected to report to Mayer, but Thalberg had a hot line to the General himself in New York. Over the next four years Schenck was personally to approve cost overruns (*Romeo and Juliet*) and astronomical budgets (*Marie Antoinette*) sought by Thalberg, apparently without prior consultation with Mayer.

Still, Thalberg took his time leaving for the coast. He and Norma saw plays, shopped, and paid a nostalgic visit to Thalberg's old neighborhood. Two weeks later, as he boarded the train, he announced his intention to organize at Metro "a production unit that will make as many pictures as I am capable of making," pictures "of the quality and type I have endeavored to make in the last fourteen years." After arriving in Pasadena four days later, he made an even more pointed reference to his commitment to quality pictures that somehow managed to convey the impression they had become an endangered cinematic species in his absence. "Quality pictures pay," he said. "The quality production which is more often than not the expensive production is the one that pays the big returns."

On the morning of August 19, photographers were on hand for the Thalbergs' return to Culver City. The San Bernardino Mountains rose slowly, tier upon tier, in the distance, their brown tones hard in the glare of the sun. But Norma wore gloves and a wool beret with her white suit, and Mayer and Thalberg were encased in jackets and ties. Mayer, his jowly face arranged into a tight, ill-fitting smile, took them to Thalberg's new office, once occupied by Cecil B. De Mille. Redone for its new occupant by Cedric Gibbons, it resembled a sumptuous Hollywood manor— beamed ceilings, a big fireplace, leather armchairs.

From Lewin Thalberg learned the Los Angeles version of his ouster: that it had actually been planned by Schenck, not Mayer, but that Mayer had embraced it eagerly. It was hardly news to Thalberg that neither prince could be fully trusted. It suited Schenck to establish a personal alliance with Thalberg independent of Mayer. For Thalberg, Mayer was now the enemy, and it was equally welcome to him not to have to be dependent on his old partner's (by now) malignant will.

Thalberg found the studio seething with internal discontent. His own removal had divided Metro into two camps—his supporters and the realists. The latter recognized Mayer as the sole power and David Selznick as his designated successor, and they adjusted their loyalties accordingly. Thalberg's supporters sat together in the studio commissary, drawing comfort from each other and solving each other's production problems. Their motto was "What would Irving have done?" To them Mayer was a despot; Selznick was cast as the hit man and son-in-law. They made jokes about him ("The son-in-law also rises") and recited bawdy verses composed by Selznick's archenemy and Thalberg's friend Charles MacArthur:

> *Someone had to marry Irene Mayer.*
> *Someone had to have the guts to lay her.*
> *Someone had to win her,*
> *Without tossing up his dinner.*
> *That's why our David was born.*

Selznick unabashedly admired Thalberg, however, and did his best to float free of studio intrigue. For his part, Thalberg recognized Selznick's creative energy and was fond of him personally, and the expected rivalry never materialized in such a way as to benefit Mayer. Three years later, intimidated by the support for Thalberg and humiliated by the public comments about his salary and the nepotism, Selznick quit to set up his own independent company, Selznick International Pictures; his supposed rival, Irving Thalberg, secretly invested $20,000 in the new venture, perhaps seeing it as the road he should have taken himself on his return from Europe.

Yet the rivalry, in some part, was unavoidable because Thalberg and Selznick tilled the same ground. When Thalberg returned, *Dinner at Eight*—Selznick's imitation of the all-star formula Thalberg had launched with *Grand Hotel*—was nearing completion. Selznick had also produced *Dancing Lady* with Joan Crawford and *Manhattan Melodrama,* which introduced the *Thin Man* team of Myrna Loy and William Powell, and both films were commercial and critical hits. At M-G-M's insistence, Selznick was reluctantly making *Anna Karenina* with Garbo—reluctantly because her last picture, *Queen Christina,* begun before Thalberg's departure and costarring a Jack Gilbert much diminished in reputation and box office popularity, had been a disappointment, and Selznick feared that the public was not interested in seeing Garbo in another historical drama.

Thalberg's own historical drama was to be *Marie Antoinette.* His other choices, however—plays mostly intended to star Norma Shearer—ran true to form. One of the last films released before his illness had been *As You Desire Me,* adapted from Luigi Pirandello's play *Così È Se Vi Pare* as a vehicle for Greta Garbo. His first production as an independent at M-G-M was *Riptide,* a screen version of the 1920s Michael Arlen's Broadway hit *The Green Hat,* starring Norma Shearer. Charles MacArthur was engaged to write the script (it evidently paid to travel with Thalberg), but inevitably his version was reworked by Edmund Goulding, who directed the picture. *The Green Hat* had been a popular Garbo silent movie as *A Woman of Affairs. As You Desire Me* and *Riptide* had something else in common: both did poorly at the box office.

As You Desire Me was an extreme example of Thalberg's fixation with filmed theater. His movie version disappointed even Pirandello himself, not, as might be expected, because it was not faithful to the original, but because it was too stagy. If the cinema merely reproduces what takes place on the stage, Pirandello wrote after seeing the picture, then the cinema has failed. In Thalberg's adaptation of the play, the Garbo character has suffered a memory loss as a result of being raped and lives in total ignorance of her real identity with a sadistic lover played by Erich von Stroheim, brought back by Thalberg as an actor. Garbo is reunited with her husband, Melvyn Douglas, and the play revolves around whether she is, or is not, his wife. The action takes place on only two sets, and the picture is not enhanced by Garbo's frizzy blond hairdo.

What may have appealed to Thalberg about Pirandello's play was its parallel with William James's view of truth as a subjective variable and not as an absolute. The original ending of the film, like the play, drew no conclusions about the woman's real identity. In the final analysis, Pirandello implied, people believed what they wanted to believe. But following its preview, *As You Desire Me* went back into production because Thalberg realized it was too static and also because the audience demanded a happy ending.

With its hard-edged upper-class sophistication, *Riptide* seemed dated and out of sync with the times. It broke even only because Shearer fans were hungry for any Shearer film, no matter how good, bad, or indifferent. But this was hardly a spectacular beginning for Thalberg as an independent producer, and for a while it seemed that it was Selznick who had his finger on the pulse of America.

Riptide was a concession to Norma's anxiety to get back to work quickly and to remind the public of her glamorous image after a year-long absence. Thalberg also wanted to feel his way in a new situation with a picture that was not too taxing. His next production, *The Merry Widow,* was closer to his announced intention of making "quality" pictures. Von Stroheim's 1925 silent version was one of his favorite films, and he had long wanted to produce a musical version. In Antibes he had secured Jeanette MacDonald's agreement to play the role. Back in Hollywood he was besieged by Grace Moore, who demanded the part, but he stuck to his original decision, teaming Jeanette MacDonald with Maurice Chevalier and signing Ernst Lubitsch to direct. To update Franz Lehar's melodies, he engaged Lorenz Hart and Richard Rodgers, at the time Broadway's leading composer-lyricist team. This distinguished array of talent pleased the critics but failed to attract the public; *The Merry Widow*, costing over $1 million, lost over $100,000.

Thalberg, however, felt that the best was to come. By the end of the year he had assigned Sidney Franklin, Norma's favorite director, to begin preliminary work on *Marie Antoinette* and Donald Ogden Stewart to start work on the film script—an undertaking that was to occupy most of his working hours for most of the next two years. Meanwhile he was able to persuade his wife to play Elizabeth Barrett in *The Barretts of Wimpole Street*.

Another source of discontent at M-G-M had been less calculable. As Franklin Roosevelt took office in March 1933, it had become clear that the nation's economy—and, eventually, the studio's—would be put on a fresh footing. In their own spirit of patriotism, early in March the movie potentates had called for a six-month "voluntary" 50 percent pay cut across the board. At Metro, Mayer announced the cut in an emotional appeal to the staff. It was immediately rejected by studio electricians, engineers, and other craftsmen who belonged to the International Alliance of Theatrical and Stage Employees (IATSE). A compromise formula was worked out whereby studio employees earning less than $50 a week would be exempt, and a sliding scale of percentages was worked out for the rest.

From New York, Thalberg had publicly denounced the pay cut. "Such desperate measures," he told reporters, would undermine morale. One of his concerns was that in the current climate of labor protest, the resentment could escalate into a unified opposition, and he was right.

Shortly after Thalberg's return, M-G-M went to war on two fronts: with the writers and with the actors. Resentment had been building up since the infamous pay cuts. Full salaries had been restored within a few months partly as a result of Thalberg's strong representations with Mayer and other studio bosses, but there was no mention of the promised retroactive compensation. The fact that IATSE members had been successful in fighting off the assault on their pay packets had dramatized the benefits of unionization, and by the middle of 1933 the Hollywood writers had formed the Screen Writers Guild under the controversial Section Seven of President Roosevelt's National Industrial Recovery Act, which granted workers the right to organize unions and bargain collectively. Hollywood actors followed suit and formed the Screen Actors Guild.

With the birth of their guild, many writers became aware for the first time of the social and economic divide between the fortunate few who prospered writing for motion pictures in Hollywood and the large number who lived within the looming specter of the breadline. On the one hand were the famous literary figures, the celebrities, well paid and socially well positioned. Irene Selznick recalled that "the Donald Ogden Stewart house was the first port of call for New York intelligentsia and café society." On Washington's Birthday 1934, the Ogden Stewarts were guests of the Thalbergs at the opening of the Santa Anita racetrack, where for the first time Whitney and Vanderbilt racing colors flashed glamorously under the California sun while their respective owners did likewise in the members' box. Long Island had at last discovered Hollywood and vice versa.

Irving Thalberg's latest literary import, humorist and playwright George S. Kaufman, was lured away from New York at a princely $5,000 a week with a guaranteed $100,000. He surprised his California friends by staying at the Garden of Allah, a once famous residential complex but by then somewhat past its prime. Why? Groucho Marx asked him. "It reminds me of Hollywood," he replied.

Kaufman did not come cheap, but Thalberg got his money's worth. Hired to work on the Marx Brothers' *A Night at the Opera,* Kaufman also found himself assigned to *Marie Antoinette* and *The Good Earth,* M-G-M's Chinese epic based on Pearl S. Buck's best-selling novel. "Don't be surprised," he once told Groucho on the set of *A Night at the Opera,* "if, when I hand you the final scene, you find you've been guillotined for not planting rice in China."

The top writers could afford to play polo, to have tabs

at Musso and Frank's, Lucye's, and the CineGrill Bar, and even to gamble at the Clover Club, although not necessarily on the same scale as their producers. They also congregated at such bookstores as Stanley Rose's on Hollywood Boulevard next to Musso and Frank's. Writers liked Rose: he was one of those colorful characters on the fringes of the motion picture community, a self-styled con man from Texas with a genuine interest in books and literature. But another part of his appeal was that he catered to their basic needs—drink and gossip. Rose was a mine of inside information as a result of his unusual entrée into all the studios: he showed up regularly to make book deliveries—twice a day at M-G-M, three times a day at Warner, as many as ten times a day at Paramount. He had a reputation for knowing everyone and everything, and eventually he became a literary agent. The back room of his store was filled with couches occupied by such legendary Hollywood drinkers as Gene Fowler and Horace McCoy.

By the mid-1930s, influenced by the sobering news from Europe, the conversation at Stanley Rose's was dominated by politics. The stream of Jewish refugees arriving from Germany, the growing popularity of communism among intellectuals, the lingering problems of the Depression, all combined to politicize Hollywood.

The successful writers—Lillian Hellman, Dashiell Hammett, Dorothy Parker—tended increasingly to see the Screen Writers Guild as a forum for their left wing political ideas. For lesser lights, however, the SWG was a timely lifeline, promising protection. Only 10 percent of Hollywood's screenwriters earned more than $10,000. Half earned less than $4,000 a year, and 40 percent received less than $3,000. The latter were part of Hollywood's firmly entrenched community of underpaid hacks who really needed the guild—the fringe people, the weary studio employees who became part of Nathanael West's grim vision in *Day of the Locust*.

The same difference in perception and purpose existed

in the Screen Actors Guild, which had met with an overwhelming response from all levels of the profession. Eddie Cantor was elected its first president. Fredric March, Robert Montgomery (both M-G-M actors), and Ann Harding were among the committee members.

March, politically a rather earnest liberal, tried to recruit Norma on the set of *The Barretts of Wimpole Street*, but she was noncommittal. The guilds were upsetting Irving, she told March. So many friends seemed to be turning against him.

It was typical of Thalberg to take the formation of the guilds as a personal affront. From the start he had voiced strong opposition to professional unionization, declaring that guild shops would be established at M-G-M "over my dead body"—a statement that was to prove sadly ironic. He was convinced, Norma told Fredric March, that the newly formed organizations were a passing fad and that support for them would soon fade once members realized they were unacceptable to the studios. Because he worked closely with writers and, in his own way, respected them, Thalberg regarded the SWG as a worse transgression than the actors' guild. One day, during a script conference with Donald Ogden Stewart and writer Salka Viertel, Garbo's confidante, the discussion turned into an argument over the guild. As the two writers heatedly defended the SWG, Stewart wrote, Thalberg "merely regarded us with the sad, reproachful eyes of a betrayed parent."

The real impact of the SWG was brought home to him on Oscar night 1934, which the guild boycotted in protest against the slow progress of recognition talks with the studios. Arriving at the Roosevelt Hotel with Norma, Thalberg was surprised and then angry to see so many familiar faces on the picket line. Actors were picketing, too, because the Screen Actors Guild had joined the boycott, but it was the writers Thalberg noticed and resented, and the evening hardened his resolve to oppose and if possible destroy the Screen Writers Guild.

In many ways the guild's demands were a direct challenge to his authority. For example, the SWG wanted producers to stop assigning a number of writers to the same motion picture simultaneously without advising them, and of course this complaint went straight to the heart of Thalberg's working style. At the time he had no less than four separate teams of writers working on *A Night at the Opera,* the Marx Brothers' first film under their new M-G-M contract. James McGuinness was writing the story, Harry Ruby and Bert Kalmar were working on comic routines, George Kaufman was writing with Morrie Ryskind in a rented cabana beside the Beverly Hills Hotel pool, and Al Boasberg, a noted gag writer, was working on additional jokes. Whether each team was aware of the others is anybody's guess. What is certain is that Thalberg felt no obligation to inform them.

Secretly or in concert, writers also proliferated on his other current projects. Disappointed with Robert Sherwood's initial efforts on *Marie Antoinette,* Thalberg had fallen back on one of his regular standbys, Donald Ogden Stewart, who was writing a new script. Jules Furthman's script for *China Seas* was handed to McGuinness and John Lee Mahin (who joined M-G-M at the age of twenty-five and was a Hollywood wunderkind) with a classic Thalberg directive: "You fellas look this over. Jim, you help John. Let John do the dialogue and some scenes here. I think there's something wrong [with Furthman's script]."

The SWG also demanded the right to determine writers' screen credits. At the time, this prerogative was vested in the producers, many of whom tended to credit "name" writers at the expense of lesser ones without regard for their respective contributions. Sometimes they simply played favorites. A writer's reputation, and therefore his worth in the market, always depended on his credits; as long as studio producers decided which of several assigned writers received public acknowledgment for a motion picture, every writer would think twice before joining a union that did not have the studio's blessing.

But another reason why Thalberg was against the guilds was his strong opposition to the Left. In this he was no different from most of his peers in the motion picture hierarchy; but Thalberg could articulate his opposition, whereas an L. B. Mayer could not. In politics as in everything else, Thalberg had achieved the status of Hollywood sage. His word was certainly gospel, if not law. No committee of top studio executives was established without him. For example, in 1934 Thalberg was appointed to head a committee of Jewish studio notables to combat anti-Semitic attacks on the movie industry by American Nazis. Given Thalberg's declared lack of concern over what was going on in Germany, and the studios' interest in hanging on to their German market as long as possible, it is perhaps not surprising that the committee's activities were very low key. "You have to face the fact that [Hollywood moguls] began to have a lot more zeal about the Nazis when the Nazis closed down distribution offices in Germany," commented Maurice Rapf.

Thalberg took his role as industry luminary in his stride, making pronouncements in his usual calm, deliberate manner whether he knew what he was talking about or not. What saved him from the ridicule directed at some of his contemporaries was that usually he did—but not always.

Music, for example, was not one of his strengths. One day he was in the projection room viewing a new M-G-M film when something on the sound track bothered him. "What is that?" he asked irritably into the darkness. "What is that in the music? It's awful, I hate it!"

Thalberg's ignorance of music was by now well known, but the tone of his voice required an answer. Someone from the studio music department leapt forward and, secure in the knowledge that he would not be challenged, replied smoothly, "That's a minor chord, Mr. Thalberg."

The next day the music department received an interoffice memo with instructions to post it conspicuously. It read: "From the above date onward, no music in an M-G-M film is to contain a 'minor chord.'" It was signed "Irving

Thalberg." Twenty-five years later conductor Andre Previn, who had worked in the Metro music department in the 1950s, remembers it still on the wall, under glass, and heavily bolted. One thing Thalberg never lacked was conviction, whether about music, the movies he made, or his politics. He was a Republican because he felt Republicanism offered him the best chance of hanging on to his acquired wealth; and no amount of reasoning could moderate his belief that socialism was a dangerous doctrine that would destroy the country.

When Budd Schulberg, son of producer B. P. Schulberg, and Maurice Rapf went to Russia on their summer vacation from Dartmouth and returned home believing that the communist system offered the best hope for mankind, their admiration for the Soviet Union alarmed their families. The instinctive reaction of Hollywood's inner circle was "Send them to Thalberg." Irving would know what to say: Irving would straighten them out.

Irving spoke to them like a wise old ruler admonishing a pair of unruly young princes. He reminded them that they belonged to a dynasty. "He told us that our politics were extremely immature, and he was concerned about us," Budd Schulberg said, "because he assumed we would eventually take over the industry. . . . We were in the line of absolute succession."

In his scheme, though, movies ranked above politics. For example, Thalberg considered the ideas of leftwing political muckraker and writer Upton Sinclair loathsome and subversive. But Sinclair had something Thalberg wanted: he had written a novel about Prohibition called *The Wet Parade*, which Thalberg wished to produce. He could not bring himself to deal directly with Sinclair and even refused to allow him into the studio. So he sent Sam Marx to the author's home to negotiate the deal, warning Marx to "Keep that Bolshevik away from me." Once the novel was in his hands, Thalberg saw to it that the screen version of *The Wet Parade* was sanitized to remove its controversial political content, and the picture was memorable only because it gave Myrna Loy, blond and shimmering in a silver paillette gown, her first important role. It goes without saying that Sinclair was not thrilled with the film.

Indirectly, Sinclair contributed to the guild's problems in gaining recognition from the studios. In 1934, he was a candidate for governor of California. He had quit the Socialist party and was standing as a Democratic candidate. But his radical plan "End Poverty in California" (EPIC), calling for tax increases to fund his social welfare programs, and his proposals for giving workers shares in public utilities and private businesses frightened not only the commercial sector, but also many moderate Democrats.

In a state badly hit by the Depression, Sinclair burst on the scene like a messiah. His social reforms promised salvation—jobs for the jobless, homes for the homeless, a future for the drifters streaming into California every day. He was a figure around whom all of the angry, disillusioned, frustrated forces in the state could rally, and he easily won the Democratic primary. Sales of his pamphlets, through which he financed his "crusade," topped a million copies, and he seemed likely to unseat the reactionary, lackluster Republican incumbent Frank Merriam, who was running against him. Following the primaries, the odds in Spring Street—the betting alley in Los Angeles, more accurate than any political poll—were seven to five on Upton Sinclair.

After trying unsuccessfully for weeks to stem the tide, Sinclair's frantic opponents finally hit upon a strategy to mobilize California's jobholders against the jobless. The message boiled down to a warning to the gainfully employed that they might find themselves without jobs if Sinclair was elected and California became the mecca for the unemployed of the rest of the country.

At the forefront of the business community's "Stop Sinclair" drive was the motion picture industry. The studios once again dug into their employees' pockets: everyone earning over $150 a week had to contribute to Frank Merriam's campaign. At M-G-M, the *New York Times* reported, "many employees were given blank checks made out to Louis B. Mayer," who would turn the money over to the Merriam campaign. In addition, the studios threatened to move to Florida en masse if Sinclair was elected, leaving thousands jobless. The threat was not taken seriously, partly because the logistical problems of such a move would have been enormous—not to say insurmountable—and the cost prohibitive, and partly because work continued at Metro on the construction of a new executive building, while the head of another studio was building himself a suite of modernistic offices at a reported expense of $50,000.

Fake newsreels employing crude scare tactics to frighten voters away from Sinclair were shown in the movie theaters. In these early political commercials, an inquiring reporter would ask "ordinary citizens" whom they would vote for. "I'm voting for Governor Merriam because I want to have my little home," an old woman replied in one of the films. "It is all I have left in the world." But most of the films played on the basic fear of a mass influx of unemployed into the state. One film showed a bearded, bedraggled immigrant saying, "Vy, I'm foting for Seenclair. . . . His system vorked so vell in Russia, vy can't it vork here?" In another, trainloads of Mexicans were seen arriving in California. They were actually extras in discarded footage from *Viva Villa!*

The films were rumored to have been made at M-G-M, but no one knew for certain until Thalberg confirmed it one night shortly after the election at a party at the home of Fredric March. The partygoers got into a heated argument over Hollywood's anti-Sinclair campaign, especially the bogus newsreels. "I made those shorts," Thalberg said quietly. When those present had recovered from their surprise, March protested, "But it was so unfair!" Thalberg replied, "Nothing is unfair in politics. I used to be a boy orator for the Socialist party on the East Side of New York.

Do you think Tammany gave me a chance to be heard? Fairness in an election is a contradiction in terms. It just doesn't exist."

Thalberg the political party trickster was a far cry from the young socialist fighting to make himself heard in Union Square. But the young socialist had borrowed his mother's ideas; the Hollywood Republican had formed his own. Given his opinion of politics, Thalberg was not a party activist the way Mayer was. Mayer sought prominence in the Republican party as a way of assimilating into the American mainstream. Thalberg had no such concern. He was a man of conservative outlook by nature, as was shown by his slow response to the introduction of sound. His innovations in the movie industry had two main objectives, the consolidation of his power and increased profits.

There is no way to gauge the impact of Thalberg's newsreels in pulling votes away from Sinclair, but the combined elements of the scare campaign had the desired effect. A week before the election, the quoted odds were two to one on Merriam. Sinclair lost by 879,537 votes to Merriam's 1,138,620.

Thalberg's role in the "Stop Sinclair" drive and his subsequent offensive against the writers show him at his most determined. It was the same single-minded pursuit of his objective that was well known to those who worked with him. The man who fired directors from pictures without so much as a second thought, and changed writers on a project with the same ease as changing his socks, was not going to be reticent in fighting off an assault on the Ruritanian kingdom of M-G-M.

"First Louis, and now the writers!" he grumbled to one of his associates. The longer the fight lasted, the more he identified the guild with the communists, and the tougher he became. Possibly, too, his reduced position in the studio hardened his mind to failure. He was no longer "what Hollywood means by M-G-M," but he could still mean a great deal to Hollywood. Throughout the studios' struggle against the SWG, it was, as usual, Irving Thalberg who did the strategic thinking.

By the middle of 1935 writer support for the SWG was widespread, but the new union was still no closer to gaining studio agreement to a guild shop. Writers all over Beverly Hills were singing "The Screen Writers Marching Song" (words and music by Henry Myers), of which the first stanza was as follows:

> *Arise, ye movie writers, and cast away your chains.*
> *Executives are human after all!*
> *Shall they still rewrite our scripts, the children of our brains?*
> *And shall we be a supervisor's thrall?*
> *No! No! No! No! A million, million no's!*
> *Not in vain our fountain pens are filled!*
> *The writers all will join*
> *And executives will loin*
> *To monkey with the Screen Writers Guild.*

The last stanza went like this:

> *Ye Gentlemen and Ladies that push the fervent pen,*
> *The time has come and Freedom is in sight.*
> *The cudgeled brain grows weary. When a bottle is your yen,*
> *Have at it! And remember, write is write!*
> *Drink! Drink! Drink! Drink! Write a masterpiece!*
> *Till twenty thousand pages have been filled.*
> *They'll all be thrown away*
> *But the producers have to pay*
> *To members of the Screen Writers Guild!*

In reality, however, neither side could find much that was amusing in the situation. The SWG's answer to the continuing deadlock after nearly three years of sporadic negotiations with the studios was to instruct its members not to sign any new motion picture contracts.

At the same time, the guild also began merger talks with the New York–based Authors League and the Dramatists

Guild—a development strongly denounced by the studios as a fiendish plot by the two New York organizations that (as Darryl F. Zanuck put it) "hate the moving pictures and hate Hollywood and make fun of it and ridicule it . . . to get a lot of writers under their control." The prospect of an alliance between the three unions alarmed the producers because it would effectively put most of the available literary material, and the majority of established writers, out of their reach except through negotiation with the Screen Writers Guild. WRITER DICTATORSHIP LOOMS ON COAST, read the grim headline in the *Motion Picture Herald,* which generally reflected the views of the motion picture establishment.

Thalberg's answer was to organize a "flying squadron" consisting of four "loyal" writers—who were instantly dubbed the Four Horsemen. In the weeks before the decisive SWG vote on amalgamation, set for May 2, 1936, they made the rounds of the studios to convince their colleagues, particularly the younger ones, that amalgamation was a closed-shop proposal engineered by communists. Screenwriting was a "soft racket" that paid extraordinarily well, as one put it; why rock the boat? The pressure on the writers was tremendous, with SWG activists such as Frances Goodrich and Lillian Hellman lobbying them to vote for amalgamation and the Four Horsemen making vague promises of rewarding assignments for those who did not.

The impending vote split the writing community. In the M-G-M commissary, guild members would sit together glaring at top-salaried writers who remained loyal—producers' favorites like James K. McGuinness, leader of the Four Horsemen, John Lee Mahin, and Howard Emmett Rogers. When S. J. Perelman, a staunch guild supporter and no admirer of Thalberg, learned that McGuinness was also contributing a piece to the *Kalmar and Ruby Song Book,* to which Perelman had also contributed a profile of Harry Ruby, he wrote an angry letter to Bennett Cerf at Random House, the book's publishers, withdrawing his contribution. Cerf pleaded with him to change his mind, but Perelman was adamant and his contribution had to be dropped from the collection. There were several such stories: it was a tense time. Long-standing friendships were destroyed in days. Feuds erupted that were still simmering decades later.

On Friday, May 1, at the Beverly Hills Hotel, a producers meeting was called by Thalberg, who also chaired it. As usual, the movie moguls were leaving it to Irving, even though his position at M-G-M was much diminished. It was a habit they found hard to break. After three hours of discussion, they agreed to his suggestion that a last minute attempt should be made to stop the amalgamation from going through, and senior producers should address the writers the next day in all the studios. During the Saturday lunch hour, about sixty writers gathered in Thalberg's projection room, where three years earlier Mayer had pleaded for a wage cut.

Thalberg came in, followed by the towering bulk of Eddie Mannix. To Maurice Rapf, who was present, it evoked images of Tammany politics or even a gangster movie—the hard guy and the Little Czar. The writers had expected a discussion, but there was none, just a thinly veiled threat to those who supported the guild that they would suffer the consequences. The threat was rendered more menacing by Thalberg's quiet, unadorned, untheatrical delivery.

Rapf later remembered Thalberg's words this way: "You've all gotten a great deal out of this industry. It's been good to you, and what you're proposing to do is give it away and turn it over to outside interests, and we are not going to tolerate it." He said he wanted them to know how the studio would feel about those who remained loyal and those who followed the guild's directive to vote for amalgamation. "We have a lot to protect here, and we are going to protect it with everything we've got," Thalberg said. Then he walked out.

Rapf added, "People who had known him and worked with him and thought he was a nice guy saw him so tough and so hard that we were absolutely shocked." Another eye-witness recalled that "Thalberg said he'd never allow a merger of the Screen Writers Guild and the Authors League because he had to protect the stockholders, some of whom were widows and orphans."

The next stage of Thalberg's offensive came that evening. In what looked like a remarkable truce, several studio loyalists, including Mahin and McGuinness himself, joined the Screen Writers Guild. At their urging, the vote was changed into a ballot on the principle of amalgamation to allow a two-week cooling-off period before a separate vote on its enactment.

The studios were buying time for their next move. Days later these same loyalists resigned as suddenly as they had joined and announced that they were forming a new group called the Screen Playwrights, which immediately denounced the SWG as a radical organization, declared itself against the idea of a closed shop, and said it was prepared to listen to "sane proposals" from the studios. It was immediately recognized by the producers.

By the end of the week 125 guild members had defected to the new group, lured by offers of good, long-term contracts, sometimes well beyond their real worth as writers. Few people doubted who had masterminded what had turned out to be an effective delaying tactic. Thalberg, like other producers, had telephoned writers individually, promising rewards for joining the new organization and warning of the consequences of sticking with the old one—options that wouldn't be picked up, free-lance employment that might be terminated. The effect of that cold, quiet voice at the other end of the line can well be imagined.

The combination of stick and carrot produced results, and in no time at all the Screen Writers Guild had lost all its momentum. Its membership had shrunk to a hard, radical core. The holdouts were branded as communists, which was certainly true in some cases (Lillian Hellman, John Howard Lawson, Donald Ogden Stewart, to name three), but not in all. In reality, the growth of antifascist activism among creative people in Hollywood had brought liberals and communists together in such organizations as the Anti-Nazi League, blurring political lines. More disciplined and well organized, the communists were in a better position to become a dominant force in the new movements and to steer them toward the Left.

Seen from the producers' perspective, what had started out as an attempt to form a writers' union now seemed more like a communist attempt to infiltrate, subvert, and perhaps ultimately control the motion picture industry. If subsequent accounts by former Hollywood communists are to be believed, the party seems not to have had specific plans to take over the movies. Its objective seems to have been the more limited one of raising its national profile by recruiting movie personalities to its cause.

Former Hollywood communist sympathizers dismiss the producers' fears as paranoia. But in the atmosphere of the time it's hardly surprising that Thalberg and the others were suspicious of communist intentions, particularly since some of the most reliable writers had joined the party or appeared to be in sympathy with it.

The worst betrayal in Thalberg's eyes was Donald Ogden Stewart's "conversion" to communism. Stewart had started out strongly opposed to the SWG, but his opposition changed to strong support and then to a passionate, blinding belief in the writers' cause and in Marxism. He joined the Communist party and became a member of the SWG board. Thalberg was first concerned and then angry. On one occasion, when Stewart was scheduled to address a peace rally that was said to be communist-sponsored, Thalberg dispatched Sam Marx to the writer's office.

"Look, Don," Marx said, "Irving has been a very good friend of yours—and he will be very hurt if you make the speech."

Stewart later wrote: "I think Irving was trying to give me some rather deeply felt fatherly advice, and it probably hurt him considerably to see one of his favorite ducklings starting to swim for himself in some dangerous unknown waters."

The fatherly advice was rejected. Stewart kept his speaking engagement, convinced that Thalberg "would not be petty enough" to fire him.

Thalberg was not going to deprive himself of one of his best writers because of politics. Still, Stewart seemed to have underestimated the depth of Thalberg's resentment. Shortly afterward Thalberg told the Federal Bureau of Investigation that his favorite writer was a communist.

The bureau had probably been in touch with L. B. Mayer, who was the one with the government contacts and personally knew J. Edgar Hoover, the legendary director of the FBI. But it was Thalberg who was in a position to supply information on left wing M-G-M writers. In March 1936, he confirmed to Agent J. H. Hanson of the FBI's Los Angeles office that Stewart was a communist sympathizer, having had Stewart's office phone tapped by studio security. Members of the Screen Writers Guild at M-G-M knew—as writer Frances Goodrich put it—that "Thalberg's boys were always listening in." Yet as a result of the tap on Stewart's phone, the FBI was able to pinpoint other Party members who were not Hollywood figures. Some SWG members were evidently less cautious than others.

Thalberg's accounts were typically precise and factual. ("Ogden Stewart has been overheard making arrangements to go to San Francisco on Thursday to attend a party meeting. . . .") The FBI had not yet, at that juncture, begun officially to regard the Communist party as a subversive movement, but Hoover had ordered files started on leading Hollywood communists, and Thalberg's revelations must have been prized. A decade later the information compiled during this period was used to build up cases of subversion in the hearings of the House Un-American Activities Committee against Hollywood's leading leftists. In 1949 Donald Ogden Stewart, ostracized by the studios for his communist past, would leave the country, settle in virtual exile in Europe, and die in England thirty years later.

When it came to employment, it was soon clear that Screen Playwrights members were receiving preferential treatment. SWG writers began to find it harder to get jobs. The producers denied the existence of any blacklist, and to the extent that there was nothing in writing this was true. But in the course of an evening of bridge or poker, a writer's name would come up in conversations and the executives around the table could scuttle his career with a negative shake of the head. Next day the writer in question would find the doors of the major studios closed to him.

Rouben Mamoulian, the director, used to dine out on a good story about the blacklist. He once complained to Thalberg about the blacklisting of Luis Buñuel, the Spanish filmmaker. Buñuel had come to Hollywood following his escape from Spain after the defeat of the Left in the Spanish Civil War. His friends had tried unsuccessfully to find him work and had concluded that he was being blacklisted by the studios because he was a communist. Mamoulian argued that the studios were throwing away an opportunity to use the services of a brilliant director. Thalberg replied, "That's nonsense, Rouben. You know as well as I do there's no such thing as a blacklist, and I'll see that his name is taken off it tomorrow." But for others the intimidation went on, and a deep bitterness divided the two factions. At Metro, Screen Playwrights members occupied the second floor of the writers' building, and SWG writers were on the third, and the occupants of the two floors met only in the elevators. This was the sad drama that Budd Schulberg would recapture so bitterly and so well in his 1941 novel, *What Makes Sammy Run?* And these were the lines of battle that demanded total allegiance to one side or the other.

Yet when two young guild writers, George Seaton and Robert Pirosh, were being harassed by Screen Playwrights members, Thalberg called them both in and said, "I understand you two were staying with the SWG. Why?" They told him they were opposed to company unions and felt that the guild responded to their needs. "Well, I disagree with you about that," said Thalberg. But he added, "If anybody tries to threaten you, to tell you your job is in danger, you come and tell me. You're entitled to your opinions." He shook hands with them and said, "God bless you both."

Thalberg's forbearance in this instance was unusual and puzzling. Possibly it was the fact that he had assigned Seaton and Pirosh to work on *A Day at the Races* and needed them. Or possibly he saw the SWG as a lost cause and was prepared to be magnanimous. By the summer of 1936, Thalberg and the other producers had successfully beaten off the Screen Writers Guild's offensive. The guild had lost almost all of its members. The enemy was crushed.

It was left to the original few to start the long process of rebuilding the Screen Writers Guild. A year later the newly created National Labor Relations Board decided that the producers had joined in a conspiracy to suppress the SWG. Then, on August 8, 1938, elections were held to determine which organization should legitimately represent the writers. Screen Playwrights were out to win at all costs and resorted to all kinds of questionable tactics, such as offering the vote to people with highly dubious credentials, among them Jean Harlow's mother. In this case M-G-M's justification was that she had written the script of one of her daughter's films.

This time the Screen Writers Guild won an overwhelming victory and with it the right to be the collective bargaining agent for screenwriters in eighteen motion picture studios. The one hollow note in the SWG's triumph was that by then Irving Thalberg, who had masterminded the producers' conspiracy and was perceived by the guild as its archenemy, had died. His vow that the SWG would enter M-G-M over his dead body had become a reality.

Ironically, Thalberg's problems in visualizing the picture

Marie Antoinette may have been influenced by his struggle against the Screen Writers Guild. Thalberg sympathized with the grievances of the revolutionaries, but he disapproved of the revolution. In the SWG conflict, the important issue for Thalberg was to defend the established order. Admittedly it had its faults, but its preservation was in the general interest. He had built the best studio in Hollywood, and to surrender control at this stage, in the making of what he must have felt could be his last films, was unthinkable.

12
MOVIES
FOR NORMA

H ow do I deal with Mayer?" The question came from Walter Wanger, a young producer newly arrived at M-G-M, and it was a valid one. In theory, Mayer was now in overall control of the studio's creative output. But if Thalberg had been cut down to size, why did his presence continue to loom as large as ever? His return to Metro on August 19, 1933, had the appearance of a total restoration. His office again became the temple of received wisdom. The ritual pilgrimage to his door was resumed as other producers, particularly old associates promoted by Mayer, sought his advice and approval. The studio machine, the organization he had so painstakingly tooled to a high level of professionalism, gave his productions first priority. Faced with this state of affairs, the newcomer was justified in asking how to deal with Mayer. Thalberg's answer made it clear whom he considered the marginal figure.

"Don't even try," was his reply. "Ignore him."

There was no shortage of people eager to report such slights to Mayer, but he steered clear of any open confrontation himself and instructed Howard Strickling and others loyal to him to do likewise. The smug, wily, dishonest infighter had not lost his capacity for vicious action, but the knowledge that Thalberg had Nick Schenck's support was doubtless a deterrent. In addition, the studio needed the kind of quality pictures Thalberg was committed to making. So Mayer watched and waited. *Riptide* and *The Merry Widow* amounted to a wobbly start. If Thalberg did not steady himself, then Mayer would doubtless strike, and strike hard. Mayer, in any case, didn't like to kick a man until he was down.

In less than a decade since the historic partnership brought M-G-M into being, their once friendly rivalry had soured into animosity and then degenerated into enmity. Their prestigious organization had become a family divided against itself, and the staff had to be very careful not to offend by appearing to favor one man over the other. To those caught in the crossfire, Mayer's theatrical outbursts were considered preferable to the cold, quiet Thalberg anger or, worse, the long, hurt stare. Mayer usually forgot: Thalberg rarely did, although he might forgive.

One second-unit director who made the mistake of preferring to work on another picture when Thalberg needed him for *Mutiny on the Bounty* found himself on Thalberg's personal blacklist. "When I told him I was going to work on another production, he looked at me sadly and said, 'Are you sure about this?' or something like that," the director recalled. "After that whenever he saw my name on a crew list for one of his productions, he would unscrew the cap of his pen and draw a line through it. I never worked for him again."

New unwritten rules came into being to cope with their rivalry. When the king of England's cousin, Lord Louis Mountbatten, and his wife, Edwina, in Hollywood as guests of Douglas Fairbanks, did the standard celebrity tour of

M-G-M studios in 1933, they spent some time with Norma and Thalberg on the set of *Riptide,* but then for balance they also made a lengthy stop on the set of another, non-Thalberg production, with L. B. Mayer. Photographers knew it was wise to avoid taking pictures of Mayer and Thalberg together on important studio occasions, because neither was pleased to be photographed with the other.

When Thalberg did steady himself with his next picture, *The Barretts of Wimpole Street,* Mayer had the satisfaction of saying, quite accurately, that the boy genius had needed the help of his former mentor and present nemesis to do it. While Norma hesitated over playing Elizabeth Barrett, William Randolph Hearst had asked Metro to give the role to Marion Davies. M-G-M had originally bought the screen rights on Thalberg's behalf, but it was now within Mayer's power to decide whether to oblige Hearst's Cosmopolitan Company or Thalberg.

Hearst's continued friendship meant favorable coverage for Metro films in the Hearst newspapers. Whatever Thalberg believed, Mayer still cared about the movies his studio produced, and he considered Norma Shearer, though admittedly no Katharine Cornell, infinitely more believable as the bedridden nineteenth-century English poet Elizabeth Barrett than Marion Davies would be. What mattered even more to Mayer was that Marion Davies's box office record was uneven at best. Between 1931 and 1933 she had starred in seven films, of which only three had made money, and M-G-M exhibitors were getting restive about losses suffered on the Davies pictures.

Hearst, who was determined to see his mistress on the screen as a dramatic actress, persuaded her to make an hour-long screen test in the role of Elizabeth Barrett. The result was a series of hopelessly contrived enjambments of mood that failed to change Mayer's view. Aware that he ran the risk of offending Hearst, he gave the film to Thalberg and the role to Norma. Hearst was extremely miffed. The order went out from San Simeon that his papers should black out *The Barretts of Wimpole Street,* and not a word about the film was printed. Hearst did, however, make a point of limiting the damage by preserving cordial personal relations with both Mayer and Thalberg.

Hearst's campaign to secure the role for Marion Davies did have one important consequence. It helped make up Norma's mind to play Elizabeth Barrett. Then, having agreed to it, she suffered a case of the jitters. For an actress with no stage training the role was a risky undertaking. Her husband gave her one of his pep talks and mustered all the protection characteristic of Thalberg's M-G-M: Sidney Franklin as director (this was his fifth film with Norma), William Daniels as cameraman, the inevitable Adrian as costume designer, and Cedric Gibbons as set designer. The production was handled with typical attention to detail; all the costumes were hand sewn, and the silverware and china, even the books were period artifacts because Thalberg believed that settings should help actors as well as create authenticity.

To play Elizabeth's sepulchral, sadistic father, Sidney Franklin wanted Cedric Hardwicke, whom he had seen on the stage in London. But Thalberg cast Charles Laughton, an actor whose work he admired and who had just come out of left field to win the Oscar for Best Actor with his performance in the British film *The Private Life of Henry VIII.* Upon arriving on the set the first day, Laughton sank to his knees and kissed Norma's hand. Fredric March, who played Robert Browning because Brian Aherne had declined to be put under long-term contract, witnessed the obeisance and saw Norma thrown momentarily off balance. But she recovered and was once again her composed, regal self.

At least on the surface. Initially, the prospect of working with an actor with a reputation for temperament as well as brilliance added to her anxiety. Norma, wrote Franklin to his friend Fred Niblo, "has found it a little difficult to get into the spirit of the picture." She was having problems with the delivery of the long speeches, "rather different from anything she's ever done before." Laughton, one may be sure, was having no such difficulty.

By the second week of shooting she had settled down and felt more secure in the part, and there was a general relaxation of tension. "She created a relaxed atmosphere, serving eggnog in her trailer at four in the afternoon," remembers Maureen O'Sullivan, who played Elizabeth's sister Harriet. Sometimes Norma would call a Los Angeles department store and order clothes to be sent over. She wasn't planning to buy anything; she just enjoyed trying on the clothes. To demonstrate her fitness and agility, she would occasionally entertain other members of the cast by turning cartwheels.

One reason for this cordiality was the blossoming friendship between the two principles, Norma Shearer and Charles Laughton. On one level they were a study in contrasts: she was the glamorous star, programmed for poise and control, a woman who, in the (perhaps envious) words of Laughton's wife, the actress Elsa Lanchester, "never steps over the edge. All her actions, movements, and gaiety are really restrained." Laughton plunged over the edge frequently and then felt guilty about it. His manner was florid, and he looked like an oversize, unmade bed in which energetic things had taken place. He was convinced that he was exceptionally ugly and fought a lifelong, losing battle with obesity.

Based on different private insecurities, their friendship became mutually reassuring. Norma and Laughton understood each other's needs for emotional release in acting and admired each other's talent.

The Laughton's became fixtures at the Thalbergs' Sunday brunches, when Irving and Charles would take long walks on the beach to discuss future projects. Thalberg had three roles in mind for the actor: Louis XVI, Marie Antoinette's impotent husband; Quasimodo in a remake of his old Universal success *The Hunchback of Notre Dame;* and Captain Bligh in *Mutiny on the Bounty.* Scared that the "moral turpitude" clause in standard M-G-M contracts could be his undoing, Laughton confided to Thalberg that he was a homosexual. Under the notorious catch-all rule, a member of the Metro "family" risked dismissal if he or she committed any act that the front office felt could "shock, insult, or offend the community, or ridicule public morals or decency, or prejudice the producer, or the motion picture, or the motion picture industry in general."

L. B. Mayer never yielded much on the "moral turpitude" clause, but though it was more honored in the breach, its enforcement was selective. Heterosexual liaisons were tolerated if they were discreet and particularly if those involved were sufficiently powerful to get away with it. Garbo's affair with John Gilbert affected the careers of neither star. Joan Crawford's string of dalliances brought no retaliation, except for the occasional warning from Mayer, who when it came to extramarital relations also considered himself above his own law.

Mayer's attitude toward gay relationships was tougher. He could deal harshly with transgressors he felt went too far. The young actor William Haines was a case in point. Haines landed in jail one night after picking up a sailor in downtown Los Angeles and taking him to the YMCA, where the house detective alerted the Los Angeles vice squad. Mayer used his connections to keep Haines out of court, then invoked the morals clause to cancel the actor's contract. And although making sure the story never reached the press, he leaked it through the grapevine. Haines was blacklisted by the major studios as a morals risk. Subsequently he forged a successful career as an interior decorator.

Laughton no doubt had Haines in mind when he made his personal confession, but the morals clause meant little to Thalberg. He actually relished hearing the gossip about his stars, which he could then pass on to Norma, just as in the old days he got a vicarious thrill out of visiting a whorehouse with his more sexually active cronies and waiting for them in the lobby.

The Thalbergs were tolerant of other people's affairs

and sexual proclivities and felt that the morals of others were their private business—as long as they stayed reasonably private. Thalberg still nursed the idea of forming his own company and was talking of putting Laughton under personal contract, where the latter would be immune from Mayer's moral rules. One element of *The Barretts* that had attracted Thalberg's attention was Mr. Barrett's incestuous fixation on his daughter. Thalberg wanted this conveyed but was worried about possible censorship problems.

"They can't censor the gleam in my eye," Laughton told him. And in the film Laughton's lustful gleam is very evident. But in the final confrontation between father and daughter, they meet on the same level of emotional power. Laughton reveals the depths of his torment, and both actors briefly invest the picture with enduring quality.

Unfortunately *The Barretts of Wimpole Street* today comes over as mannered and stagy, another of Thalberg's filmed plays rather than the film version of a play: more theater than cinema. When it was released *The Barretts* was an enormous box office success, earned Best Picture and Best Actress Academy Award nominations, and the *Photoplay* medal. Laughton's performance is brilliant but theatrical, but Norma's Victorian spinster is closer to understated contemporary screen acting. Inside the pale, sick, repressed invalid with the dangling ringlets and wan smile, she shows us glimpses of the passionate spirit waiting to be freed. One of the problems with the pictures is Thalberg's choice for the poet Browning. Fredric March does not come across as the liberator one envisions. Brian Aherne would have been better.

Norma poured her own anxieties and sexual frustrations in the role, which was not unusual for her. Maureen O'Sullivan found her studied, charmingly flirtatious, and yet "underneath it there was something else. She was a very passionate woman." Norma was better than her material, but that wasn't unusual, either. Her presence saved more than one of her husband's movies from mediocrity. That was the essence of the star system.

Thalberg felt that Norma Shearer had blossomed into

an outstanding actress. He developed something of a fixation about her performances. He would show one and often two of his favorite Shearer films for dinner guests at 707 Ocean Front—*Strangers May Kiss, Private Lives, Smilin' Through, The Barretts,* but not the more risqué roles that were *her* favorites, *The Divorcee, A Free Soul, Lady of the Night*—and watch intently as though seeing the picture for the first time. According to Sam Marx, Thalberg's choice of roles for her was conditioned by the belief that she had transcended mere stardom and could tackle any role. Even Shakespeare.

On a spring afternoon in 1934, Howard Dietz, who led a double life as Loew's publicity executive and a successful lyricist (whose hits included "Dancing in the Dark"), received a call from Thalberg that he remembered this way:

Thalberg said: "Howard, answer me yes or no. Do you think we should make *Romeo and Juliet?*"

"Offhand, no," Dietz replied.

"What do you mean, 'no'? It's the greatest love story ever told, it's a work of art."

When Dietz asked, "Who'll play Juliet?" he knew the answer before Thalberg gave it: Norma Shearer. Dietz said, "I doubt she would be right for it. She's not that young."

"Juliet can be any age," Thalberg said.

"I don't think *Romeo and Juliet* is good box office," Dietz argued.

"With Norma, it will be a cinch." "Cinch" was one of Thalberg's favorite words.

Thalberg was looking for arguments he may not have thought of against making the picture. Katharine Cornell had played Juliet on Broadway, and this had prompted him to revive an old idea of a screen version of what was in fact his favorite Shakespeare play. The prevailing wisdom that Shakespeare was not good box office he had already dismissed. Douglas Fairbanks's production of *The Taming of the Shrew* and Warner's *A Midsummer Night's Dream* had been fine films as far as they went, but they didn't have Norma

Shearer as the star and Thalberg as producer. But Dietz was not alone in his doubts about Norma as Juliet.

When Thalberg came home one evening and told his wife that he wanted her to play the role, she had one of her most serious anxiety attacks. She didn't have the stage training to handle Shakespeare, she told him. She could never look young enough (she was then a few months short of thirty-three). Besides, she was pregnant.

Thalberg first learned that Norma was expecting a second child from Louella Parsons's column, where the news was first reported. It was hardly the most intimate form of communication between husband and wife, and it revives the old residual doubts about Norma's real feelings for Irving. Considering the care she lavished on him, this is perhaps unfair. Still, Irving was certainly not the first person to hear that he was going to be a father. Norma had taken Helen Hayes aside at a dinner party and confided: "I'm pregnant again. Irving's going to be furious with me. He's got my next picture all lined up, and I'll never be able to finish it if I start now." Well, replied Helen Hayes, she had better let Irving know at once. "I know I'll have to tell him," Norma said. "But first I must tell Louella Parsons. I promised to let her know the minute I got pregnant—that she would be the first to know."

More likely Norma was secretly furious at this further interruption of her career, coming so close to her five-month absence while nursing Thalberg in Europe. As before, there was the worry about the effects of motherhood on her figure and the deeper concern of having eventually to bring up two children without a father.

Thalberg received the news with quiet satisfaction. He had counted himself lucky to have survived long enough to have had a son. A second baby—which he took for granted would be a daughter—was a bonus, the unplanned result of a burst of sexual energy following his recovery.

The pregnancy postponed Norma's confrontation with the rigors of Shakespearean performance and put back the start of *Marie Antoinette* after that, but Thalberg remained busy on her behalf as well as his own. The writing of the script of *Marie Antoinette* had become a saga in itself. By early 1935 it had undergone four major revisions, plus a few minor ones. Thalberg assigned Claudine West, a Metro contract writer, to produce one draft. This was subsequently rewritten by the playwright Robert Sherwood. Unhappy with the Sherwood version, Thalberg again passed the assignment back to Donald Ogden Stewart with instructions to find a new approach. One problem, as Thalberg explained to Stewart, was to ensure that Norma kept the audience's sympathy. At his instigation, successive drafts stressed the enmity of those around her and her husband's lack of interest in sex; Marie Antoinette was thus portrayed as a woman without friends and without sexual release.

Stefan Zweig had written a full biography of the Austrian empress Marie Theresa's daughter, but Thalberg's picture picked up the story from the point where she is chosen as the wife of the future King Louis XVI of France. Like all Hollywood producers, Thalberg had difficulty confining himself to historical fact. He wanted a powerful romantic story; he also wanted to make the role memorable for Norma, a role guaranteed to establish her once and for all as queen not merely of the M-G-M lot, but of the screen. As originally conceived by him, the movie had audience allure as he knew how to fashion it: dutiful young princess weds boring foreign prince in arranged royal marriage. Homesick, surrounded by court intrigue, alienated from her husband, who turns out to be impotent, she falls deeply in love with dashing nobleman and has an affair.

Boring husband becomes king, and she queen, but they are deposed in violent revolution. Caught with the king in attempted escape (arranged with her lover's help), she accepts her historic destiny and goes to her execution together with her husband, dying regally on the guillotine. Thalberg toyed with the idea of suggesting that the queen might have escaped execution and found happiness in exile with her nobleman. When successive writers persuaded him that the plot was too well known for the public to accept such distortion, he contented himself with a tender—but apocryphal—last meeting in jail between the queen and her lover.

Crucial to Thalberg's storyline was the revelation in Zweig's biography that Louis XVI was impotent as a result of phimosis, a condition in which the foreskin cannot be drawn back to uncover the penis. Marie Antoinette, sexually frustrated, sought release in a variety of amorous adventures. Zweig suggested that the queen had sex with dwarfs, hinted strongly at a lesbian relationship with her closest confidante, the Marchioness de Polignac, and—his most important claim—described a love affair with the Swedish count Fredrik Axel von Fersen. This was the kind of sexual undertow that appealed to Thalberg and had attracted him to the subject in the first place. But he had reckoned without opposition on two fronts: from French historians who challenged the accuracy of Stefan Zweig's book and from the movie industry's censorship code.

Looking for further material to develop this aspect of Marie Antoinette's life, Thalberg consulted three French authorities on the queen, including French academician Henry Lavedan, author of a play about the royal couple's attempt to escape from revolutionary France. The French scholars saw little merit (surprise!) in the Austrian author's book. All three strongly challenged the historical accuracy of Zweig's portrayal of Marie Antoinette and her husband. Each stressed that there was no evidence whatsoever to suggest a lesbian relationship between the queen and her confidante. Each warned Thalberg that the Polignac family, still in existence in France, might not take kindly to Zweig's characterization of their ancestor and could take legal action.

It was not what Thalberg wanted to hear, so he ordered three more expert French opinions through M-G-M's Paris office—with almost identical results. Historian Alain Byer called Zweig's portrait of Louis XVI and Marie Antoinette "exaggerated and deformed," and the story of the king's phimosis "ridiculous." Another writer, Alain Aleinet, wrote that "Marie Antoinette was not the royal 'grisette' that appears on every page of Zweig's book. She was frivolous, and like all frivolous women, probably did have love 'aspirations' . . . but she was always gentle, a real queen." Besides, he added, "the Queens of France . . . have never been physically adulterous, and this may not be exclusively by nature or duty, but for fear of bringing a bastard into the dynasty."

Thalberg was annoyed and Norma disappointed. She had been looking forward to developing the sexual side of Queen Marie Antoinette—a welcome change of mood and pace from Elizabeth Barrett Browning and Juliet. Heedless of the French historians' objections, scripting went ahead according to Zweig's version of events. There was more than one love scene between the queen and Fersen ("I shall be queen and have you, too," Marie Antoinette triumphantly tells the count following the death of King Louis XV). The relationship with the marchioness was suggested by a couple of long, meaningful looks and a few sharp remarks from Marie Antoinette's villainous royal brother-in-law, the Comte d'Artois. At one point the script also calls for the queen to stroke the head of a dwarf in her entourage.

But Thalberg also had to contend with the censor. In the fall of 1934 he held several lengthy conferences with Joseph I. Breen, head of the movie industry's so-called Production Code, over the *Marie Antoinette* script. Breen's main objections coincided with those of the French, not as historical inaccuracies, but as infringements of Hollywood's self-imposed, strict rules of moral conduct. After long arguments Thalberg promised that the king's sexual problem would be "very delicately handled, referred to once, and then dismissed." The script, he assured Breen, would "make the point and then get away from it." Furthermore, Thalberg agreed to remove any suggestion that Marie Antoinette was having a lesbian relationship.

Breen also banned the adulterous affair between the queen and Count von Fersen. Thalberg disputed this point, arguing that the affair had to be seen in the context of the king's condition and the queen's unhappy end. He meant that since Marie Antoinette dies at the guillotine, the story complied with the code's rigid stipulation that adultery must not go unpunished. But Thalberg argued in vain. Breen ruled that the affair was not "necessary to the proper telling of the story" and therefore violated the code. Thalberg had to agree to delete most of the love scenes between the queen and her alleged Swedish lover.

Thalberg regarded the production code as a necessary inconvenience. He had, after all, helped set it up and realized its value in keeping at bay outside control that could be even stricter. But he spent accumulated hours arguing with the decisions of its administrator. Once he lost the dispute, he tended to comply with its decisions. On this occasion his determination to give Norma her strongest role overruled his usual pragmatism. His commitment to Breen was largely ignored. Advance publicity for *Marie Antoinette* continued to focus on the romance between the doomed queen and her handsome count. Furthermore, when shooting began in 1937, a year after Thalberg's death, the script was essentially the one he had discussed with Breen. It still included six references to King Louis's impotence, and the queen's romantic dalliance was almost intact.

His main concession had been the removal of any hint of sex with the dwarf. Dwarfs, in any case, stirred unpleasant memories for him. A couple of years earlier, *Freaks,* a circus thriller directed by Tod Browning, his old colleague from Universal, had been released to a chorus of accusations of tastelessness. To film this circus story, Thalberg had recruited a large cast of dwarfs, midgets, Siamese twins, and other physically deformed characters. *Freaks* is generally regarded as an early horror movie, but the public was not ready for it. Audiences ran out of the theater during its climax in which the circus freaks mutilate the lovely trapeze star (Olga Baclanova) after she has cruelly jilted one of the clowns. Mayer was so enraged by the picture that the studio withdrew it and rereleased it without the M-G-M logo.

Freaks perhaps represented Thalberg's biggest mistake

in gauging public taste. He had always been fascinated with the bizarre, but in this case he had sadly misjudged what mass audiences would tolerate. But *Freaks* could represent something deeper than a miscalculation. It could be an indication of an emergent dark side. Despite his good looks, his intelligence, and his gifts as a producer, Thalberg may have come to think of himself as something of a freak. Without evidence, however, this is not a line of thought that can be pursued effectively. Thalberg kept no diary, nor does he appear to have spent much time discussing the lengthening shadows.

Making pictures dominated his thoughts and energies, and he expected everyone else to share his interest at all times. Kitty Carlisle, who met him about this time and would soon have a singing role in one of his films, remembered him years later as "very stressed, very nervous, very pushy. One had the feeling that he was very driven." One morning in the fall of 1933, he instructed his secretary to track down Sidney Franklin. When she found the director at the dentist, Thalberg immediately went there to talk about *Marie Antoinette*. While the dentist worked on Franklin's teeth, Thalberg discussed the picture, pacing the room as he did in his own office. Their strange conference became something of a standing joke between them. "I am thinking of having my teeth cleaned after the first of the year," Franklin once wrote to Thalberg. "I want you to be there."

Meanwhile Thalberg had acquired the rights to the play based on Jane Austen's *Pride and Prejudice,* with the role of Elizabeth Bennet in mind for Norma. He filmed a theatrical performance of it and assigned a writer to prepare a script. This project, like *Romeo and Juliet,* promised to be a costly "quality" picture. Once Norma returned to the screen she seemed destined to remain encased in period costume for at least the next four years. Other M-G-M actresses had good reason to be envious of this formidable lineup. If they had expected any diminution of Norma's status as a result of Thalberg's removal as head of production, they were clearly disappointed, and Joan Crawford's gripe about being the permanent second choice—"Big budget, costume, meant Norma; low budget, ex-shopgirl, meant me"—rang true.

But besides his program for Norma, Thalberg had two other productions in the filming stage. One was the Marx Brothers film *A Night at the Opera* and the other *Mutiny on the Bounty,* the movie version (the first of several) of a best-seller based on an actual uprising by the crew of a Royal Navy frigate in the late eighteenth century. Thalberg was interested in its portrayal of the reality behind the swash-buckling image usually shown in adventure fiction. He had also noted the hint of a homosexual relationship between Bligh and Fletcher Christian, the officer who eventually supports the mutiny, as he had caught the undertone of incest in *The Barretts of Wimpole Street;* and once again he had Charles Laughton ready to convey it with the glint in his eye.

But there was no room for a subtext of this nature once Thalberg realized (with strong prodding from Mayer) that a mutineer was a risky hero for a major production. To make Christian sympathetic to the audience he felt he needed to portray Captain Bligh as a villainous sadist who cruelly mistreated his crew and Christian as the idealistic champion of the lower deck, which meant nothing but ha-tred could pass between the two men. He also needed a magnetic star to play opposite the magnetic Charles Laughton. He needed Clark Gable.

Mayer, who had voiced strong objections to the project in the first place, had even stronger ones to Gable appearing in a costume picture. He felt Gable's image as a thoroughly modern American male would be undermined if he were to be seen with his hair in a pigtail and wearing breeches. Moreover, the studio was experiencing one of its periodic allergies to costume dramas: *Operator 13,* a Civil War drama starring Marion Davies, had fared badly at the box office. Please, one exhibitor from Uvalde, Texas, had pleaded to

Metro, "no more pictures where they write with feathers." *Photoplay* magazine, in one of its recurrent appeals to the studios to keep the screen's heroes and heroines out of crinolines and suits of armor, commented, "One bo-bo-bo from Bing Crosby is more exciting than a whole screenful of Crusaders."

Gable himself needed to be persuaded to play the role of Fletcher Christian, fearing that his fans would find his English accent and period costume effeminate. Thalberg enlisted the help of Eddie Mannix, and Gable was slowly won around. On one point he remained adamant: no English accent.

To cast the remaining leading role, Thalberg approached Cary Grant, who was then under contract to Paramount. Grant agreed immediately, attracted by the part and by the prestige attached to appearing in a Thalberg production. But the decision was up to the studio head, Adolph Zukor, and he refused to loan out Grant, ostensibly because the young actor was too busy. The real reason was that Zukor nursed a grudge against Mayer and Thalberg. Some years earlier M-G-M had demanded an exorbitant price for a loan-out just when Zukor was hard-pressed for cash and Paramount seemed on the verge of going out of business; Zukor had not forgotten.

So Thalberg cast Franchot Tone in the role denied to Grant. By the time M-G-M approached Grant for another picture, Zukor had relented; and the irony was that on the day *Mutiny on the Bounty* received its Academy Award, Cary Grant would be working at M-G-M in *Suzy*, a charming but forgettable comedy-drama that also starred Jean Harlow—and Franchot Tone.

=13=

GROUCHO, CHICO, AND HARPO— AND IRVING

In keeping with M-G-M's institutional aversion to location work, *Mutiny* was filmed on Catalina Island, off the California coast. The lush, tropical verdure of the South Seas shore was reproduced on the leeward side of the island, and on the windward side appeared the rain-washed waterfront of eighteenth-century Portsmouth. A replica of Bligh's British fighting frigate HMS *Bounty*, meticulously reproduced by Cedric Gibbons and looking as if she had come off the slipway of an English shipyard, was anchored off Catalina's western reefs.

Cast and crew were housed in barrackslike quarters and bungalows according to their status. They were awakened at dawn by a bugle call, then fed in a large mess hall while assistant directors with loudspeakers intoned their schedule for the day. They walked in the dawn light of the California summer to the pier area, where makeup men covered them generously with cocoa butter to simulate sweat. Those who wore period wigs collected them from refrigerated boxes, and everyone was then ferried by water taxi to the *Bounty,* which was a floating set. The sea was often rough, and a young cameraman was drowned when he fell off a boat while filming in a storm. Some members of the crew and cast suffered from sea-sickness, notably Charles Laughton.

Bounty was far from a trouble-free production, and Thalberg had to fly to Catalina by seaplane more than once to calm rough waters of another sort. Laughton and Gable were in agreement only on one thing: their antagonism toward Frank Lloyd, the veteran director from the silent era who had owned the movie rights to the book and insisted on making the picture in return for transferring the rights to Thalberg (another condition was that Laughton's makeup replicate Lloyd's bushy eyebrows). Both actors felt that Lloyd was paying more attention to filming the hardships of life on His Majesty's ship than to the two principal characters. When they telephoned Thalberg to protest, he flew to the island and ordered Lloyd to follow the script and stop unsettling the stars.

But in other respects, life imitated art as the tension between them mirrored the tension between Bligh and Christian. Laughton was difficult, Gable touchy. Jealous of, and perhaps a little intimidated by, his co-star's good looks, Laughton retreated behind a wall of stiff British reserve. Off the set he ignored Gable totally, and in their scenes together he deliberately and systematically avoided eye contact. When Captain Bligh addressed Fletcher Christian, he stared out across the Pacific or up at the rigging, anywhere except at the man in front of him. Gable conversed with the back of Laughton's head for a few days and then protested to Lloyd: "He's not playing to me, he's ignoring me!"

On Gable's side there was a distaste for Laughton's homosexuality. Gable did not hide his dislike for gays, but the intensity of his feelings against them may have been due to a homosexual experience in his own past. According to a biography of director George Cukor, it was well known among Cukor's gay friends that Gable had had a one-night stand with William Haines in the 1920s, when the still undiscovered star was working as an extra in a Haines movie. Haines was a lifelong friend of Cukor. If true, the episode was almost certainly the macho actor's only foray into gay sex, but the fact that other homosexuals might know about it (which apparently some did), and the consequent fear of what it would do to his image, and even his career, if they went public with that knowledge, could further explain why Gable was so obviously aggressive and uncomfortable in their company. Laughton had a good-looking young masseur with him on the island, and the two were intensely devoted. Seeing them together, Gable would turn away in disgust—and, unhappy about his costar, he became quarrelsome and uncooperative, arguing with Lloyd, the crew, and the rest of the cast.

Soon all three were complaining to Thalberg about one another, and he again crossed over to the island to investigate. He found tempers raging; and after listening to charges and countercharges from Gable, Laughton, and Lloyd, and the independent testimony of Franchot Tone, he told Gable to stop complaining and follow Lloyd's directions (but sweetened the pill by giving Gable the weekend off). Then he took Laughton aside and warned him to stop avoiding eye contact with Gable in their scenes together. Privately, though, Thalberg was not as bothered by the existing tension as he pretended to be. The footage already filmed held the promise of a powerful drama; the scenes between Laughton and Gable that he had screened were electric. To Thalberg that was more important than harmony among the actors. If the tension-filled atmosphere on Catalina improved the picture, he was not too anxious to restore peace on the set.

But the atmosphere did not change, and neither did the quality of the footage. *Mutiny on the Bounty* was a spectacular critical and commercial success. The film won the Academy

Award for Best Picture of 1935, plus Oscar nominations for Laughton, Gable, Frank Lloyd, editor Margaret Booth, and scenarists Talbot Jennings, Carey Wilson, and Jules Furthman, and it lives on as one of Hollywood's all-time greats.

The Marx Brothers were a departure from Thalberg's usual area of interest, but one of his last actions as head of production before his heart attack had been to persuade L. B. Mayer to let him put the comedy team under contract to M-G-M. In so doing, he gave the brothers' collective career a new lease on life and may well have rescued them from obscurity. Today the Marx Brothers are enshrined as immortals of film comedy, but at the time they were well on the way to becoming half-forgotten relics of the silent era. *Duck Soup,* their fifth film for Paramount, had been well reviewed but, like its two predecessors, was a disappointment at the box office, and the word was that they were all but washed up in Hollywood. They were middle-aged, and many of their routines seemed that way as well. With money still scarce, Paramount had shown no interest in investing in another Marx Brothers movie.

The Marx Brothers may not have known the modern term *networking,* but they were expert practitioners of it. Groucho was a founder-member of the Hollywood Literary and Asthma Club, which consisted almost entirely of leading writers, especially humorous writers, among them Gene Fowler and Robert Benchley. Its members met for lunch every Thursday to grouse about their various employers and destroy reputations. Harpo, always mute in their act but the most articulate of the three in real life, was a favorite of the New York literary crowd, with his own place at the Algonquin Round Table. But Harpo also had powerful friends in top movie circles, including Sam Goldwyn, and on the basis of that friendship, Goldwyn had stepped in with a halfhearted offer to produce the Marx Brothers' next picture. Chico, who had cultivated studio executives for years, played bridge regularly with Thalberg and now appealed to him for help.

Thalberg screened *Duck Soup,* watched other Marx Brothers movies, and then pressed a very reluctant Mayer to sign up the comedy trio. "If Irving wants you, go with him," Goldwyn told Harpo, possibly a little relieved to be off the hook himself. "He knows more in one finger than I know in my whole body."

Irving wanted them in part because at the time M-G-M had no star comedian. Buster Keaton, the great stone face of silent screen comedy, was fired by Mayer in 1932 after the studio chief raided Keaton's dressing room in the middle of a wild party; but that was only the final debacle. Relations between Keaton and the studio had been worsening steadily because of Keaton's drinking and the difficulty he had in adjusting to Thalberg's structured production system.

When he'd come to M-G-M in 1928, Keaton was warmly welcomed by Thalberg, who admired him just as Keaton admired Thalberg. Thalberg assigned Larry Weingarten to supervise the Keaton productions and provided him with writers and all the other backup available to Metro stars. Keaton wasn't accustomed to having a supervisor. For years he had chosen his own team and made all the creative decisions. Thalberg's attempt to fit him into the system made him increasingly temperamental, and he blamed M-G-M for the declining quality of his pictures. Perhaps, as Keaton contended, Thalberg should have let him do things his way, for that was when he turned out his best work—namely, *Doughboys,* his most successful sound picture.

But M-G-M was interested in using Keaton as a performer, not as a producer, for the simple reason that in the time it took him to develop a project, he could have appeared in two or three pictures set up by the studio's production staff. When Mayer burst in on one of Keaton's parties with his cronies and their girlfriends, the star's resentment at the studio boiled over and he angrily ordered Mayer to get out. Shortly afterward he refused to be on hand to meet a group of distinguished visitors. These visits were an important public relations exercise that was taken very seriously by Mayer and the studio. Within forty-eight hours Keaton had been fired. By then Thalberg was already negotiating with the Marx Brothers.

He was confident that the Marx Brothers could successfully fill the gap in the studio's production lineup. He had a personal motive, too, and this was to prove to himself as well as to others that broad comedy was not beyond his scope. Hal Roach had once told him that he had no comedy sense, and Thalberg had never forgotten how the position Roach had all but promised him had gone to an executive with experience in comedy production. He had brooded over the rejection, but Roach had been right. Thalberg recognized and appreciated sophisticated wit, and delivered the occasional good line himself, but he tended to dissect rather than enjoy humor. If he watched a comedy alone, he would sit there quietly breathing through clenched teeth; if he was in company, he would be counting the laughs, but his manner serious and broody. I once asked Sam Marx how often had he heard Thalberg laugh out loud. It was not a question he had confronted before. A minute went by as the story editor who had known and worked with Thalberg for decades searched his memory, and then he said: "Never." It did happen, but rarely, and then it was the gleeful laughter of a young boy—an echo, perhaps, of happier times.

When Thalberg met the Marx Brothers to discuss his offer of a contract early in 1934, he began, typically, by telling them what was wrong with their earlier pictures. His diagnosis was that they were having difficulty adjusting their performing style to the new realities of sound movies. On stage they were masters of timing, but on screen they were not "holding" their lines. Result: The audience was laughing through some of their best gags. The answer, in Thalberg's view, was improved timing and (what else?) better editing.

Second, their pictures had no stories. "I don't agree with the principle 'Anything for a laugh,'" he told them. "For my money, comedy scenes have to further a plot. The comedians have to help someone who's a sympathetic character. With a sound story, your pictures would be twice as good and you'd gross three times as much."

There was also a gender problem. "Men like your comedy, but women don't," Thalberg said. It was an article of faith in Hollywood that the audience for slapstick was predominantly male. Women, Thalberg pronounced, "don't have that kind of humor. So we'll give the women a romance so they can become interested."

The Marx Brothers were signed by Thalberg's production company, and the whole bewildering gallimaufry of Metro's creative and technical skills closed in around them as work began on *A Night at the Opera*. Their bottom pinching and prankish behavior around the studio angered Mayer, and when they suggested that the film should open with their heads in the circle instead of the lion's, Mayer's refusal was colorful and lengthy. Fortunately Thalberg removed them from Culver City and sent them on the road for six weeks with the completed *A Night at the Opera* script.

The basic screenplay was written by James McGuinness, but George S. Kaufman, Morrie Ryskind, and Al Boasberg, among others, had worked on the comedy. Thalberg had the idea of testing the material in performance, so a vaudeville show had been put together consisting of the main big comedy sequences. *Scenes from "A Night at the Opera"* opened on April 13, 1934, at the Orpheum Theatre in Salt Lake City, one of the few surviving vaudeville houses going back to the days when moving pictures were program fillers in variety shows; thus it had a screen as well as a large stage.

The Marx Brothers tried out their routines in live sketches, and a narrative was projected on a movie screen to provide continuity for the audience. Ryskind and Boasberg accompanied the Marx Brothers, and they would sit in the audience at each performance, making notes. Ryskind was small, wiry, and very funny. Boasberg, who was well over six feet tall and weighed about three hundred pounds, was a well-known gag writer who supplied jokes to virtually every comic in show business. He got his best ideas in the bathtub, in which he spent the better part of his life. Every day the two writers created new routines and pieces of business to replace the material that had failed to work the previous night.

Boasberg wrote the famous stateroom scene in *A Night at the Opera,* in which more and more people squeeze into the four-by-four cabin on an ocean liner until there is no room to move. But what ended up as one of the funniest comic sequences ever filmed flopped in the early performances and the Marx Brothers wanted to cut it. When Thalberg was told he sent instructions: "Leave it in." Throughout the tour the Marx Brothers worked on it and eventually brought out the comedy in it.

Scenes from "A Night at the Opera" wound up its six weeks at the Golden Gate Theater in San Francisco. The show had improved steadily since its opening in Salt Lake City. The stateroom scene was now getting bigger laughs than anything they had previously done on the stage, and they were playing to packed houses. Nevertheless, on closing night the Marx Brothers were in a state of great anxiety. Thalberg was in the audience to give his verdict, and the future of their picture hung in the balance. If he did not like the material, there would at the very least be the further delay of writing a fresh script.

Thalberg sat in the first row, and Groucho watched him anxiously through the performance. To his growing dismay Thalberg never smiled once, not even when the stateroom scene was bringing down the house. The Thalberg in the audience sat poker-faced, but the Thalberg who came backstage after the show was smiling and enthusiastic.

"We're going to have a great picture," he told Groucho. But you didn't laugh once, Groucho told him.

"Well, this isn't the first time I've seen [the show]," Thalberg admitted. "I've been out front watching you for the past four days. I didn't tell you I was there so as not to make you nervous."

Most of the time the Marx Brothers looked upon Thalberg as their savior, but that did not stop them from occasionally regarding him as a mixed blessing. The enlightened prince could sometimes turn out to be a benevolent despot. As spokesman for the Marx Brothers' collective angst, Groucho would complain that Thalberg's obsessive overorganization was killing their spontaneity. After sailing for years in unchartered waters, they found Thalberg's detailed maps too confining. Surprises were part of the Marx Brothers' stock in trade; for Thalberg they were a nuisance.

The problems began with Thalberg's choice of Sam Wood to direct the picture. Wood was not the most brilliant director in Thalberg's stable, but he had qualities Thalberg probably appreciated as much as brilliance in his filmmakers. No Ernst Lubitsch, Wood was nonetheless a competent technician, and—as Thalberg told Groucho when he protested—"he'll take suggestions better." In other words, he would follow orders. Wood was a former officer in the U.S. Marines. He was also a right wing reactionary of the most determined kind.

He had learned his craft as Cecil B. De Mille's assistant and had more than fifty movies to his credit at the time, ranging from several Wallace Reid pictures in the early 1920s to such recent Metro successes as *Red Dust*. On the set he was unpopular with cast and crew; he was grumpy and complaining, and his idea of geniality was to boast that he had three testacles.

Six years after directing *A Night at the Opera,* Wood gained some fame as one the marginal unsung heroes involved with the making of *Gone With the Wind*: he had been called in by David Selznick to direct part of the picture but received no screen credit. Some years after that, he earned the more dubious distinction of having founded the Motion Picture Alliance for the Preservation of American Ideals, ostensibly dedicated to "the continuance of the . . . American way of life" in the movies, but in reality an organized, fanatical right wing crusade against Hollywood liberals. It was intensive lobbying by Wood's alliance that eventually persuaded the House Committee on Un-American Activities (HUAC) to open its infamous investigation of communists in the motion picture industry.

Aware of the Marx Brothers' unease, Thalberg supplied constant reassurance—the daily footage was excellent, the previous day's routines were among the funniest they had ever done, the film was going to be a smash, and so on. When they complained to him that Wood, whom they regarded as the enemy, filmed take after take of every scene, his standard reply was that he would look into it. In reality, however, Wood was following Thalberg's instructions. Thalberg had asked him to make sure that he had a large number of takes for editing.

A pretty young New York opera singer named Kitty Carlisle made this discovery herself when, with Allan Jones, she was cast as the movie's romantic interest. Thalberg gave her the role after pianist Oscar Levant took her to a Sunday brunch at 707 Ocean Front and assured his host that her soprano voice was as outstanding as her looks. Carlisle and Jones prerecorded the arias for the opera sequence, intending to mouth the words to the playback during filming. Their first day of shooting took place in a replica of the Metropolitan Opera House, with an audience of extras in full evening dress. The opera was *I Pagliacci,* and Carlisle was on stage in costume, ready to sing the Ballatella to her own playback. At the shout of "Action" she began to mouth the opening bars—but suddenly stopped. The voice on the playback did not sound like her own. A second take was started, and this time she was certain: the voice belonged to someone else. Kitty Carlisle stormed off the set.

She then learned that Thalberg had arranged for an additional recording to be made by two leading soloists from the real Metropolitan Opera, and Wood was supposed to film the scenes two ways: first with Kitty Carlisle and Jones mouthing the arias to the other soloists' voices and then again to their own. Thalberg liked Kitty Carlisle's voice and looks. He respected Oscar Levant's judgment. But—typically—he wanted insurance.

The production was held up for three days while Carlisle's agent tried to persuade Thalberg to film the sequence with her voice only. On the fourth day she was herself summoned to the presence, and, "I cried all over his office. I cried in his wastebasket; I cried on his desk; and I cried all over the top of his head. In the end he gave in . . . and when I see the movie now I have the satisfaction of knowing that the high C in the Miserere is mine!" But her agent's reward for all his efforts on her behalf was somewhat different. Thalberg barred him from the studio for a year.

The preview of *A Night at the Opera* was attended by the studio brass en masse. The train went north to Riverdale, where the cans of film were carried into Loew's Mercury Theatre. In their wake came a procession of M-G-M executives led by Louis B. Mayer. When the film was shown the laughter was scattered, and afterward Thalberg held a sidewalk conference with his colleagues. "That wasn't a Marx Brothers audience," he declared. Mayer looked smug. The Marx Brothers looked miserable.

Across the street was another theater, and Thalberg had no difficulty persuading the manager to show the film. But the second preview was no better: more sporadic laughter and long stretches of silence; the most frequent comment from the audience afterward was that the gags were too far apart. By now Groucho was almost suicidal: Mayer could hardly conceal his delight. But Thalberg had been there before. The following morning he shut himself in the cutting room with one of his favorite editors, William Levanway. Three days later they finished the process of tightening up the picture. The Marx Brothers, of course, had been left out of the editing room, but they sent in word that they wanted to cut Allan Jones's song "Alone," which they felt slowed down the film. For some reason Thalberg ignored the request, and "Alone" became one of the top songs of 1936.

Marx Brothers purists miss the zaniness and spontaneity of the earlier films, but *A Night at the Opera*, the first Marx Brothers film for Thalberg, has not been dislodged from its position as the most profitable and most critically successful picture made by the Marx Brothers. Its success, together with that of *Mutiny on the Bounty*, which was released about the same time, completed the restoration of Irving Thalberg. He was, once again, the movies' leading producer.

He was also overworked. To Norma's distress, he was once again pushing himself to dangerous limits. He put in a long day in his studio and insisted that they also keep a high social profile. The Thalbergs attended premieres, overnight dinners at San Simeon hosted by Hearst and Marion Davies, and major parties. They were high on the A list, and much sought after by leading society hostesses such as the very wealthy Countess Dorothy di Frasso, a noted party giver who was something of a swinger. Born Dorothy Taylor in 1888, the daughter of a Wall Street operator who left her $10,000,000, she had acquired an old-style Italian title via an old Italian husband, a Roman palazzo with a ceiling by Raphael, and a piano lid covered with autographed photographs of European royalty and Mussolini. She had spent considerable sums restoring her husband's family home, Palazzo Madama, only to have it confiscated by the Fascist government. So she moved to Hollywood with her husband, the count, to join her lover Gary Cooper, whom she had met in Rome. Her rented mansion close to Coop's had become a glittering focal point for Hollywood society. Later, when Coop's ardor cooled, she took up with Bugsy Siegel.

Though not particularly gregarious, Thalberg believed that attendance at big social occasions was an important aspect of his and Norma's position in the motion picture community. Besides, it provided an opportunity to maintain contact with other studio executives, who were notorious at parties for huddling together in one corner all evening talking movies. But to Thalberg such behavior made eminent sense, even if it was antisocial. The movies were life. The movies were truth. The movies were beauty. This belief conditioned his existence, and he expected the same fervor in everyone else. When he needed someone for a picture, refusal was unthinkable. His was the burning determination of the fanatic, the iron single-mindedness of the visionary, the rocklike conviction of the converted.

In the spring of 1934, long before Thalberg had informed the FBI of his activities, Donald Ogden Stewart broke the news to his boss that he had decided to quit writing for the movies to resume his career as a playwright. His contract with Metro had long since expired, but he had gone on working month after month "because Irving and Marie Antoinette needed me." With Marie Antoinette beheaded (at least on paper: filming would not begin for another two years), Stewart planned to make the move back to New York. Thalberg, Stewart said, gave him a look "that made me feel that he hadn't heard what I'd said, but that he'd forgive me if I signed for just one more year. I shook my head sadly and went home to pack. Irving telephoned. I was still firm." Thalberg upped the offer from good to very good. Stewart declined.

At seven o'clock on the morning of his departure, Stewart was awakened by the doorbell. His wife peeked out of the window. "It's Irving," she whispered.

"If you don't want me to sign that contract," Stewart warned, "don't let him in."

But it was too late: the maid had opened the door. They heard Thalberg's voice calling, "Don, are you upstairs?" Stewart signed the contract.

Thalberg once telephoned Helen Hayes in the middle of the night in Pittsburgh, where she was on tour. "Charlie's missing," he said, referring to her husband. Missing? Hayes was puzzled.

Thalberg said, "The message he left said he was seeing you. Isn't he with you?" No, replied Hayes.

"He left yesterday," Thalberg went on. Hayes thought

Thalberg "sounded distressed, as if Charlie's sudden departure using me as an excuse had hurt him."

MacArthur, it turned out, had committed the unpardonable sin of deciding to take off on a trip to get away from the studio. Before long, both the actress and her husband were to quit Hollywood and move back east. "Thalberg," Hayes said, "never understood our defection."

=14=
A HEAVY LOAD

Thalberg spent the week-end of his thirty-sixth birthday, May 30, 1935, with Norma at the Oasis Hotel in Palm Springs. She insisted that he bring no scripts to read, but their conversations inevitably centered on film projects and travel plans. After *Romeo and Juliet* and *Marie Antoinette,* he talked of returning to Europe—perhaps to Germany to see Dr. Groedel, still there in Bad Nauheim despite the gathering storm, but certainly back to their favorite haunt, the Hotel du Cap in Antibes. In his mind the scene of his earlier recovery had become a magical place with special restorative powers. He believed his time was running out and that he had about five years left, but perhaps a return to Antibes could pro-long his life.

He was now discussing medicine as decisively as movies, questioning Jessie Marmorston on her latest research into heart disease, exchanging symptoms and remedies with David Perla, who against all medical predictions was still living and working. Thalberg took glycerine pills and chewed candy for extra energy. In winter he was cocooned in a muffler and topcoat to protect himself against further deterioration of his condition through colds.

Even so, his physical appearance could sometimes be alarming. Arriving for a story conference, George Oppenheimer, the writer, noted his "look of frailty, his thin form, the pallor of his cheeks, his hunched posture," but said he came alive when he talked about movies, as if the subject revitalized him. Cole Porter, invited to Metro to play and sing his score for a new picture in the presence of senior studio executives, thought Thalberg "looked more dead than alive. But after the finale, he leaped from his seat, rushed over to me, grabbed my hand, and said, 'I want to congratulate you. . . . I think it's one of the finest scores I have ever heard.' "

He often came home so exhausted that he had to lie down to ease the throbbing in his forehead. Solicitous as ever, Norma was always on hand with the weak Scotch and soda that Dr. Newmark recommended. She checked that he had taken his medicine and tried to persuade him to get more sleep. At her request he began to hold some script and production conferences at home instead of at the studio.

Yet he continued to ignore the one course of action that offered the best chance of prolonging his life—to drastically reduce his workload or even stop work altogether. His wife cut down on their social engagements, but what she should have been doing was forcing him to cut down on his work commitments. Although he no longer was responsible for forty productions, as he once had been, even the demands of the six big-budget pictures he was now supervising at any given time were too much for him. It was not in the nature of their relationship for Norma to be assertive with Thalberg, but a display of forcefulness at this juncture might have helped. On the other hand, Norma was convinced that life without movies would have been intolerable for him, no better than living in a coma or on a life-support system.

So Thalberg continued to work himself to a standstill. He does not appear to have fallen back on religion for consolation, as some would have done in similar circumstances. But then the movies were his religion, into which he poured his energies—indeed, his life. The one important distraction was the birth of his daughter.

On the drive back from Palm Springs, Norma had suffered an attack of nausea and acute discomfort. The Thalbergs went immediately to the obstetrician, who discovered that the sac of amniotic fluid enclosing the baby had begun to tear. There was, however, no danger. On June 13 Norma was admitted to Good Samaritan Hospital, having first urged Thalberg's secretaries to distract him with work. Later that day he was told that all had gone well and that he had a daughter. Once again Norma had lived up to her reputation as the perfect wife and given him what he wanted. The Thalbergs named their new daughter Katharine, after Cornell. "Father and child are doing very nicely," Norma wrote to Sam Marx.

Having done her duty, Norma started a rigorous shape-up program to regain her figure in preparation for playing Juliet. Thalberg's choice of Shakespeare's romantic tragedy for his sixth independent production once more brought him into conflict with L. B. Mayer. Convinced that Thalberg's film would fare no better commercially than earlier cinematic versions of Shakespeare's plays, he tried to persuade Thalberg to drop the project. When Thalberg, following his own advice to Walter Wanger, ignored Mayer, the studio boss refused to approve the budget for what he saw as a high-risk, high-cost venture. But Thalberg went over Mayer's head to Nick Schenck, who released M-G-M funds for the picture in return for a commitment that the cost not exceed $1 million. A producer with Thalberg's experience must have known that, given the scope of the production he was planning, it was a promise he could never keep.

His first task was to build up Norma's confidence. She still had misgivings about her ability to cope with the challenge, but Thalberg brought her around by engaging

Constance Collier, a veteran British stage actress living in Hollywood, as her acting coach and George Cukor as her director. Thalberg had long admired him, but from afar because David Selznick, who had brought him to M-G-M, monopolized his time and talents and at first Thalberg had prudently avoided competing with Mayer's son-in-law for Cukor's services. However, Cukor seemed ideal for the delicate task of directing Norma as Juliet. He had been a theater director; he had a special gift for breathing fresh life into the popular literary classics much favored by Selznick and Thalberg (the pictures he had made for Selznick included *David Copperfield* and *Little Women*); and above all, he handled women stars with unusual skill and insight, even though his label as "woman's director" was also 1930s code for a stigma, the open secret that set Cukor apart from the generally macho, swaggering fraternity of movie directors. He was, in fact, the only homosexual among his colleagues—a fact widely known in movie circles but never publicly mentioned until several decades later.

With Selznick and Thalberg both wanting Cukor, the director became the object of an unusual tug-of-war between Metro (on Thalberg's behalf) and David Selznick, who was then on the point of leaving M-G-M to set up his own company and wanted Cukor to join his new organization. In the summer of 1935 it came down to a choice between the two producers, and rather than favoring his friend and mentor, Cukor favored Thalberg, whose offer had been too tempting both financially and in professional terms. In the end a compromise was worked out whereby Cukor signed contracts with both producers, except that his one-film-a-year deal with Thalberg took precedence over his obligations to Selznick, and this arrangement, according to some of Thalberg's contemporaries, may have been the real reason behind Thalberg's investment in Selznick's new production company.

The fact that Selznick was willing to surrender first call on his favorite director to Thalberg may also have reflected the way Thalberg's movie friends now saw him as a man in the final countdown of his life. Selznick, in blunt terms, did not expect the arrangement to last for very long. Indeed, the grim possibility of another heart attack, this time perhaps fatal, was not forgotten in Cukor's contract with M-G-M. An extraordinary clause inserted in the agreement stated that Cukor's services were "to be assigned by and rendered under supervision of Thalberg. If Thalberg is incapacitated or severs relations with M-G-M, we [that is, M-G-M] advise Cukor in writing promptly and on condition that Cukor advises us within thirty days after Thalberg is incapacitated or severs relations, he may cancel agreement. . . ." That reference to Thalberg severing relations with Metro was included because, while everyone else was writing him off as a doomed man, Thalberg was still planning to start an independent production company once *Romeo and Juliet* was completed, and he contemplated taking a number of key personalities with him.

His condition had certainly not limited his sense of scope. For a while he toyed with the idea of filming *Romeo and Juliet* on location in Verona, but this time Mayer put his foot down—invoking the memory of *Ben-Hur*, drawing Thalberg's attention to the political tension in Europe, and reminding Thalberg of the studio's highly successful policy of bringing the world and its history to Hollywood. Thalberg gave in and, on Cukor's recommendation, sent the distinguished British designer Oliver Messel with a camera crew to Verona, where they photographed its fifteenth-century architecture.

From the outset, Thalberg's *Romeo and Juliet* was burdened with its own significance. With "important" casting, lavish expenditure, and a solemn approach to Shakespeare's text, Thalberg was clearly out to impress public and critics alike with the film's artistry. Besides Cukor and Constance Collier, Thalberg imported Harvard scholar John Tucker Murray, an authority on the Elizabethan theater, and (at Lewin's suggestion) Professor William Strunk from Cornell

University. Strunk owes his posthumous fame to his text-book *The Elements of Style,* but he was also an authority on Shakespeare and had been adviser on Katharine Cornell's much admired stage production of *Romeo and Juliet.* Thalberg wanted him to assist writer Talbot Jennings in turning the play into a movie script and later to be on hand to help actors with the interpretation and delivery of their lines.

Thalberg insisted on a British actor for Romeo. His first choice was Brian Aherne, who was by now under personal contract to Thalberg. Aherne tested for the role but decided that he was too old to be convincing as Juliet's youthful lover. Then Thalberg approached Leslie Howard (later Ashley Wilkes in *Gone With the Wind*), probably inspired by news stories that the handsome blond actor was planning to play Hamlet on Broadway in a production he was to finance himself in the fall of 1936.

Howard, like Aherne, was reluctant. At forty-two he did not see himself in the role of "a boy, a rather tiresome, headstrong boy at that." Yet thinking about it, he came to the conclusion that "this part of Romeo . . . could be turned to advantage." He began to see Romeo as a kind of embry-onic prince of Denmark—"a baby Hamlet," as he put it. Two stronger motives conditioned his acceptance: first the experience he would gain in a classical role, and second the money he would make to help pay for *Hamlet.* So he let himself be persuaded, and Warners, the studio where he was under contract, agreed to lend him to Thalberg in ex-change for the loan of Norma Shearer for one picture.

For Mercutio, Thalberg signed John Barrymore on the strength of their past association, without seeing him. When they eventually met for the first time since the filming of *Grand Hotel,* Thalberg noted the damage that alcohol had done in the intervening two years and began to worry. Barrymore had aged more than twenty years and was some-times vague and forgetful. Thalberg was still willing to hire him but insisted that he move into a sanatorium for the duration of filming. Basil Rathbone, who was Katharine Cornell's Romeo in the New York production, was cast as Tybalt, and Edna May Oliver, M-G-M's resident dragon, got the role of the Nurse.

Oliver Messel's designs for costumes and sets were sabotaged by the M-G-M bureaucracy, which closed ranks against the outsider. Cedric Gibbons complained that Messel's drawings were impressive but impossible to execute, but the dispute was over territorial preserves, and Thalberg sided with the home team. Thalberg allowed Gibbons to change the designs. He was not about to antagonize his longtime collaborators by backing Messel, and the vision of Verona seen in the picture belongs mainly to Gibbons, whose sets are on a characteristic M-G-M scale, detailed and colossal architectural behemoths that tend to dwarf the actors.

The centerpiece was an exterior reconstruction of the Piazza San Zeno in Verona, with its surrounding streets and balconies. It stood on five acres of the M-G-M lot. Juliet's balcony was so high, wrote Graham Greene in his review of the movie, "that Juliet should really have conversed with Romeo in shouts like a sailor from the crow's nest sighting land." The surrounding garden took up the whole of stage fifteen, which had a glass roof and was then the largest sound stage in the world. There were fountains, a three-story Romanesque tower, sculpted shrubbery, and so much vegetation that when it was watered the moisture sometimes formed a cloud over the set. The interiors, which included the vast Capulet ballroom, Juliet's bedroom, and the fatal crypt, occupied other sound stages.

Mayer watched the costs spiral, saw them outpace the film's million-dollar budget, complained to anyone who would listen, and in the end protested to Schenck. Thalberg countered by arguing that "quality" pictures justified the heavy investment, and the General continued to back him against Mayer's objections. Yet as expenses continued to mount, Thalberg seemed to have crossed the line between costly, and justified, expenditure and obsessive extravagance. The production acquired an even richer cultural glow when Thalberg engaged the New York dancer Agnes de Mille as choreographer of the dance sequences. Yet what appeared on the screen hardly required the creative talents of one of the leading dancers of the time. Thalberg was buying prestige for his picture, as when he'd hired William Faulkner as a writer.

Most of the gigues, gavottes, and saltarellas devised by de Mille to music by Byrd, Morley, and Dowling, Shakespeare's musical contemporaries, were never even filmed. For the Capulet ball at which Juliet first meets Romeo, she created a slow, elaborate pavane to a fifteenth-century French ballad. But only parts of the dance were shot, as Cukor had explained to her that too much choreography would slow down the pace of the picture. De Mille got prominent billing as dance director, and the studio released photographs of her teaching Norma the dance steps, with Norma looking remarkably trim in her dance outfit despite the recent birth. "The disappointment was blasting," Agnes de Mille said, "but I had eight thousand dollars in the bank." In the last two years of his life Thalberg sometimes seemed not to be producing movies, but building monuments to himself. Not simple memorials of classic dignity, but large baroque creations, overblown, overexpensive, and overboard on size and grandeur.

To help Norma, Thalberg asked Cukor to lay out the filming schedule in very long takes and as much as possible in sequence, far from the most economic way to film a picture. The balcony scene took five weeks to shoot because Thalberg wanted the widest-possible choice of takes for editing.

"I had five versions of it," says Margaret Booth, who with Thalberg edited the picture. "One with tears, one without tears, one played with close-ups only, another played with long shots only, and then one with long shots and close-ups cut in." Toward the end the balcony itself had begun to crack under the combined weight of Norma

Shearer and Leslie Howard, but it was reinforced and the takes went on.

By November 1935 Norma had immersed herself totally in the role of Juliet. She felt more confident about speaking blank verse, but long speeches still frightened her, and she studied daily with Constance Collier to make them sound more natural.

"Norma was wonderful," Leslie Howard recalled. "The public didn't care if she said, 'Wherefore *art* thou, Romeo,' or 'Wherefore art *thou,* Romeo.'" But Norma cared; and as usual she insisted on take after take until she felt she had got it right. For years afterward, whenever Norma was mentioned to George Cukor, he would join his hands together in an attitude of prayer and roll his eyes skyward.

Thalberg spent hours on the set, not directing operations but standing in the shadows, hands deep in his pockets, intently watching Norma act her scenes. The lighting was designed to hide her age: a mystic white light suffused her while the other actors were in shadow, prompting that caustic grande dame of nineteenth-century English theater, Mrs. Patrick Campbell, who had a small part in the movie, to refer to the cast as "Norma Shearer's Ethiopians." Norma was living the role off the set as well as on it. She moved more lightly, like a young girl, and spoke rapidly with an unusual cadence, as though she were still reciting iambic pentameters. In December she attended a dinner at San Simeon for H. G. Wells and wore an embroidered Renaissance gown with a billowing skirt. Around her throat was a silver ruffle and on her head a "Juliet's cap" designed for her by Adrian, who had copied it from a Renaissance painting.

But if Thalberg the husband was entranced by his wife's performance, Thalberg the producer retained his sense of judgment. When Cukor gave Norma her head in Juliet's farewell to the banished Romeo, the producer found the emotion exaggerated and laid down a Thalberg law. Heartbreak must always be underplayed. He became progressively more unhappy with John Barrymore. Sober or drunk—and Barrymore managed to go on an occasional bender even though he was confined to the sanatorium—his erratic behavior on the set was occasionally funny, always costly, but also a sad reminder of his physical decline.

He was frequently late on the set, and his chronic problems included forgetting his lines and losing his voice. Mercutio's famous Queen Mab speech had to be filmed in takes because Barrymore couldn't memorize it in its entirety. One morning he fell asleep on the couch in his dressing room and refused to get up. Crew and cast waited idly while the makeup man shaved him, made him up, and put on his hairpiece, and all the time Barrymore remained in a recumbent position. Several assistants then dressed him. At noon a studio car rushed him to the set—but he had lost his voice.

On another occasion he took exception to Mercutio's line about Romeo, "He heareth not, he stirreth not, he moveth not." Long pause, and then he added with much relish: "He pisseth not."

Cukor groaned. "Jack, please." But Barrymore refused to speak the line correctly and claimed to have improved Shakespeare's text.

Thalberg was sent for and came onto the set. Very gently he pleaded with Barrymore to speak the line as it was written.

"Very well," declared Barrymore. "Just once I will say it that thou mayst see how it stinketh." And he did, and the camera was running. That was the only take they got from him that day and, of course, the one used in the picture. Barrymore complained furiously that he had been tricked and vowed vengeance.

Eventually Thalberg decided that Barrymore had to go. He approached William Powell to take over the role, but Powell refused, partly out of loyalty toward Barrymore, who had given him his first movie part, but also because he thought Mercutio was outside his range. So Thalberg was stuck with Barrymore. To help his erratic actor with the role, he engaged Margaret Carrington, a well-known voice coach who had worked with Barrymore on other Shakespearean stage productions. Barrymore called her "Christ's elder sister," but he trusted her and she had some success in keeping him under control. But the end result was hardly what Thalberg had envisioned. Barrymore's portrayal of Romeo's kinsman as a testy, middle-aged queen, though colorful, is overacted and at odds with the rest of the picture, an ornate Victorian couch in a roomful of contemporary furniture.

The picture took 108 days to film and was completed in July 1936. Then Thalberg immediately set about supervising Margaret Booth's editing until the 140-minute movie was ready for preview. The film was shown to an audience of college students in Pomona, and when the lights went on after the final fade-out, there was some scattered polite applause, and the rest was silence. Deeply disappointed, Thalberg pinned his hopes on the New York premiere but felt too tired to attend.

Even in New York, though, attendance was respectable but not overwhelming. The film received a boost from several fashion columnists who popularized Norma's "Juliet cap," copies of which were sold in the department stores. But *Romeo and Juliet* was far from the "cinch" Thalberg had predicted, failing by some $900,000 to recoup its final cost of about $2,000,000, which was double its original budget.

To Thalberg, the biggest blow was not that *Romeo and Juliet* proved a commercial failure, but that it failed to impress the critics. His prestige pictures were not necessarily expected to be box office successes; they were, however, required to have a certain critical resonance. Reviewers were polite, with "dignified" and "tasteful" as the recurring adjectives. The two leads were surprisingly plaintive and moving, and Norma and Leslie Howard—as Graham Greene says— "spoke the verse as verse should be spoken and were satisfying in the conventional and romantic and dreamy mode."

After seeing the picture, Joan Crawford—not, admittedly, an impartial judge—remarked to a friend, "Christ, I couldn't wait for those two old turkeys to die, could you?" The Metro publicity department, which never knowingly rejected a cliché, used as its campaign theme the headline BOY MEETS GIRL, 1436. What was missing, however, was exactly that: a pair of lovers hot with energy, lust, youth, and Italian temperament. It was, on the contrary, a sedate, adult drama: with his thinning hair and deliberate manner, Leslie Howard is a mature Romeo who should have known better, and as Juliet's suitor Paris is not youthful but well past early manhood. Nor is Basil Rathbone a fiery young man, but a calculating courtier. In earlier pictures Norma had shown herself capable of transmitting sexual energy: in this instance she was too busy making the verse sound "natural." Leslie Howard was just too busy. In the final analysis there was little in *Romeo and Juliet* to show that Irving Thalberg was a producer of uncommon talent, and if he'd been looking for a suitable epitaph, it was going to have to be some other picture. This was the price he'd paid for his obsession with establishing Norma as the screen's Katharine Cornell. At best, producing *Romeo and Juliet* was a calculated risk. Casting Norma as Juliet, given her age and lack of stage experience, was an error in judgment.

Rumors that he planned to set up an independent production company had been circulating in Hollywood since before his most recent heart attack. Although able to choose his own stories, he was still subject to M-G-M's financial control. In theory, at least, this gave L. B. Mayer a strong say in, even veto over, Thalberg's productions. While Thalberg enjoyed Nick Schenck's support, Mayer could be kept at bay. If that support was ever lost or even wavered, however, Thalberg knew he would be exposed to Mayer's antagonism.

The rivalry between the studio and Oliver Messel, which had turned Thalberg's visual concept into something of an oversize jumble, helped to concentrate his mind on the advantages of an autonomous operation. The departure from M-G-M of his (more or less) friendly rival David Selznick to set up Selznick International Pictures further encouraged him to take the plunge. Early in 1936 Thalberg went to Mayer and told him that he wanted to form the I. G. Thalberg Corporation, which would release films through Loew's but would be free from any supervision by Mayer and M-G-M. He said he wanted to take with him under exclusive contract Norma, George Cukor, Charles Laughton, the Marx Brothers, and a few other M-G-M stars.

Once again Mayer was rendered initially speechless at the effrontery of Thalberg's latest proposal for self-advancement. Then the meeting soon degenerated into a shouting match. Mayer was not about to accept this encroachment on his power without a fight. He accused Thalberg of wanting to destroy the studio they had built up together not only because he would be deserting it himself and raiding it for talent, but also because he would be setting a tempting precedent that other producers would want to follow. Thalberg made the countercharge that Mayer had lost interest in the business that had once been his ruling passion; that he had forgotten their commitment to quality pictures. Mayer reminded Thalberg that his contract did not expire until 1938, but Thalberg brushed that aside. M-G-M couldn't hold him against his will.

After days of internal tension, Schenck intervened once again and supported Thalberg's request. An agreement was drawn up, with Mayer fighting over every clause as if each were a trench on a World War I battlefield, and when the smoke cleared Thalberg had achieved most of what he wanted on condition that he remain at the studio until his contract expired. The I. G. Thalberg Corporation was to come into being in 1939. It would thereafter be financed by, and release its films through, Loew's Inc.

Thalberg was allowed to sign on any five or six Metro stars, but when he asked for Garbo the answer was a flat no. Under the new agreement he would no longer share in the Loew's profits but was to receive a sizable percentage of the gross on his own pictures, as well as a salary of $2,000 per week. When Mayer protested to Schenck that he was giving away the store, the General's reply was that the I. G. Thalberg Corporation was a luxury M-G-M could afford.

While Thalberg negotiated with Mayer, his production schedule proceeded at full pace. At the beginning of 1936 he had no less than nine pictures in various stages of production: apart from *Marie Antoinette* and *Pride and Prejudice* for Norma, there was *China Seas* (which had evolved into a more sophisticated version of *Red Dust*), *A Day at the Races, Camille, Maytime* (another musical starring Jeanette MacDonald and Nelson Eddy), and adaptations of three best-sellers, Franz Werfel's *The Forty Days of Musa Dagh*, James Hilton's *Goodbye, Mr. Chips*, and Pearl S. Buck's Pulitzer Prize–winning Chinese saga, *The Good Earth.*

There was by now a certain inevitability in Mayer's strong opposition to filming *The Good Earth*, which was the most controversial of Thalberg's projects. Even though it was a best-selling book and a successful Broadway play, he felt its account of the vicissitudes of a Chinese peasant family was too somber and downbeat to appeal to a mass movie audience and consequently did not justify the cost he had come to expect from a Thalberg production. But Thalberg was attracted by the story's heroic sweep and its universal theme of human suffering and survival, which he thought had echoes in the contemporary mood of the world. Besides, he felt he had the perfect actress to play O-Lan, the submissive slave woman who marries the young, upwardly mobile Chinese peasant Wang, played by Paul Muni.

This was Luise Rainer, an Austrian-born newcomer to M-G-M, whom Thalberg cast on the strength of what was virtually a cameo role in *The Great Ziegfeld*. Released contemporaneously with *Romeo and Juliet*, *Ziegfeld* turned out to be the studio's most successful picture of the year. In it, Luise Rainer played Anna Held, and her one big scene was an emotionally charged telephone call in which Held, still in love with Ziegfeld (played by William Powell), forces herself to congratulate him on his marriage to Billie Burke (Myrna Loy). The camera sees her agitation and her forced gaiety: but when she hangs up she dissolves into tears. Thalberg was impressed, but so, to his intense displeasure, were the members of the Motion Picture Academy. Despite his efforts to secure the award for Norma as Juliet, the Oscar for Best Actress went to Luise Rainer.

Once again Schenck overruled Mayer, and *The Good Earth* went into production. L.B. had lost another battle. Verona was dismantled on the back lot, and a section of Shanghai went up in its place. Thalberg also bought five hundred acres of suitable terrain in the San Fernando Valley, where, in the shadow of a section of the Great Wall, Chinese farmers created the Wang family farm, complete with rice paddies and Chinese livestock. With his passion for authentic detail, Thalberg imported tons of artifacts from China: everything from teak furniture to bone needles and opium pipes.

When it came to choosing a composer to write the score, Thalberg again showed that music was one of his blind spots. The German composer Arnold Schönberg had just joined the growing colony of European refugees in Hollywood, and Thalberg decided—probably at someone else's suggestion—that he would be just the man to compose *The Good Earth* score. Having listened only to some of the composer's earlier, and more conventional, pieces, Thalberg had no inkling that Schönberg had since become an exponent of the starkly dissonant twelve-tone idiom. So he arranged a meeting.

"Last Sunday when I heard the lovely music you have written—" Thalberg began.

"I do not write lovely music," Schönberg interrupted him curtly.

Somewhat taken aback, Thalberg persevered and explained his offer. If he'd expected the composer to jump at the chance of composing for the movies—Thalberg's movies—he was mistaken. Instead Schönberg said he hated the way movies employed music and would agree to write the score only on condition that he had complete control over the sound.

"What do you mean by complete control?" Thalberg asked incredulously.

"I mean that I would have to work with the actors," Schönberg replied. "They would have to speak in the same pitch and key as the score I compose. It would be similar to *Pierrot Lunaire,* but, of course, less difficult."

A less determined soul would at this point have given up. But Thalberg was confident that he could teach Schönberg there was a world of difference between composing for films and composing an opera, and he continued to press for an answer. By the time Schönberg replied, demanding twice as much money as Thalberg had offered, Thalberg had lost interest. He had found some Chinese folk music that had inspired Herbert Stothart, head of the music department, to compose some "lovely" music.

For the picture's climax, the plague of locusts, filmed on location in the valley, M-G-M bought swarms of grasshoppers and used wind machines to make them fly in dense clouds in the right direction for the camera. When Thalberg viewed the sequence, which had cost $250,000 to film, he discarded most of it. Not enough locusts. So an additional $200,000 was spent on refilming the sequence with even denser clouds of grasshoppers.

As O-Lan, Luise Rainer barely spoke any dialogue or raised her eyes to look directly at the camera. Perpetually huddled in submission, she gave a low-key performance that, depending on the point of view, was either a tour de force or colorless and wooden. The critics hailed it as the former, and Luise Rainer was to gain the distinction of being the only actress to win an Academy Award in two successive years. Many moviegoers must have seen her portrayal as the latter, for the film was not a commercial success.

Sam Marx said Thalberg would occasionally talk about *The Good Earth* as a metaphor of the storm scudding down on Europe in the thirties. The theme was sufficiently familiar to strike a responsive chord, but the setting distant enough not to give offense. For in 1936, Hollywood—and M-G-M perhaps in particular—was still careful not to stir trouble in its big European markets.

In February of that year, M-G-M abruptly stopped production of a movie version of Sinclair Lewis's book *It Can't Happen Here* about the rise of a fascist dictatorship in the United States. According to reports circulating at the time, cancellation of the production a week before filming was scheduled to begin was the result of a sudden attack of cold feet. The studio was afraid the film might offend the Hitler and Mussolini regimes. Sinclair Lewis claimed the Hays Office had vetoed the film because of "fear of international politics and fear of boycotts abroad." In an angry statement Lewis said; "Are we to be delivered over to a film industry whose every step must be governed by whether or not the film will please or displease some foreign power?"

The Hays Office denied having banned *It Can't Happen Here* and said the decision had been Metro's. Metro, on the other hand, said it had not scrapped the picture. L. B. Mayer explained smoothly that production had been postponed because the existing script (by Sidney Howard) would have "cost too much." *It Can't Happen Here* would be made, he said, but in a less expensive version once a new script was completed. The film was never made, of course—and nobody believed it ever would be—and both the Italian and German governments publicly welcomed the cancellation. The German government in Berlin declared that by not making the picture, the United States had saved itself the embarrassment of an official protest.

Meanwhile refugees arriving in Hollywood from Germany had provided an irrefutable picture of the scope of Hitler's anti-Semitic drive. The purge of Jews in the German film industry was so systematic that even foreign movie companies were not allowed to send Jews to Germany as their representatives. Thalberg continued to believe that by opposing communism, Hitler was performing a service for the Western democracies. Prince Hubertus von und zu Lowenstein, a prominent German refugee, tried to convince him that Hitler was in reality the more immediate danger, but he failed.

Prince Lowenstein had barely managed to evade the pursuing Gestapo and escape to the United States. At a reception in his honor at the Ogden Stewarts', he gave Thalberg an account of what was happening inside Germany. Some fifty years later in Bonn, the prince recalled his conversation.

"Everybody crowded around us to hear what Thalberg had to say," he said. Thalberg listened in silence, "then he shrugged his shoulders and said, 'When a dictator dies his system dies, too, but once communism is allowed to spread it will be hard to root out. What's at stake is our whole way of life, our freedom. They will have vanished forever.' Well, I was opposed to communism, too, but I felt the Nazi threat was more urgent. So I decided to appeal to his emotions. I said, 'Mr. Thalberg, your own people are being systematically hunted down and rooted out of Germany.' He replied that the Jews would survive long after Hitler was gone." However, the prince did point out in Thalberg's defense that the full impact of Hitler's anti-Semitic drive had not yet become clear to the world.

At the time of Thalberg's meeting with Prince Lowenstein, who had been a cabinet minister in the last democratically elected government before the Nazi takeover, Metro's office in Berlin still kept Dr. Goebbels regularly supplied with newly released M-G-M movies. The films were sent to the Nazi propaganda chief with the compliments of L. B. Mayer or Irving Thalberg, and there is no evidence that either man attempted to dissociate himself from this public relations exercise. Goebbels, like Adolf Hitler himself, was a movie fan and screened all the pictures. After screening

Viva Villa! (one of David Selznick's Metro productions), Goebbels sent word through a Metro representative that no film since Sergei Eisenstein's *Potemkin* had impressed him so much. But he still denied the picture a German import license because it condoned revolution.

In its efforts to remain in good standing with Mussolini's government in Rome, Metro appointed Mussolini's eldest son, Vittorio, head of M-G-M in Italy. Vittorio, a former Italian air force ace, visited Hollywood to discuss M-G-M co-productions with Italy, including a movie version of Rigoletto. He was lionized by society hostesses and heckled by anti-Nazi activists. At receptions he regaled bemused guests with stories about bombing missions over Abyssinia, which the Italians had invaded and conquered.

In the long run the studio's policy of conciliation toward Germany and Italy did not stop censorship in either country from reducing the number of movies imported from Hollywood. By 1935 the number of Hollywood films shown in Germany had been slashed to half of what they had been five years previously, and distribution was being choked off. But movies from Hollywood remained immensely popular. The top box office film in 1935 was *One Night of Love,* and the year before that it had been Garbo in *Queen Christina.* Early in 1936, the Warner Brothers representative, a Jew named Joe Kauffman, was chased by a gang of thugs in Berlin and murdered. Warners immediately closed its German office, and other studios gradually followed suit. M-G-M's German operation was the last to be shut down.

15

A DEATH
FORETOLD

Thalberg had originally intended *Camille* to go into production in the winter of 1933. In December, with Greta Garbo still in Sweden on vacation, he received a memo from L. B. Mayer informing him that Garbo had "requested an extra month in Sweden to recover fully from a serious illness. Her request has been granted and all contract obligations suspended for one month." Perhaps anticipating Thalberg's irritation at the delay, Mayer added, "In the circumstances there seems no alternative but to agree." Mayer didn't have to elaborate on the circumstances: Garbo's contract was for two pictures with the studio at $250,000 per picture. She had personal approval of directors, cameramen, costar, and virtually everything else in the production. She had days off during her menstrual period, a not uncommon concession in studio contracts with leading ladies. If Garbo was still working after twelve weeks, she was to be paid an additional $10,000. In short, Garbo was at the peak of her star power and economic muscle. Except for a star-producer like Chaplin, who made his own pictures, Garbo was now the highest-paid talent in Hollywood. Mayer had no choice other than to give her the extra time she wanted.

Camille was the stage and screen title for Alexandre Dumas's *belle époque* novel *La Dame aux Camélias*. When Thalberg decided to make it, the story was already regarded as an old warhorse that had been trotted out on the screen three times before—in 1915 starring Clara Kimball Young, two years later as a vehicle for Theda Bara, and in 1921 with Rudolph Valentino and Nazimova. Could it stand yet another version?

Hollywood was still going through its phase of remaking silent movie successes. But *La Dame aux Camélias,* with its popular "classic" origins and solid commercial track record not only as a novel and motion picture, but as a play and a Verdi opera (*La Traviata*), had irresistible appeal for Thalberg, particularly since the heroine is a woman with a past who redeems herself beautifully in the last reel by dying of a wasting disease. In Garbo he felt he had the perfect star for the role of Marguerite. Plus, the novel was part of his boyhood reading. His mother had, improbably, borrowed it for him from the library when he was about twelve. He had wept when Marguerite died of consumption, then consulted a medical encyclopedia to check whether he had tuberculosis.

As usual, writers converged on the production from all directions—Carey Wilson, Morduant Sharp, Tess Schlesinger, Ernest Vajda, Austrian playwright Vicki Baum, Mercedes de Acosta, and the three who eventually shared the screen credit: Frances Marion, Zoë Akins, and James Hilton. The latter was on hand to write the script of his novel *Goodbye, Mr. Chips,* and at the time Thalberg was trying to interest Brian Aherne in playing the title role.

A script of *Camille* was submitted to the Hays Office and duly returned bleeding from a thousand cuts. The climate had changed significantly since the last film version. The numerous deletions demanded by the censor transformed Marguerite from a courtesan into a member of the Salvation Army. Thalberg immediately began one of his marathon negotiations with the Hays Office, but he was unsure enough of the outcome to secure Garbo's consent to another picture. After much haggling, the Hays Office gave its grudging consent, and so the world never saw Garbo in *The Woman in Spain* (apparently a version of Prosper Mérimée's *Carmen*).

To direct the film, Thalberg engaged George Cukor. He regarded Cukor's gift for painting everything with a generous veneer of glamour as highly suitable for the picture— indeed, for any of the high-grade pictures he wanted to make. Cukor was a real find for Thalberg because he displayed none of the temperament that Thalberg, from experience, associated with talented filmmakers. George Cukor, who maneuvered through Hollywood with the skill, political savvy, and discretion of a courtier in the court of the Borgias, was not only talented, but also accommodating, at any rate toward his studio bosses. Nevertheless, talented as he was, he was prepared to transmit Thalberg's ideas and to do Thalberg's bidding without dramatics or confrontations.

Cukor spoke of Thalberg as having "a taste for refinement" and of being "in his own way . . . an artist." The latter was a qualified compliment, but Cukor did not refer to any other producer as an artist, not even his friend David Selznick. When Thalberg, dissatisfied with the footage of Marguerite's death scene, ordered the scene shortened and reshot with Garbo lying on a chaise longue instead of in a bed, Cukor did it Irving's way. For years afterward Cukor would describe a story conference in which he and Thalberg and writer Zoë Akins were discussing the scene in which Marguerite and Armand (Robert Taylor) planned their elopement. Not too much sentiment, Thalberg warned them: "They should play the scene as though they were plotting murder." And that was the way the scene was filmed.

Thalberg's retakes rang alarm bells in the Metro executive office because of Garbo's twelve-week deadline. But he pressed on in his usual style, steering the film in the direction he intended it to take, indifferent to the warning phone calls and memos about the importance of keeping to the shooting schedule. Thalberg never mentioned his health, but to more than one of his collaborators he now seemed to be working on every picture as though it could be his last, his epitaph. The effort he put into *Camille* would have exhausted a man in perfect physical health; his secretary would sometimes find him slumped facedown on the surface of his large desk, awake but too drained to move.

After the high cultural tone of *Romeo and Juliet* and the refinement of *Camille*, Thalberg's production of *China Seas* was aimed at more basic tastes. To placate the Hays Office Thalberg warned John Lee Mahin that "after the trouble we had with Vantine [the Harlow character in *Red Dust*], such as protests from women, the China Doll should be less obviously a tramp," and as a result, Harlow as China Doll is softer, more sentimental, than her earlier, hard-boiled screen persona.

But Thalberg was initially also concerned about the star's frame of mind so soon after Paul Bern's death, and he visited the set frequently until he was sure that she was fully recovered. Possible fallout from the Bern scandal continued to worry him, and he told Howard Strickling to arrange for Harlow to put flowers on Bern's grave from time to time and then tip off the press that she was doing so.

China Seas fulfilled his hopes of being a profitable movie. "The hell with art this time," he commented when filming started, "I'm going to make a picture that will make money." Its success, together with that of *A Night at the Opera*, released about the same time, was welcome after the less-than-satisfactory performances of *Romeo and Juliet* and *The Merry Widow*. But, judged by Hollywood's bottom-line standards, Thalberg's performance in three years as an independent producer was uneven.

Over roughly the same period, M-G-M distributed David

Selznick's last three pictures made at the studio under a similar arrangement to Thalberg's, and the contrast was obvious. *David Copperfield, Anna Karenina,* and *A Tale of Two Cities* were tasteful, reasonably faithful condensations of popular classics, combining quality and commercial success.

Moreover, Thalberg's less successful "artistic" productions could hardly be defended as bold attempts to widen the scope of Hollywood mainstream filmmaking. *Romeo and Juliet* was less an experiment in bringing Shakespeare to the screen than a vehicle for Norma. The as-yet-unmade *Marie Antoinette* was another lavish exercise in his wife's glorification rather than the serious portrayal of one of the most turbulent periods in modern history. And in his heart Thalberg must have known that despite the success of the novel, *The Good Earth* was neither a mass audience movie nor a serious look at social conditions in China.

The widening feeling that Irving had lost his touch is said to have been a source of satisfaction to L. B. Mayer, his mentor-turned-rival. Relations between them were now so awkward that Thalberg went out of his way to avoid the studio boss so that he would save himself an argument.

Although it may have looked that way, Mayer did not lose all the battles. His view prevailed on one occasion when Thalberg, because of his long-standing interest in Freud, toyed with the idea of producing a biography of the father of psychoanalysis, a picture that would go beyond his tentative attempt to come to terms with Freudian material in *Strange Interlude.* Psychoanalysis—later the movie colony's religion—was still unfamiliar ground in Hollywood. Mayer put his foot down and Thalberg found no allies, not even the faithful Al Lewin.

However, Mayer's main worry was *Marie Antoinette.* The relentless preproduction spending was making the project look increasingly like Thalberg's *folie de grandeur.* As Norma told her biographer, Gavin Lambert, even though filming did not start until after his death, "Irving produced it. . . . He was dead, but it was still his." Much of the $500,000 already spent in preproduction costs went to purchase period furniture, some from Versailles itself. Adrian was sent to France on a shopping expedition and returned with original fabrics and jewelry.

Aside from the cost, however, *Marie Antoinette* once again put Mayer in a tough situation with William Randolph Hearst. Early in 1935, when Hearst learned that *Marie Antoinette* had had to be postponed on account of Norma's pregnancy, he instructed his executive secretary to send Thalberg a telegram: DEAR IRVING ARE YOU WORKING ON MARIE ANTOINETTE THE CHIEF WANTS TO KNOW IF IT WOULD BE POSSIBLE FOR MARION TO DO THIS PICTURE IF IT IS GOING TO BE DONE.

Irving was not going to be drawn into a direct conflict with Hearst, so he asked Mayer by memo to comment on the Hearst situation. Mayer admitted that he could not see Marion Davies as Marie Antoinette any more than he could see her as Elizabeth Barrett, but he dreaded the fallout from Hearst if M-G-M denied her another important role. So everything depended on how the matter was handled: aware that Hearst was short of ready cash, he came up with what he hoped was an ingenious ploy. He told Hearst that although he could not envision Marion in the role, she could play Marie Antoinette provided Hearst agreed to finance the entire production.

The ingenious ploy backfired. Hearst took offense, seeing the offer not only as an attempt to break the terms of his movie company's agreement with Metro, but as a vote of no-confidence in Marion's box office appeal. He broke off his long-standing relationship with M-G-M and negotiated a deal over the telephone to move Cosmopolitan Pictures and Marion to Warner Brothers.

In the spring of that year, Marion Davies's famous fourteen-room bungalow, the setting of so many celebrity luncheons, was broken into sections and transported over the hill to Burbank. Mayer stood and watched with Marion as the caravan of ten flatbed trucks rolled away from the studio. Marion wept as she left M-G-M, and Mayer, trying to comfort her, wept, too.

"The queen is leaving the lot," he murmured.

"Not the queen," Marion replied. "The king."

Marion Davies was genuinely sorry to leave Metro. Incapable of harboring a grudge for very long, she had taken Mayer's successive refusals to give her coveted roles philosophically and had been happy at the studio, as she never was subsequently at the more macho Warner Brothers. In 1937, just as *Marie Antoinette* finally began shooting at Culver City, Marion Davies took a hard, realistic look at her reflection in the mirror, saw the inroads that booze and time had made on her face and figure, and decided to retire from the screen.

Once again, although the estrangement between Hearst and Mayer lasted several years, Thalberg managed to distance himself from the controversy over *Marie Antoinette* as if it had been solely Mayer's doing. He escaped the lash of Hearst's legendary vindictiveness, and their friendship remained undamaged. Within a few weeks of Marion's departure from M-G-M, she had persuaded Hearst to invite the Thalbergs to a beach party, where Hearst once again asked him to find a good dramatic role for Marion. It was a touching and fatal obsession, for he was still too infatuated to admit that Marion was losing her looks.

Preparations for *Marie Antoinette* trundled on like one of the tumbrils in the movie, but meanwhile Thalberg pressed on with other productions, including a second Marx Brothers movie, *A Day at the Races,* and a remake of *Maytime,* the latter based on the Aida Johnson Young–Sigmund Romberg operetta (B. P. Schulberg had produced a silent version in 1923). Mayer objected to the story of *Maytime:* two big stars in an important "family" picture were not supposed to be in love with each other while they were married to others, particularly when one of the stars was Jeanette MacDonald, a Mayer favorite. Worse, Thalberg tampered with the original romantic story of a love affair between a great opera star and a young baritone who sadly go their separate ways, spicing it up with racy touches of turn-of-the-century Vienna, faint but distinct echoes of Erich von Stroheim's *Merry Widow,* and a strong suggestion that the lovers had something more substantial to remember than merely holding hands. In addition, only the song "Will You Remember?" survived Thalberg's overhaul of Romberg's original score.

Thanks to Thalberg, *Maytime* was not the story of "pure love" that Mayer hoped for—and even more distressing, Thalberg was shooting the picture in Technicolor. The process was new and still far from perfected—why was Thalberg running unnecessary risk by using it in a high-budget production? Thalberg explained he was using Technicolor partly because other studios were already using it, and he did not want to see M-G-M left behind as it had been when sound was introduced. In addition to that, he wanted to get a closer look at the system, which he was thinking of using in *Marie Antoinette.*

There were times when Thalberg regretted his split with Mayer. He said as much to Norma on at least one occasion early in 1936, recalling the early days of Metro-Goldwyn-Mayer when the formidable Mayer-Thalberg partnership had been the talk of Hollywood. As he counted his blessings and also his losses, he was sorry he had not spent more time with his children. He was more demonstrative in his affection toward Irving Jr. than was Norma, and he was deeply fond of his baby daughter, a fondness perhaps intensified by the knowledge that there was very little chance he would see her grow up. With her dark skin, eyes, and hair, she resembled her aunt, Thalberg's sister, Sylvia, and had a more openly demanding temperament than her quiet, fair-haired brother. Worried about her frequent crying spells, Thalberg consulted a pediatrician and, on the latter's advice, hired a child care specialist as a live-in nurse.

His enduring wish was to found a Thalberg movie dynasty. Both John Lee Mahin and Sam Marx heard him say on separate occasions, and only half-jokingly, of one of his productions, "Irving Jr. can remake it in color." Occasionally Thalberg would take his son to Culver City to watch the filming on the studio sound stages, where the little boy was treated with suitable deference. Norma, however, was not enthusiastic about being visited on the set by her five-year-old son.

On August 30, 1936, the Thalbergs attended the Los Angeles premiere of *The Great Ziegfeld* at Grauman's Chinese Theatre, and three days later they were there again for a special performance of *Romeo and Juliet*. The audience was roughly the same, the reaction different. *Ziegfeld* received a prolonged ovation, *Romeo and Juliet* warm applause. This was a crowd that knew a winner when it saw one, and the difference could not have been lost on Thalberg.

Publicly he continued to justify *Romeo and Juliet* as a "prestige picture" intended to bring kudos, not grosses, to M-G-M. Privately he was deeply disappointed, not that *Romeo and Juliet* was unlikely to make money, but that Norma's Juliet was not receiving the public acclaim he apparently felt she deserved. He had already declared that "*Romeo and Juliet* and *Marie Antoinette* will mark the end of Norma's acting career. Too many stars stay on camera too long. I want her to bow out at her highest point." The two pictures, in other words, were to be the twin pillars of Norma Shearer's reputation as first lady of the screen.

But *Romeo and Juliet* was not proving to be Norma's highest point. Her Juliet was good, but not the stuff that grand exits were made of. *Marie Antoinette* remained a mountain still to be scaled, although Cedric Gibbons was building Versailles on M-G-M. This could be why, having announced Norma's retirement, Thalberg had bought *Pride and Prejudice*. Norma's departure from the screen now seemed farther off than Thalberg had indicated. If there was any departure in the offing, it seemed more likely to be that of her husband. As Gloria Swanson noted, "All Hollywood was whispering about Irving Thalberg's health, saying he was mortally ill."

The object of these whispers spent the Labor Day weekend at the Del Monte Lodge in northern California, where nine years earlier he and Norma had honeymooned. Several of his regular bridge partners joined them, including the director Sam Wood; Jack Conway and his wife, Virginia; and Chico and Helen Marx. Besides the bridge, Thalberg wanted to talk to Chico and Wood about the filming of *A Day at the Races*.

In the evenings, when they sat down to a couple of rubbers, the air was brisk on the hotel verandah overlooking the Pacific and the temperature unseasonably cool. Norma kept urging Thalberg to move indoors or wear a sweater, but Thalberg refused to be coddled in front of his friends.

When he returned to work on Tuesday, September 8, he had a bad head cold. But he worked all day and then drove to the Hollywood Bowl for a dress rehearsal of Max Reinhardt's production of *Everyman*. Again the air was damp and chilly, but the medieval mystery play was being performed to benefit Jewish charities and Thalberg was one of the sponsors, so he felt obliged to stay on and offer his suggestions to Reinhardt. Two nights later he and Norma attended the premiere, and Thalberg took a bow along with the other sponsors. He was in good spirits, but the cold was very evident.

Next morning he woke up with fever and chills. Norma sent for Dr. Newmark, who diagnosed a strep throat. But it failed to respond to treatment, and twenty-four hours later Thalberg seemed to be much weaker, breathing with difficulty. Deeply concerned, Norma got in touch with Dr. Groedel, who had left Germany and set up practice in New York. Groedel caught a plane to Los Angeles the same day and diagnosed lobar pneumonia but noted one encouraging sign. Thalberg's heart appeared to be unaffected.

There was talk of flying Irving to the Mayo Clinic in Rochester, Minnesota, where he could be treated with recently discovered sulfonamide drugs not yet on the market. But by the time arrangements could be made to charter a plane, both doctors decided that Thalberg was too ill to be moved.

That Sunday, for the first time in memory, Thalberg missed the annual M-G-M picnic at Clarence Brown's ranch in the San Fernando Valley. The mood of the boisterous cookout was briefly serious as Eddie Mannix read out a telegram sent by Norma in Thalberg's name: ONLY ILLNESS KEEPS ME FROM BEING WITH YOU. The climactic tug-of-war that had acquired symbolic overtones in recent years lost much of its tension with Mayer leading one team, as usual, but with Mannix substituting for the traditional opposing leader, Irving Thalberg.

Later that day some of Thalberg's Metro colleagues visited him. He was clearly very ill. When Bernie Hyman made the usual comforting remarks, Thalberg shook his head. "I'm not getting the right treatment," he told him after a coughing spell. "They don't know what they're doing. They're killing me." Hyman protested, but Thalberg said with the same quiet conviction with which he made production decisions, "No, Bernie. This time I'm not going to make it." Then he smiled. "Nearer my God to thee. . . ." The scene distressed Norma, who quickly left the room.

She telephoned Merle Oberon, who had become a close friend, and told her Thalberg believed he was dying. But with other visitors she kept up a hopeful front. Henrietta Thalberg arrived and sat staring silently at her son. Norma's mother, Edith, also came and took charge of running the household. And, surprisingly, a car stopped outside the Ocean Front house, bringing someone from his past. Rosabelle Laemmle had come to visit him. Thalberg smiled but could not speak to her.

Throughout Sunday night he coughed a great deal. There was blood in his sputum, and he had violent chills. In the early morning he rallied and asked for one of his secretaries to be sent for so that he could work in his bed. To humor him, Norma sent for Margaret Webster, but by the time she arrived his fever was higher and he had slipped into a coma. Dr. Newmark was setting up an oxygen tent when Norma brought in Irving Jr. and little Katharine to see their father, but if he recognized either of them or his wife, he gave no sign of it.

At ten-fifteen in the morning he had been in a coma for two hours inside the oxygen tent. Gathered in his bedroom were Norma; Henrietta and William Thalberg; Edith; Thalberg's sister, Sylvia, and her husband, Larry Weingarten; and Bernie Hyman. Legend attributes various famous last words to Thalberg. The story that he had died in splendidly ambivalent Hollywood fashion reciting the Lord's Prayer is certainly apocryphal and was probably invented by the studio to give Thalberg's death broader religious appeal. So was the rumor that at the very last he whispered to Norma, "Don't let my children forget me." In reality, his mumblings were disconnected lines of dialogue from his pictures. His life ended, not with an immortal pronouncement, but in a slow, incoherent fade-out.

Mayer was waiting in his office with other studio executives when Norma called with the news. Replacing the receiver, he said quietly, "Irving's dead." Then he drove to the Thalberg home, where Norma was waiting. As they embraced, tears flowed down their faces. On the set of *A Day at the Races*, Sam Wood was called to the telephone. He returned with tears in his eyes and announced, "The little brown fellow has just died." As the news spread around the studio, work stopped and hundreds of people wept—stars, writers and directors, studio employees, all sharing a sense of loss at the death of a man who had been a part of their working lives, in some instances a significant part, and yet remained a mysterious, haunting figure, even to his closest collaborators.

They buried him two days later, on September 17, 1936, with all the ceremony M-G-M could muster. The studio remained closed that day, and at ten A.M., when the service was due to begin, the other studios throughout Hollywood observed a five-minute silence. Outside the Wilshire Boulevard Temple in Los Angeles, which Irving had occasionally attended, a star-gazing crowd of thousands gathered as if for a premiere. They watched the arrival of every M-G-M contract player from Garbo to Harlow to the Marx Brothers, of Freddie Bartholomew in one of his velvet suits from Little Lord Fauntleroy, of Chaplin, Mary Pickford, and Douglas Fairbanks, Sr. Guards checked their invitations ("Admission by this card only"), and the ushers who led them to their seats included Clark Gable, Fredric March, and the playwright Moss Hart.

The arrival of Thalberg's widow reduced the crowd to sudden silence, as if all sound in the vicinity had somehow been shut off. Still recognizable despite the black veil covering her face, Norma Shearer walked inside, leaning heavily on the arm of Howard Hawks, and took her place with Henrietta and William Thalberg.

Irving was gone, and the industry's living monuments— Louis B. Mayer, the brothers Warner, Adolph Zukor, Nicholas Schenck—sat hard-faced, shoulder to shoulder, as Rabbi Magnin praised "Irving's creative mind" and his high principles and called him "sweet and kind and charming." Was that the Irving they were remembering? Or was it the Irving who consolidated the power of the producer, pressed creativity into the service of the box office, put down the writers' attempt to unionize, and lived, breathed, talked, and in the end died for the movies? The Irving who seemed to know what they were going to say before they said it, who usually outwitted them in business and won huge sums of money off them at poker?

When Rabbi Magnin spoke of the love between Norma and Irving—"a love greater than in the greatest motion picture I have ever seen, *Romeo and Juliet*"—Norma could be seen sobbing. She broke down a second time when Grace Moore, herself in tears, sang the Psalm of David, "The Lord is my Shepherd; I shall not want." But after the service, she walked unaided behind the massive coffin of burnished copper covered in flowers, and her limousine headed the procession to Forest Lawn Memorial Park, where Thalberg was buried in a grandiose marble pavilion in the Sanctuary of the Benediction. At the rear of the motorcade were two truckloads of floral tributes, the most lavish being Mayer's, a throne-shaped display of white gardenias with a caged dove suspended above it.

Leaving the mausoleum following her son's burial, Henrietta collapsed and had to be helped to her car. Norma walked slowly away with her brother, Douglas, and en route to 707 Ocean Front paid two calls. One was to thank Grace Moore, the other to visit her husband's friend and admirer Sam Goldwyn, who was at home recovering from an operation.

The official tributes from such colleagues as Jack Warner and Darryl Zanuck stressed Thalberg's contribution to the prestige of motion pictures. Selznick called him a genius, and Mayer said he had lost "the finest friend a man could ever have." But malicious gossip reported that, leaving the mausoleum, Mayer was overheard saying to Eddie Mannix, "Ain't God good to me?" And the trouble is that, true or not, it didn't sound out of character for Louis B. Mayer.

Whatever he did or did not say, Mayer quickly tightened his control over the studio. He dismantled Thalberg's production unit and took over control of Thalberg's productions. Thalberg would have appreciated the decisive, clean sweep! The filming of *Maytime* was stopped, the color footage scrapped, director Edmund Goulding sacked, and two key supporting players replaced. A new script was written, scrubbed clean of innuendo. Songs, costumes, even some of the characters' names, were changed, and the film was reshot in black and white. Jeanette MacDonald had been Peggy van Dyck in the film; she became Marcia Mornay. Nelson Eddy was Richard Wayne and became, inexplicably, Paul Allison.

Bernie Hyman was assigned to supervise *Camille*, with orders to bring the picture to a rapid conclusion. Hyman stationed an assistant on the set whose sole job was to force Cukor to speed up the filming. Hyman also ordered several new scenes, but hardly any of the footage was added, and

Camille remains the outstanding achievement of three people, Irving Thalberg, George Cukor, and Garbo herself. Films about intelligent women in love are not all that common, and it takes an actress of exceptional talent to portray both states simultaneously. What gives *Camille* its freshness is the unbroken line of Garbo's performance and the way she plays against all expectations, substituting a ruthless self-scrutiny for the flirtatiousness of the grande cocotte, and it was to Thalberg's credit that he encouraged this approach.

Because *The Good Earth* was ready for release, it was singled out to carry a dedication to Thalberg. That, and the naming of the new administration building after Thalberg, was the extent of M-G-M's tribute to its dead co-founder, who deserved much more. The faithful Albert Lewin resigned to protest the way Thalberg's memory was being expunged from M-G-M, and L. B. Mayer blacklisted him for the rest of his life.

Shortly after Thalberg's death, the Motion Picture Academy introduced the Irving G. Thalberg award to be presented each year on Oscar night. Inauguration of the award was postponed a year while squabbling producers decided who should be the first to receive it. Eventually a majority was persuaded to agree that it should be Darryl Zanuck. His nomination was strongly opposed by Jack Warner because of Zanuck's defection from Warner Brothers to 20th Century–Fox; and when Zanuck received the award, his old boss filed a formal protest with the academy. Born in controversy, the Thalberg Award was to have a checkered life, marred by disputes over candidates and even an attempt to abolish it on the grounds that it was inappropriate. On at least three years it was not awarded because academy members failed to agree on a recipient.

16

A HELL
OF A HOLE

L ouis B. Mayer continued to battle Irving Thalberg's ghost long after Thalberg had been laid to rest. For several years he used to complain about his former partner, blaming him for unsuccessful M-G-M pictures that had gone into production after Thalberg had died. His most frequent label for Thalberg became "the man who lost the studio *Gone With the Wind*." In reality it was Mayer who rejected the novel, on Thalberg's advice: by then Thalberg was an independent producer. But Mayer would then go on to say that thanks to his astuteness in holding out for the distribution rights of the picture in return for the loan of Clark Gable to play Rhett Butler, M-G-M would still profit handsomely from *Gone With the Wind*'s phenomenal success.

Thalberg's imagined offenses no doubt helped justify Mayer's decision to terminate the long-standing profit-sharing agreement whereby each of the three original partners, Mayer, Thalberg, and J. Robert Rubin received 6 percent of the studio's continuing gains. Thalberg had barely been dead two weeks when Mayer made his move. With Rubin's support, he argued that Thalberg's death invalidated the deal, and Thalberg's share should be divided between the two surviving partners.

Thalberg died leaving an estate of $4,469,013, half of which went for taxes. His will, which he had updated and modified at half-yearly intervals, named Norma as his principal heir, with trust funds of $100,000 each for his two children and lesser sums for his mother and sister. Even after taxes, Norma, who, of course, had money of her own from her pictures, was very well off. But that did not stop her from challenging Mayer and Rubin's attempt to cut her out of her late husband's share of the profits.

Moreover, she also demanded payment of Irving's hefty 37.5 percent of Loew's Inc. profits on the pictures he was producing when he died—*Camille, A Day at the Races,* and *The Good Earth.* Thalberg himself could not have handled the ensuing legal fight any better. Norma, it turned out, had learned a thing or two about going for the jugular while at the same time keeping up a facade of civility and good manners.

She sailed into battle supported by a good lawyer and a good public relations man. The public relations man, Russell Birdwell, had worked for David Selznick, and he immediately put it about that Norma was being considered to play Scarlett O'Hara in *Gone With the Wind.* While the lawyers argued, Birdwell also arranged for Norma to give interviews to a few well-placed columnists, to whom she vowed that she would not go back to work for a studio that insulted Thalberg's memory by depriving his estate of money he had worked so hard to earn. And yet, as she told Louella Parsons, "I must go back to work or face the poorhouse."

In Hollywood movie circles, Mayer was cast as the heavy and Norma the damsel in distress. At the time, half the town was receiving black-edged cards that Norma sent out after Irving's death:

Irving Thalberg's Wife
and Family
thank you for your kind expression
of sympathy, the memory of which
will remain always

The situation was bad for Metro's image: if Norma did not return to the studio, loss of the sizable investment to date in *Marie Antoinette* would make the company's balance sheet look even worse. But it was April 1937—seven months after Thalberg's death—before Nick Schenck succeeded in pressuring Mayer into backing down. The Thalberg estate was granted all continuing profits from M-G-M movies produced between April 1924 and December 1938, when Irving's contract would have expired.

Shortly afterward Norma's own contract was renegotiated, giving her $150,000 per picture—plus a $900,000 bonus for staying at Metro. "Poor Norma," remarked Fredric March when he heard the story of her legal struggle. "No, rich Norma," Ouida Rathbone corrected him. "Rich Norma."

Having successfully avoided "the poorhouse," Norma launched her own off-screen version of *The Merry Widow*. As Thalberg's wife she had been the model of propriety. "I don't believe any true woman permits her eyes to wander once she has pledged herself to her husband," she wrote in a fan magazine article on Juliet in 1935. After Thalberg's death she astonished her friends by embarking on a hyperactive love life that for a while bordered on promiscuity. Her sexuality released like a tightly coiled spring, she bounced from (among others) David Niven to George Raft, the quintessential screen gangster, to young James Stewart, to Howard Hughes, and even to Mickey Rooney, M-G-M's randy sixteen-year-old screen brat, whom she seduced in her trailer on the studio lot.

Only the affair with Raft, who was then married, was widely reported; but in the movie community her liaisons with a succession of men were followed with fascination.

The impression of someone making up for lost time was hard to avoid, throwing a different light on what had been seen by many as an ideal Hollywood relationship. Then, on August 23, 1942, twelve days after her fortieth birthday, she married a Sun Valley ski instructor twelve years younger, Marti Arrouge.

Marriage for the second time had followed another landmark decision to end a dwindling career by not renewing her contract with Metro. For nine years the most important choices of her life had been dictated by a quietly compulsive manufacturer of illusions who knew his time to live was limited. Without Thalberg, Norma faced the prospect of making her own career decisions at least post–*Marie Antoinette*, because in that picture, as she remarked to Sidney Franklin, Thalberg was there, "tapping me on the shoulder."

What happened to Norma's career in the wake of that last picture Thalberg had chosen for her showed how indispensable he had been to her rise to superstardom. Left to her own devices, she made one questionable choice after another. She turned down the key role in *Mrs. Miniver*, preferring to work on *We Were Dancing*. She rejected *Now, Voyager* in favor of *Her Cardboard Lover*.

We Were Dancing was a thin Noël Coward confection about a pair of society hangers-on in Palm Beach. The film's attraction for Norma was obvious, but would Thalberg, with his talent for judging public mood, have let her make the choice? Filming began a week after the Japanese attack on Pearl Harbor. When it was released in 1942, it played poorly in a country mobilizing for war. *Mrs. Miniver*, on the other hand, earned the studio a $4 million profit and Greer Garson an Academy Award.

Her Cardboard Lover was a virtual remake of *We Were Dancing*, with the setting transposed to the French Riviera, but once again Norma had chosen a story that was out of tune with current events, and the picture did little business. *Now, Voyager* was a box office success and further boosted the career of its star, Bette Davis.

Her Carboard Lover was Norma's last movie. She was now almost forty and no longer queen of the lot—a fact brought home by Mayer's insistence that Garson play opposite Laurence Olivier in *Pride and Prejudice,* a film Thalberg had intended for Norma. Interestingly, the failure of *We Were Dancing* was noted by Greta Garbo, who put it together with a perceptible chilling in audience warmth toward herself, and she, too, decided that it was time to go. Thus Metro lost two of Thalberg's biggest stars within the same year.

Both women lived on for many years, becoming progressively more reclusive, Garbo alone and Norma with Marti, whom she frequently addressed as "Irving." Both women shunned the press and—above all—the camera lens, which could record the passage of time. In 1977, Norma's sight began to fail. An examination revealed that she was suffering from insidious chronic glaucoma. In 1980, white-haired, her memory failing and close to blindness, she entered the Motion Picture Country Hospital, the home for aged movie people in the San Fernando Valley, where she died three years later, frail and diminished, of bronchial pneumonia, the same disease that had killed Irving.

On her instructions, she was buried beside her first husband in his marble mausoleum at Forest Lawn. And on his instructions, Irving Jr. was not: when he died of cancer of the liver in 1987 at the age of fifty-seven, he was cremated.

Irving Jr. had not, after all, followed his father into movies, but Thalberg would not have been able to fault his son's distinguished career as a philosophy professor. After attending Le Rosay, an expensive Swiss boarding school for the sons of the international rich, and then going on to Stanford University, he taught philosophy first at his alma mater and then at the University of Illinois's Chicago campus, publishing several studies in philosophy.

His father would have been less pleased with Irving Jr.'s liberal politics. During the so-called Chicago Seven trials in 1969, the trial of seven left wing extremists for their role in the riots at the Democratic party convention in the same city the previous year, Irving Jr.'s apartment became a hideaway for several of the defendants and their attorneys. Tom Hayden, Rennie Davis, and William Kunstler, their leading defense lawyer, all bunked there at one time or another, out of reach of the press. The Thalberg name still has ties with the movies, however, because Irving Jr.'s daughter, Marian, is a movie actress. Irving Thalberg's daughter, Katharine, twice divorced and almost totally alienated from her mother since her rebellious teens, lives in Aspen, Colorado, where she owns and runs a bookstore.

Both children were at the Dorothy Chandler Pavilion on March 28, 1986, when the Motion Picture Academy's Oscar presentations observed the fiftieth anniversary of Thalberg's death. Neither Irving Jr. nor Katharine spoke about the father they had hardly known, but George Lucas, the young producer of *Star Wars* and *Raiders of the Lost Ark*—both, incidentally, pictures Thalberg was not likely to have considered making—lauded his genius as a producer and his central role in the emergence of a powerful industry out of what had been an amusement park side show.

Irving Thalberg was in effect a leading architect of a unique system of picture making that was efficient, derivative, and profitable—derivative because the movie studios showed a strong preference for recycling already successful material and put tight constraints on creativity. Of all the movies with which Thalberg was most intimately connected, starting with his days at Universal, only a handful were based on original subject matter. This was the Hollywood process from which he, more than any other, could have departed, but which, by following it, he strengthened and perpetuated.

His concept of quality was often defined by glamour and bigness, expensively packaged, but that did not mean he couldn't tell the difference between glamour and style. Nor did it mean that he did not recognize and appreciate distinguished filmmaking when he saw it. Few foreign-made films were shown commercially in the United States, but Thalberg screened films from Europe regularly. He once ordered his writers to see Fritz Lang's masterly thriller *M*. The writers watched the unforgettable picture, filmed in Berlin in 1931 before Lang emigrated to Hollywood. Now there was a film, Thalberg told them. The writers were puzzled.

Lang's picture was the very opposite of a Thalberg production: A psychopathic child murderer (played by Peter Lorre) evades police capture but is trapped by the city's criminals because his activities are giving them a bad name. Lang's setting is a mean, unglamorous city full of menacing shadows and dark corners. There is no hero, no love interest, not even a woman's part. One writer asked Thalberg how he would have reacted if the writer had brought him the same story. Thalberg laughed. "I would have told you to get the hell out."

Thalberg believed he knew what the paying public expected from M-G-M, and it wasn't *M*. To him motion pictures were a high-yield business aimed at a mass market. Built into his concept of the occasional "prestige" production was the inference that films should make a profit. He expected to make money on his pictures. His contemporary, David Selznick, approached money as a means of living well and producing the pictures he wanted to make. Thalberg used the studio's money to produce the pictures, and their profits to get rich.

But Thalberg was not merely the ringmaster of the collaboration required of filmmaking; he was a filmmaker himself. We have seen him writing films, casting them, devising special effects, supervising the filming even to the point of directing sequences himself, and finally editing them. So it is fair to talk of "Thalberg's" pictures, just as it is fair to say that not all of them stood the test of time. His Shearer films have not, on the whole, stood up well. For example, *The Barretts of Wimpole Street* is stiff and dated today, and *Riptide* looks self-conscious and mannered, as much a period piece in its way as *The Barretts*. Many of Thalberg's non-Shearer films, on the other hand, have fared better: *Camille,* for example, is as vivid today as when it was filmed, and *Mutiny on the Bounty* is superior to any of its Technicolor successors.

Thalberg's deep and unfaltering interest in Norma's career was a beacon for those who wanted to capture his attention: he always had time to listen to a new idea for a Shearer picture, and when he died there were three other Norma Shearer movies being prepared or under consideration besides *Marie Antoinette* and *Pride and Prejudice.* So at the very least, Norma's requirements, as he saw them, diverted his attention from other projects, in the process limiting the scope of his achievement.

His strong commitment to stage material was partly the result of his quest to legitimate the movies. He wanted motion pictures to gain broad acceptance as an institution commensurate with their growing financial importance. By 1936 Hollywood had a multimillion-dollar annual turnover, but Wall Street continued to maintain a cautious distance. The studios relied for major backing mainly on California banks—notably the Bank of America in San Francisco, which was owned by the Giannini brothers—and also on the First Boston Bank, which had been a pioneer in movie investment. Thalberg saw himself as the great "civilizer," a man who could make pictures as literate and European and classy as the theater despite Hollywood's natural tendency toward crassness. "Artistic" was a word he used often in connection with pictures. The 1930s offered a period of innovation in the arts, ablaze with such controversial names like Picasso and Braque in painting, Stravinsky in music, Auden and Eliot in poetry, Sartre and Cocteau in the theater. But Thalberg's notion of art was conventional, dignified, glamorous, and profitable. "Dignified" was another Thalberg word. He planned to call his company the I. G. Thalberg Corporation, instead of something glitzier such as Thalberg Pictures or Thalberg Productions. In a community haunted by its fairground past, this attitude alone was enough to make him a hero.

He even thought comedy should be dignified because he felt that upset dignity was an effective comedy situation. "Hit a fellow in old clothes with a snowball, and it won't mean a thing," he told Groucho Marx. "But dress a man up in tails and a silk hat and then knock his hat off with a snowball, and you'll get a laugh." He chose grand opera as the background for *A Night at the Opera* solely because it was a dignified setting.

The *Fortune* magazine article about M-G-M, published four years before Thalberg died, reported: "He is called a genius more often than anyone else in Hollywood, which means that the word is practically his nickname." At thirty-seven he had left an indelible personal imprint on a new American art form that was also a vast new industry, and his influence lingered long afterward.

"The movies have been rolling through the cameras into theaters for ten years without Irving Thalberg, but no single frame of celluloid has slipped into focus without his influence," Sam Marx wrote on the tenth anniversary of Thalberg's death. "A great many men who knew him well are still producing pictures. And a great many of those, walled in by insurmountable problems of production, must often clap a moisty hand to a fevered brow and wonder, 'What would Irving do?'" Which, after all, is what genius is all about.

Had Irving Thalberg not met and impressed Carl Laemmle and not been employed by him, the chances are that the cinema would have lost its favorite genius. But he was fortunate enough to lock on to his destiny and to emerge as a key Hollywood figure in its heyday. Because Thalberg, unlike other producers, never included himself in the screen credits of his pictures, his name lives on thanks to that surprisingly generous and enlightened collective decision by the studio moguls at the time of his death to establish the Irving G. Thalberg Achievement Award. Being remembered at the Academy Awards ceremony has probably saved him from oblivion, even if, ironically, most people have forgotten the exact nature and extent of his achievement.

The industry is not likely to forget that Thalberg elevated the producer to the post of creative master of moviemaking. And although the marriage between Thalberg and Norma Shearer seems not to have been the stuff of romance, there is no doubt that his real romance was with the celluloid muse. Thalberg was the matchmaker in the nation's love affair with the movies. Beyond that he was, quite simply, the best of what Hollywood did best.

SOURCE NOTES

INTRODUCTION

PAGE

2   Thalberg and *Gone With the Wind:* Norma Shearer to the author, September 1974. Also Roland Flamini, *Scarlett, Rhett and a Cast of Thousands,* pp. 3–4.

4   Editorial: *New York Times,* Sept. 16, 1936.

5–6   Retakes invented by Harold Lloyd: Kevin Brownlow, *The Parade's Gone By,* p. 40

6   M-G-M's profit: *Fortune* magazine, December 1932.

8   Annual film production statistics: *Motion Picture Almanac* for years 1929–1936.

8   "that's what you're going to wear": James Kotsilibas-Davis, *The Barrymores,* pp. 288–289.

9–10   Cedric Gibbons complains: Samuel Marx, *Mayer and Thalberg: The Make-Believe Saints,* pp. 8–9.

11–12   *China Seas:* Transcript of Thalberg script conference, May 17, 1933.

12   Howard Dietz didn't remember: Howard Dietz, *Dancing in the Dark,* p. 157.

1. IN THE OLD COUNTRY

14–15   The founders of the American film industry: Main sources; Neal Gabler, *An Empire of Their Own: How the Jews Invented Hollywood;* Philip French, *Hollywood Moguls;* and various biographies.

15   The Thalbergs came: Marx, op. cit. p. 39; see also profile of Irving Jr. by Grant Pick in the *Los Angeles Free Weekly,* June 17, 1988; also author's interview with Deborah Pellow.

15–16   Sigismond Thalberg: Entry in *Grove's Musical Dictionary.*

16   Musical gifts not passed on to Irving: Andre Previn, *No Minor Chords,* p. 86.

17   "Dark, menacing eyes": Irene Selznick, *A Private View,* p. 49.

17   Norma Shearer mentioned: Author's interview with Eddie Lawrence.

17   Thalberg's boyhood and illness: Irene Selznick, op. cit. p. 49; Charles Higham, *Merchant of Dreams: Louis B. Mayer and the Secret Hollywood;* Gary Carey, *All the Stars in Heaven: Louis B. Mayer's MGM,* 51–64; Samuel Marx, op. cit. p. 8; Neal Gabler, op. cit. p. 146; author's interview with Howard Strickling.

18   Henrietta nursed him: Gavin Lambert, *Norma Shearer,* pp. 67–68, et al.; author's interview with Samuel Marx; Neal Gabler, op. cit. p. 73.

20   William James: Interview with Deborah Pellow.

20   "You've been sick long enough": Gary Carey, op. cit. p. 132.

2. THE LITTLE FELLOW AT UNIVERSAL

22   SITUATION WANTED: *New York Journal of Commerce,* September 7, 1917.

22   The Hudson Trading Company: Samuel Marx, op. cit. p. 72.

23   Thalberg's uncles: Author's interview with William Wyler.

23   His mother introduced him: Samuel Marx, op. cit. p. 14; Pat McGilligan, *Backstory: Interviews with Screenwriters of Hollywood's Golden Age,* p. 63

23	Hillquit was impressed: Irwin Ross, *The Image Merchants,* p. 132.
24	"We could sit down": Gabler, op. cit. p. 84.
24	Convinced him of the importance: Director William Wyler to the author.
24–25	Thalberg meets Laemmle: Samuel Marx, op. cit. p. 20; *Hollywood Reporter* obituary, Sept. 15, 1936; see also Gary Carey, op. cit. p. 154.
25	The president of Universal: Kevin Brownlow, op. cit. p. 416 et seq.
27	Sam Marx remembered: Gary Carey, op. cit. p. 211.
27	Thalberg goes to California: Kevin Brownlow, op. cit. p. 38; Samuel Marx, op. cit. p. 123.
28	He took a room: Samuel Marx, op. cit. p. 33; and William Wyler to the author.
30–31	Thalberg's confrontation with von Stroheim: Samuel Marx, op. cit. p. 33; Kevin Brownlow, op. cit. p. 417; Richard Kozarski, *Von Stroheim: The Man You Loved to Hate,* p. 75; John Barna, *Von Stroheim,* p. 222.
33	Set in prewar Vienna: Richard Kozarski, op. cit. pp. 91–102; John Barna, op. cit. p. 223; Kevin Brownlow, op. cit. p. 38.
36	Rouben Mamoulian: Richard Kozarski, *Hollywood Directors, 1914–1940,* p. 65.
37	Louella Parsons: Quoted in Gary Carey, op. cit. p. 145.
37	Touchy about his age: Ethan Mordden, *House Style in the Golden Age of the Movies,* p. 104.
38	In a sense: Kevin Brownlow, p. 56.
38	Ingram: Kozarski, op. cit. p. 83.
38	Part of the learning experience: William Wyler to author.
39	Thalberg's script: Samuel Marx, op. cit. p. 36.
40	Two days was all: Samuel Marx, op. cit. p. 42.
40–41	Cast the hunchback: Gary Carey, op. cit. p. 156.

3.   FATHER AND SON

43–44	Thalberg and Rosabelle: Irene Selznick, op. cit. p. 111; Samuel Marx to author.
45	"shrewd and inclined to be harsh": Irene Selznick, op. cit. p. 48.
46	"Geniuses we have all we need": Gary Carey, op. cit. p. 55.

46   Thalberg meeting with Mayer: Irene Selznick, op. cit. p. 83; Howard Strickling to the author; Samuel Marx, op. cit. p. 141; Bosley Crowther, *Hollywood Rajah: The Life and Times of Louis B. Mayer*, p. 89.

48   Hidden partnership: Real estate files for 1924 in the Los Angeles Hall of Records.

48–49   Thalberg and Mayer's daughters: Irene Selznick, op. cit. p. 67.

49   Thalberg and Henrietta: Irene Selznick, op. cit. p. 68.

50   Serendipitous sequence of events: Bosley Crowther, op. cit. p. 89; Charles Higham, op. cit. p. 102; Gary Carey, op. cit. p. 56; Howard Strickling to the author.

51   Profit-sharing deal: Gary Carey, op. cit. p. 145.

52–53   On April 26, 1924: Irene Selznick, op. cit. *Variety,* April 27, 1924.

54–56   *Greed:* Kozarski, op. cit. p. 148, 163; Lewin quote from interview with Lewin in Bernard Rosenberg and Harry Silverstein, *The Real Tinsel,* p. 235.

57   "a footage fetishist": Kevin Brownlow, op. cit. p. 417.

58   "This is filth": Richard Kozarski, op. cit. p. 167.

58–59   *The Merry Widow:* Curtis, Thomas Quinn, *Von Stroheim,* p. 254.

4.   MORE THAN ALL THE DOCTORS

61   "It is almost beyond my conception": Thalberg to Niblo, Sept. 24, 1924, M-G-M Collection, University of Southern California Cinema-Television Library.

62   "The whole company": Kevin Brownlow, op. cit. p. 36.

62   Niblo telegram dated July 4, 1924, from MGM Collection, USC. Published sources on filming of *Ben-Hur* include Gary Carey, op. cit., Samuel Marx, op. cit., Italian newspapers *Roma* and *Corriere della Sera;* also, J. J. Cohn to author.

63   "We are making great progress": Thalberg letter to Fred Niblo quoted above.

64   THINGS GOING SPLENDIDLY: from M-G-M Collection, USC.

64–65   On his return: Correspondence on Niblo's possible dismissal in USC files.

65–66   Chariot race: Account principally from Samuel Marx, op. cit. p. 134; Charles Higham, op. cit. pp. 97–98.

67, 68   Thalberg's protest: Telegram to Nick Schenck, Dec. 15,

1925, in M-G-M Collection, USC, as is Schenck's wire
WELL KID . . .

68   MORE THAN ALL THE DOCTORS: Thalberg to Niblo in M-G-M Collection, USC.

69   Ramon Novarro poster: Howard Strickling to author.

72   Thalberg wanted $2,000 a week: Gary Carey, op. cit. p. 222.

73   Strickling was a blunt, quick-tempered man: Strickling to the author.

75   Always "present at conferences": Neal Gabler, op. cit. p. 154.

75–77   Bern: See Irene Selznick, op. cit. pp. 176–177; Samuel Marx to author.

5.   IRVING'S WOMEN

79   Thalberg and sex: Eddie Lawrence to author.

79   Thalberg at Lee Francis; Samuel Marx, op. cit. p. 56.

79   Thalberg's women: See Irene Selznick, op. cit. pp. 78–79.

80   It happened when Thalberg: Gary Carey, op. cit. p. 231.

81   Thalberg meets Norma Shearer: Gavin Lambert, *Norma Shearer,* p. 56.

83   "Irving's spare tire": Irene Selznick, op. cit. p. 79.

83   Norma's early career: See Gavin Lambert, op. cit. pp. 25–29.

84   Raced through six pictures: Howard Strickling to author; J. J. Cohn to author.

87   "In my many years": Thalberg to Brian Aherne, June 3, 1932, in the M-G-M Collection, USC.

88   "Close to despair": Anita Loos, *Kiss Hollywood Good-bye,* p. 32.

89   "She's frivolous": Irene Selznick, op. cit. p. 78.

90   "Everyone has a lot to learn": Gavin Lambert, op. cit. p. 90.

90   Noticeable absence of passion: Eddie Lawrence to author.

92   It was during this summer: Eddie Lawrence to author. For more on Norma's repressed sexuality see Gavin Lambert, op. cit. pp. 139–140 and elsewhere.

6.   MRS. IRVING THALBERG

96   One passerby that night: John Bainbridge, *Garbo,* p. 91,

and John Gilbert, p. 105; see also Alexander Walker, *Garbo,* p. 110.

100   "Irving's decided": Irene Selznick, op. cit. p. 79.
100   Norma would move in: Eddie Lawrence to author.
102   Rabbi Magnin suggested: A. Scott Berg, *Goldwyn: A Biography,* p. 164.
103–104 Years later: Eddie Lawrence to author; besides being Strickling's deputy, Lawrence was assigned as Norma Shearer's publicity agent.
104   On Friday: Howard Strickling to author.
105   Norma's cartwheels: Gavin Lambert, op. cit. p. 104.
106   "Letters and credentials": Mayer to Herbert Hoover, Feb. 10, 1928, in Herbert Hoover Presidential Library.
107   Eva von Plentzner: Hubert Voight in *Saturday Review,* March/April 1985.

7. QUALITY TALKING PICTURES

109   "terror in all their faces": A. Scott Berg, op. cit. p. 173.
112   Norma Shearer had to face the anxiety: Gavin Lambert, op. cit. p. 121.
113   "The making of pictures": Thalberg to Aherne, op. cit.
114   Sent Bessie Love: Eddie Lawrence to author.
116   "Norma's dress": Basil Rathbone, *In and Out of Character,* p. 131.
117   Fox's takeover bid: Gary Carey, op. cit. pp. 121–124, Upton Sinclair papers at Indiana University at Bloomington.
117–118 His hostility toward Thalberg: Higham, op. cit. p. 143.
118   Thalberg letter to IRS: quoted by Samuel Marx, op. cit. p. 127.
119   Loew's stock: *Variety,* Oct. 31, 1928.
120   "What I would like": *Grand Hotel* script conference. Dec. 9, 1931, M-G-M Collection, USC.
121–122 One day he got: David Thompson, *David O. Selznick: The Man Who Made Gone With the Wind,* p. 168.
122–123 Thalberg says: Conference notes, Dec. 4, 1931, M-G-M Collection, USC.
124   Thalberg usually sat: Dean Dorn to the author.
126   *The Sin of Madelon Claudet*: See Gary Carey, op. cit. p. 231; see also Helen Hayes to the author.

8. INTO THE THIRTIES

131   "Very strong": Gavin Lambert, op. cit. pp. 129–130.

134   Thalberg's "prestige" movie: See interview in *Variety*, June 12, 1932; see also lecture at University of Southern California, May 11, 1933.

136   The shooting script: See Pat McGilligan, op. cit. Introduction; see also Samuel Marx to author.

137   "There isn't one thing": Script conference, Dec. 26, 1931, M-G-M Collection, USC.

138   Initially wanted Clark Gable: References to Gable in *Grand Hotel* script conferences in M-G-M Collection, USC.

138–139 "In the play there was this mood": Conference notes, Nov. 18, 1931, M-G-M Collection, USC.

140   Several scenes were reshot: Conference notes, March 18, 1972, M-G-M Collection.

142   To Joan Crawford's not very secret delight: Howard Strickling to author.

142   Alexander Korda: Michael Korda, *A Charmed Life*, p. 167.

142–143 Mayer questioned the wisdom: Telegram quoted in Alexander Walker, *Garbo*, p. 167.

144   On the day she met Thalberg: Anita Loos, op. cit. pp. 39–40.

146   He had suggested: Samuel Marx to the author.

9.   707 OCEAN FRONT

147   Douglas Fairbanks, Sr.: Grant Pick, op. cit.

147–148 Descriptions of 707 Ocean Front: See Gavin Lambert, op. cit. pp. 144–145 et seq.; see also Richard Schickel article on the Thalberg house in *Architectural Digest*, June 1981.

150–151 Fitzgerald at the Thalberg brunch: See account by Dwight Taylor, *Joyride*, and Aaron Latham, *Crazy Sundays: F. Scott Fitzgerald in Hollywood*.

153   The sex in their marriage: Eddie Lawrence to the author.

153   "Irving could spot": Anita Loos, op. cit. p. 38.

154   Thalberg's only sexual oddity: Eddie Lawrence to the author, quoting a confidence from Norma Shearer.

155   Thalberg letter to David Perla: Letter from David Perla's daughter, Norma Pisar.

155   "Then I'm riding in Thalberg's car": Neal Gabler, op. cit. p. 252.

10.   THE HEART OF THE MATTER

157   "How does Irving stand it?": Gavin Lambert, op. cit. p. 178.

"I work my butt off": Gary Carey, op. cit. p. 160.

158   "The single most beloved person": Irene Mayer, op. cit. p. 128.

158–159   Bern's suicide: See Samuel Marx. op. cit. p. 231 et seq.; Charles Higham, op. cit. pp. 185–187; John Douglas Eames, *The MGM Story;* interviews with Howard Strickling, Eddie Lawrence; *Los Angeles Times* and other press accounts.

160   Los Angeles District Attorney considers indictment: Howard Strickling to author.

161   Harlow refused outright: Gavin Lambert, op. cit. p. 322.

162–163   Bern's funeral: *Los Angeles Times* and Donald Ogden Stewart, op. cit. p. 253.

163   Bern's death shattered Thalberg: Samuel Marx, op. cit. p. 175.

165   Once even at a funeral: Philip French, op. cit. p. 57, and Samuel Marx, op. cit. p. 156.

165–166   He spent half a day: Conference notes on these productions, M-G-M Collection, USC.

166   "He made his points by mumbling": Kevin Brownlow, op. cit. p. 331.

166   "He would never praise you": Patrick McGilligan, *Backstory:* interview with Donald Ogden Stewart.

166   "The most unpleasant of guys": Patrick McGilligan, ibid.: interview with James Cain.

166   "We never got a clear reading": Dorothy Herrmann, *S. J. Perelman: A Life,* p. 234.

167   Perelman on difficulty of seeing Thalberg: Dorothy Herrmann, op. cit. p. 234.

168   Frank Orsatti and L. B. Mayer: Gary Carey, op. cit. p. 179.

169   Thalberg-Mayer dispute: Bosley Crowther, op. cit. p. 276; Howard Strickling and Eddie Lawrence to author; Charles Higham, op. cit. p. 245; see also Gary Carey, op. cit. 161; Barry Brennan to author.

171   If Thalberg wanted to interrupt her career: Gavin Lambert, op. cit. p. 214.

171–172   Faulkner in Hollywood: Joseph Blotner, *Faulkner: A Biography,* one-volume edition, pp. 307, 309; and Frederick R. Karl, *William Faulkner: American Writer,* pp. 470, 479, 487.

174 Thalberg's condition: Lawrence Quirk, *Norma: The Story of Norma Shearer,* p. 132.

174–175 Thalberg suffered a serious reminder: Neal Gabler, op. cit. p. 167; Howard Strickling to author.

175 "A mild coronary": *Variety,* Jan. 5, 1932.

175 Louis Mayer appeared: Howard Strickling, who accompanied Mayer, to author; letter quoted by David Thompson, op. cit. p. 145.

177–178 Mayer letter and Thalberg's reply: David Thompson, op. cit. p. 146.

178 A warmer leavetaking: *Hollywood Reporter,* April 23, 1932.

179 After passing through the Panama Canal: Helen Hayes, *On Reflection: An Autobiography,* p. 125.

180 Thalbergs in Bad Nauheim: Eddie Lawrence to author.

181 "A lot of Jews": Neal Gabler, op. cit. p. 338.

181 German film industry: Howard Strickling to author. Thalberg met German film officials in Berlin.

181 Tightening Nazi control: U.S. embassy, Berlin, commercial attaché's reports from late 1932 indicated the direction Nazi regime was going.

182 "Censorship has become so severe": U.S. embassy report to Washington, June 6, 1934.

11. MAYER'S PURGE

183 Norma saw him read it: Gavin Lambert, op. cit. pp. 193–195; Bosley Crowther, op. cit. p. 178. Interestingly, Charles Higham, op. cit., doesn't mention this development.

183 "They knifed me": Helen Hayes interview in Turner Entertainment television documentary *When the Lion Roars.*

185 In Antibes the Thalbergs: Basil Rathbone, op. cit. p. 111; Fred Laurence Guiles, *Jeanette MacDonald,* p. 67.

186 Thursday nights: Scott Berg, op. cit. p. 245.

186 "Fellows, I've got to go": Neal Gabler, op. cit. p. 258.

187 The scheme had been Mayer's: Samuel Marx, op. cit. p. 184; Bosley Crowther, op. cit. p. 211; Barry Brannen to the author.

189   Thalberg found the studio: Howard Strickling to author.

189   Charles MacArthur's verse: John Robbins, *Front Page Marriage*, p. 176.

189   Thalberg's secret investment: Irene Mayer, op. cit. p. 167.

192–193 Hollywood unions: Michael Shnayerson, *Irwin Shaw*, p. 67; Nancy Lynn, *The Hollywood Writers' Wars*, p. 34.

193   "It reminds me of Hollywood": Harold Arce, *Groucho*, p. 224.

194   Writers liked Rose: Nancy Lynn, op. cit. p. 67.

194   The successful writers: Lillian Hellman to author.

195   It was typical of Thalberg: See Nancy Lynn, op. cit., pp. 115–118; see also Donald Ogden Stewart, *By a Stroke of Luck*, pp. 224–228; Stewart to Pat McGilligan, op. cit. p. 345.

196   At the time: Arce, op. cit. p. 225.

197   "You have to face the fact": Neal Gabler, op. cit. p. 167.

198   When Budd Schulberg: Maurice Rapf confirmed published reports to author.

199   After trying unsuccessfully: Upton Sinclair, *The Autobiography of Upton Sinclair;* on his campaign, *New York Times* reports October 23–26, 1934, which include description of newsreels.

202   "The Screen Writers Marching Song": quoted in full in Nancy Lynn, op. cit. p. 221.

203   Thalberg's answer: Lillian Hellman to author; see also Nancy Lynn, op. cit. p. 245.

203–204 S. J. Perelman: Dorothy Herrmann, op. cit. p. 109.

204   Thalberg came in: Nancy Lynn, op. cit. p. 231; John Lee Mahin to author.

206   "Look, Don": Donald Ogden Stewart, op. cit. p. 224.

207   But it was Thalberg: Frances Goodrich, quoted by Nancy Lynn, op. cit. p. 234; Lillian Hellman told the author that the writers had inside information Thalberg was in touch with the FBI, and Eddie Lawrence told the author that Thalberg was interviewed by the FBI at Mayer's recommendation.

208   Rouben Mamoulian: Mamoulian to author.

12. MOVIES FOR NORMA

212 On divisiveness at M-G-M: Samuel Marx to author.

212 One second unit director: Ridgeway Callow to author.

213 Hearst's continued friendship: W. A. Swanberg, *Citizen Hearst,* p. 117; Fred Laurence Guiles, *Marion Davies,* p. 145.

214 Her husband gave her one of his pep talks: Gavin Lambert, op. cit. p. 205.

214–215 "found it a little difficult": Letter quoted in Gavin Lambert, op. cit. p. 206.

216 William Haines's homosexuality: Patrick McGilligan, *George Cukor: A Double Life,* p. 132; Eddie Lawrence to author.

217 "They can't censor": Gavin Lambert, op. cit. p. 208.

218 Thalberg said: Howard Dietz, op. cit. p. 159.

219 Norma had taken Helen Hayes aside: Helen Hayes, op. cit. p. 72.

221 French authorities: Reports forwarded to Thalberg from Laudy Lawrence, M-G-M representative in Paris, July 24, 1934, from M-G-M Collection, USC.

222–223 But Thalberg also had to contend with: Thalberg's earlier problems with the censor mentioned in Joseph L. Breen to Louis B. Mayer, Dec. 30, 1937, in M-G-M Collection, USC.

224 When she found the director: Franklin to Thalberg, Dec. 19, 1933, in M-G-M Collection, USC.

225 Mayer, who had voiced strong objections: Howard Strickling to author.

225–226 "where they write with feathers": Roland Flamini, op. cit. p. 4.

226 To cast the remaining leading role: Charles Higham, *Cary Grant,* p. 70.

13. GROUCHO, CHICO, AND HARPO—AND IRVING

228–229 On Gable's side: Patrick McGilligan, *George Cukor: A Double Life,* p. 150.

229 Laughton had a good-looking masseur: Charles Higham, *Charles Laughton,* p. 63 et seq.

231 Thalberg screened: A. Scott Berg, op. cit. p. 231.

232–233 When Thalberg met: Arthur Marx, *My Life with*

Groucho: A Son's Eye View, p. 159 et seq.: Hector, op. cit. p. 222 et seq.: Howard Strickling to author.

236   A pretty young: Kitty Carlisle Hart, *Kitty,* pp. 72–73.

238   Countess Dorothy di Frasso: Hector Arce, *Gary Cooper: An Intimate Biography,* pp. 241–243.

239   With Marie Antoinette: Donald Ogden Stewart, op. cit. p. 211.

239–240   "Charlie's missing": Helen Hayes, op. cit. pp. 73–74.

14.   A HEAVY LOAD

241   He believed his time: Norma Pisar to the author.

241–242   He was discussing: Norma Pisar to the author.

242   Cole Porter: Charles Schwartz, *Cole Porter,* p. 156.

243   The studio boss refused to approve: Gary Carey, op. cit. p. 239.

244   Choice of Cukor: Patrick McGilligan, *George Cukor: A Double Life,* p. 104 et seq.

245   An extraordinary clause: Patrick McGilligan, op. cit. p. 105.

245   From the outset: Gary Carey, op. cit. p. 241.

245–246   William Strunk: Gavin Lambert, op. cit. pp. 224–225.

246   "a boy": *Trivial Fond Records,* p. 127.

246   John Barrymore as Mercutio: Arthur Brown, *Cads and Cavaliers,* p. 52; Gene Fowler, *Goodnight, Sweet Prince: The Life and Times of John Barrymore,* p. 178.

247   Mayer watched: Howard Strickling to author.
Most of the gigues: Agnes De Mille, *Speak to Me, Dance with Me,* pp. 347–351.

248   "I had five versions": Kevin Brownlow, op. cit. pp. 302–303.

249–250   He became progressively unhappy: Basil Rathbone, op. cit. pp. 133–135; Gene Fowler, op. cit. p. 211.

251   Reviewers were polite: Graham Greene, *The Pleasure Dome,* p. 109.

253   After days of: Howard Strickling to author; Samuel Marx to author; see also Arthur Marx, op. cit. p. 169.

257   Sam Marx said: Samuel Marx to author.

257   Sinclair Lewis claimed: *New York Times,* Feb. 15–17, 1936.

258   Prince Hubertus: Prince Hubertus von und zu Lowenstein to the author, recalling his visit in Bonn in 1985.

258	The films were sent: Howard Strickling to the author; see also Berlin embassy commercial attaché's report to Washington, Jan. 21, 1936.
259	Vittorio Mussolini: *New York Times*, Sept. 15, 1937, and other trade press reports.
259	In the long run: Berlin embassy reports, Jan. 26, 1935, and Nov. 6, 1935; see also *Variety*, March 13, 1935. Joe Kauffmann: Neal Gabler, op. cit. p. 206.

15. A DEATH FORETOLD

260	Mayer added: Alexander Walker, op. cit. p. 187.
262	When Thalberg, dissatisfied: Patrick McGilligan, op. cit. p. 110.
263	But Thalberg was initially: Eddie Lawrence to the author.
264–265	Much of the $500,000: Gavin Lambert, op. cit.. p. 241.
265	DEAR IRVING: Telegram quoted by Gavin Lambert, ibid. p. 218.
266	Marion Davies was: Fred Lawrence Guiles, op. cit. p. 267.
266	Mayer objected: James Robert Parrish, *The Jeanette MacDonald Story*, pp. 92–93.
266	A Mayer favorite: Charles Higham, op. cit. p. 209. Higham mentions that Mayer and MacDonald may have had an affair.
268	"All Hollywood": Gloria Swanson, *Swanson on Swanson*, p. 334.
269	Next morning: Account of Thalberg's last days drawn from Arce, op. cit. p. 344; for Thalberg in Monterey, Norma Pisar (Norma sent for Dr. Newmark), Howard Strickling to author.
270	"They're killing me": Gavin Lambert, op. cit. p. 232.
270	Rosabelle Laemmle: Eddie Lawrence to author.
271–272	Thalberg burial: *New York Times* and other press reports.
273	Mayer tightens control: *Jeanette MacDonald*, pp. 92–93.

16. A HELL OF A HOLE

276	Thalberg's will: *New York Times, Los Angeles Times*, Oct. 12, 1936.
277	"I don't believe": *Photoplay* magazine, July 1935.

279   His father would have been: *Los Angeles Free Weekly,* June 17, 1988.

283   "Hit a fellow": Arthur Marx, op. cit. p. 156.

283   Sam Marx wrote: *Hollywood Reporter,* Sept. 14, 1946.

BIBLIOGRAPHY

Arce, Harold. *Groucho.* New York: William Morrow & Co., 1979.

Bainbridge, John. *Garbo.* London: Macmillian Publishing Co., 1954.

Behlmer, Rudy. *Memo from David O. Selznick.* New York: Viking Press, 1972.

Berg, A. Scott. *Goldwyn: A Biography.* New York: Alfred A. Knopf, 1989.

Blotner, Joseph. *Faulkner: A Biography.* One-volume edition. New York: Random House, 1974.

Brownlow, Kevin. *The Parade's Gone By.* . . . London: Secker and Warburg, 1968.

Carey, Gary. *All the Stars in Heaven: Louis B. Mayer's MGM.* New York: Dutton, 1981.

Cole, Lester. *Hollywood Red.* Palo Alto, Calif.: Ramparts Press, 1981.

Crichton, Kyle. *Total Recoil.* Garden City, N.Y.: Doubleday & Co., 1960.

Crowther, Bosley. *Hollywood Rajah: The Life and Times of Louis B. Mayer.* New York: Henry Holt & Co., 1960.

Curtis, Thomas Quinn. *Von Stroheim.* New York: Farrar, Straus & Giroux, 1971.

Davies, Marion. *The Times We Had*. New York: Bobbs Merrill, 1975.

De Mille, Agnes. *Speak to Me, Dance with Me*. New York: Little, Brown & Co.–Atlantic Monthly Press Books, 1972.

Dietz, Howard. *Dancing in the Dark*. New York: Quadrangle/Times Books, 1974.

Eames, John Douglas. *The MGM Story*. New York: Crown Publishers, 1976.

Fitzgerald, F. Scott. *The Last Tycoon*. New York: Charles Scribner's Sons, 1941.

Flamini, Roland. *Scarlett, Rhett and a Cast of Thousands: The Filming of Gone With the Wind*. New York: Macmillan Publishing Co., 1978.

Fountain, Leatrice Gilbert. *Dark Star: John Gilbert*. New York: St. Martin's Press, 1985.

French, Philip. *Hollywood Moguls*. Chicago: Henry Regnery Company, 1969.

Gabler, Neal. *An Empire of Their Own: How the Jews Invented Hollywood*. New York: Crown Publishers, 1988.

Guiles, Fred Lawrence. *Jeanette MacDonald*. New York: McGraw-Hill, 1975.

———. *Marion Davies*. New York: McGraw-Hill, 1975.

Hart, Kitty Carlisle. *Kitty*. New York: Doubleday & Co., 1988.

Hayes, Helen. *On Reflection. An Autobiography*. New York: M. Evans & Company, Inc., 1968.

Herrmann, Dorothy. *S. J. Perelman: A Life*. New York: Doubleday & Co., 1976.

Higham, Charles. *Merchant of Dreams: Louis B. Mayer and the Secret Hollywood*. New York: Donald I. Fine, 1993.

Jobbes, Gertrude. *Motion Picture Empire*. Hampton, Conn.: Archon Books, 1966.

Kobal, John. *People Will Talk*. New York: Alfred A. Knopf, 1985.

Kotsilibas-Davis, James. *The Barrymores*. New York: Crown Publishers, 1981.

Kozarski, Richard. *Hollywood Directors, 1914–1940*. New York: Oxford University Press, 1976.

———. *Von Stroheim: The Man You Loved to Hate*. New York: Oxford University Press, 1983.

Lambert, Gavin. *Norma Shearer*. New York: Alfred A. Knopf, 1990.

Latham, Aaron. *Crazy Sundays: F. Scott Fitzgerald in Hollywood*. New York: Viking Press, 1971.

Loos, Anita. *Cast of Thousands*. New York: Viking Press, 1977.

————. *Kiss Hollywood Good-bye*. New York: Grosset & Dunlap Publishers, 1975.

————. *The Talmadge Girls*. New York: Viking Press, 1978.

Marion, Frances. *Off With Their Heads! A Serio-Comic Tale of Hollywood*. New York: Macmillan Publishing Co., 1972.

Marx, Arthur. *My Life with Groucho: A Son's Eye View*. London: Pan Books, 1991.

Marx, Samuel. *Mayer and Thalberg: The Make-Believe Saints*. New York: Random House, 1975.

Mayer Selznick, Irene. *A Private View*. New York: Alfred A. Knopf, 1983.

McGilligan, Patrick. *George Cukor: A Double Life*. New York: St. Martin's Press, 1991.

————. *Backstory: Interviews with Screenwriters of Hollywood's Golden Age*. Berkeley, Calif.: University of California Press, 1986.

Mordden, Ethan. *House Style in the Golden Age of the Movies*. New York: Alfred A. Knopf, 1988.

Peters, Margot. *The House of Barrymore*. New York: Alfred A. Knopf, 1990.

Previn, Andre. *No Minor Chords: My Days in Hollywood*. New York: Doubleday & Co., 1991.

Rathbone, Basil. *In and Out of Character*. London: Collins, 1955.

Rosenberg, Barnard, and Harry Silverstein. *The Real Tinsel*. New York: Macmillan Publishing Co., 1970.

Ross, Irwin. *The Image Merchants*. New York: Doubleday & Co., 1983.

Schatz, Thomas. *The Genius of the System: Hollywood Filmmaking in the Studio Era*. New York: Pantheon Books, 1988.

Schwartz, Nancy Lynn. *The Hollywood Writers' Wars*. Completed by Sheila Schwartz. New York: Alfred A. Knopf, 1982.

Sinclair, Upton. *The Autobiography of Upton Sinclair*. New York: Harcourt Brace and World, 1962.

Stewart, Donald Ogden. *By a Stroke of Luck*. New York: Paddington Press, 1975.

Swanberg, W. A. *Citizen Hearst*. New York: Charles Scribner's Sons, 1961.

Swanson, Gloria. *Swanson on Swanson*. New York: Random House, 1981.

Taylor, Dwight. *Joy Ride*. London: Victor Gollancz, 1959.

Thompson, David. *David O. Selznick: The Man Who Made Gone With the Wind*. London: Andre Deutsch, 1991.

Walker, Alexander. *Garbo*. London: George Weidenfeld, 1986.

Zierold, Norman. *The Moguls*. New York: Coward McCann, 1969.

PERIODICALS

New York Times
Los Angeles Times
Variety
Fortune magazine, December 1932

UNPUBLISHED SOURCES

Cinema and Television Library, University of Southern California
M-G-M Collection
Norma Shearer Collection
King Vidor Collection
Turner Entertainment, Inc., Atlanta, Georgia, M-G-M files
National Archives, Washington, D.C.
Berlin Embassy Reports

INDEX

Shearer, Norma (*cont.*)
fights for better roles, 86–87
and Victor Fleming, 84, 86
legal battle with M-G-M and
Loew's, Inc., 276
love life as widow, 277–278
marriages of, 100–101, 103, 104,
278
movie costumes, 128
religion of, 101
retires, 279
and *Romeo and Juliet*, 218, 219,
243, 249, 251, 252
son born, 131
star buildup, 130–131
and Henrietta Thalberg (mother-
in-law), 91, 92, 100, 104, 115,
175
meets Irving Thalberg, 81–82,
88, 89
voice test, 112
Shenberg, Margaret. *See* Mayer,
Margaret Shenberg
Sherwood, Robert E., 55, 167, 196,
220
Sinclair, Upton, 198, 199, 200, 201
Sinners in Silk, 69
Sin of Madelon Claudet, The, 126, 127
Smilin' Through, 156, 157, 173, 218
Snob, The, 84, 86
Stallings, Laurence, 69, 101, 165
Stealers, The, 83
Stewart, Donald Ogden, 113, 136,
166, 167, 179, 192, 193, 220,
258
and Screen Writers Guild, 195,
196, 205, 206, 207, 208
and Thalberg pressure, 239
Stewart, James, 277
Stiller, Mauritz, 64, 93–96, 97, 98
Strange Interlude, 133, 141, 264
Strangers May Kiss, 132, 174, 218
Strickling, Howard, 73–74, 159,
160, 162, 212, 263
Stroheim, Erich von, 4, 5, 26,
30–35, 38, 53, 60, 135, 190,
267
and *Greed*, 54, 55, 56
and *The Merry Widow*, 56–59
Stromberg, Hunt, 77, 121, 122, 184
Strunk, William, 245, 246
Student Prince, The, 90, 99
Suzy, 226

Talmadge, Constance, 79, 80, 82,
83, 88, 111
Talmadge, Norma, 79

Temptress, The, 95, 96
Thalberg, Henrietta Heyman
(mother), 16, 17–20, 21, 38,
44, 48, 49, 59, 66, 79, 118,
175
and Norma Shearer, 91, 92, 100,
104, 115
and son's death, 270, 271, 272,
273
Thalberg, Irving Grant
aides, 74–77
and his children, 267–268
contract negotiations, 169–170,
179, 183–185, 187–188
daughter born, 243
death of, 271
and directors, 135–136, 262
earnings of, 6, 7, 51, 71–72, 99,
119, 120, 157, 281
engagement of, 99–100
estate of, 276
European trips, 106–107, 178,
179–181, 183, 185, 186
family history, 15, 16, 17
and *Gone With the Wind*, 1, 2, 275
health problems, 17, 18, 19, 59,
174–175, 180, 181, 183, 241,
242
independent production company plans, 253–254
investments, 48, 119
and Jews in Germany, 180–181,
197, 257–258
last illness, 269–271
and Rosabelle Laemmle, 43–45
marriage of, 100–101, 103, 104
and Louis B. Mayer, 46–47, 73,
117, 118, 142–143, 168–170,
175–177, 183–184, 211–213,
253–254
and M-G-M reorganization,
183–185, 187–189
and music, 197, 198, 255, 256
ouster from M-G-M, 183–185,
187–189
politics of, 197, 198, 199, 200,
201, 207
religion of, 67, 243
and Screen Writers Guild,
195–197, 201, 202–210
as scriptwriter, 39
meets Norma Shearer, 81–82, 88,
89
son born, 131
star buildup, 130–131, 133
story conferences, 123, 136–140
and Constance Talmadge, 88–89